Sometimes We Walk Alone

{*notes from a pilgrimage*}

Ankur Shah

2008

for Ramachandra Gowda

Author's Note
(worth reading first)

Welcome to India.

On March 12, 1930 Mohandas K. Gandhi began walking with 78 *satyagrahis* from his *ashram* at Sabarmati, through the Gujarati countryside, to the Indian ocean at Dandi, to break the law. When he did so, on April 6th, through the simple act of making salt from seawater, millions of his soon-to-be countryfolk broke the law with him, and the Indian independence movement entered a stage of massive non-violent civil disobedience.

That's the short version of the story. Clearly, there's a lot of pregnant background. Thousands of years of pregnant background that this book will not provide.

Instead I have chosen to focus on another journey. On March 12, 2006, I began walking from Gandhi's *ashram* at Sabarmati, through the Gujarati countryside, to the Indian ocean at Dandi, to understand a little of Gandhiji's life and message.

I have provided definitions and footnotes that I consider necessary to understand the text. Please use them. It is an extremely limited introduction to the vast and unified territories of Indian philosophy and culture.

There is a mountain in the South of Indian that is Shiva (a God). We call it Arunachala, *arun* being the color between the black of night and the first reds of the dawn. Since Arunachala is Shiva and the rocks on Arunachala are Shiva and the dirt shimmying down the side of Arunachala, too, is Shiva then she who would seek the end and extent of Shiva should walk, it seems, unto the sea. And then even, she, in her dedication, may not be sure to stop.

So it is with the pregnant background.

In the text you may also note a frustrating diversity of titles and suffixes to peoples' names. In general, it is impolite to refer to an elder only by their first name, *sans* respectful suffix. It is the suffix that shows the relation involved in an interaction, much more important than the names of the participants. For historical personages, such as Gandhi, I tend to use the '*ji*' of respect when I am referring to him as a personal influence, and to leave it out when I am referring to him as a historical figure.

As for the text that follows, it is a transcription and translation of the scragged journals I kept while walking. Over the last two years, I have occasionally had a week or two, here and there, to correct, to clarify, and to otherwise translate from my private dialect to something more comprehensible for public digestion. It is not a 'literary' work.

I have resisted a great deal of temptation to insert sentiments, reflections, and supposed wisdoms that I have accumulated over the past two years – I want the book to reflect the pilgrim's progress at the time.

The epigraphs I have used to precede each chapter come from a book of Gandhiji's writings entitled *My Non-violence*, published by Navajivan in Ahmedabad. It was the only guide I carried with me through the evolving moral and physical topography of rural Gujarat.

Finally, a note on the title. The most common question I fielded during my pilgrimage was "You are walking alone?". I would be asked over and over by the same person, in flat disbelief. I should normally have said 'Yes' – I had set out with the intention to walk alone, in the footsteps of Mahatma Gandhi, to Dandi. However, I was required in the interest of Truth to say 'No' – for anytime I was being asked if I were alone, I was not alone. And – remember, this is India, mystic and sacred and super-populated – I was always being asked. Hence the title, *Sometimes We Walk Alone*, from the song *Eyes of the World*, written by Robert Hunter and first performed live at Maples Pavilion, Stanford University, on February 9th, 1973.

> Sometimes we ride on your horses
> Sometimes we walk alone
> Sometimes the songs that we sing
> Are just songs of our own

- ankurbhai

ACKNOWLEDGMENTS

A great deal of thanks are in order, for those who have helped this become whatever it is.

I would first like to thank all the Gods, all those who have walked before, and all my relations.

I never would have gotten started without the kindness of Jayeshbhai and Anarben, and never would have made it without the help of everyone mentioned in the journeys that follow. My community in Ahmedabad has only grown stronger since the pilgrimage, and I look to them as a constant source of love and inspiration. Special thanks to Anarben for culinary advice and to Anjali for many of the linguistic and cultural translations that appear in the glossary.

I want to thank everyone who has inspired and supported me through the years, and, specifically, those who told me to keep a journal, to type my journal, and to edit those journals. Especially Neilu Naini and Christopher Holmes. I did most of the revision at two places of safety and reflection: Ishwardada's Environmental Sanitation Institute in Sughad, Gujarat, and Nash's Organic Farm in Sequim, Washington. My friends and their computers, at both locations, have been too open, too giving, and too kind.

My editors, Erik Uzureau, Denali DeGraf, and Chris Pierson, were instrumental in helping me to clean, shape, and translate these fevered writings.

Special thanks to all those who developed LaTeX, especially the 'glossaries' package, and to Pat Linehan for teaching me how to use it. May open-source software and natural farming prevail, together.

Thanks also to Max Edleson for the drawing, Tomas Werner for the cover photography, and to Scott Chichester for graphic design consultation.

The printing of this book was made possible by numerous generous investments, some from dear friends, some from new acquaintances, and some from people I have never met. Indeed, the flow of events regarding the financing process left me with the same cocktail of disbelief and gratitude that I felt during the entire pilgrimage. Truly fractal.

It was in Argentine Patagonia, years ago, that I became interested in India and the lessons she had for me. I owe so much to my community there, and especially to Ramachandra Gowda.

I will say, in closing, that no harm was intended in the writing of this book, and that I acknowledge all errors to be my own.

Contents

Day 1

March 12, 2006

"My soul refuses to be satisfied as long as it is a helpless witness of a single wrong or a single misery."

1.1 to Chandola Lake

"Did you bring any money?"

I wake up at 4h30 in the morning, following Gandhiji's example, perform my morning practices, and am ready to leave the house before 6h00. Seventy-six years ago, to the day[1] , Gandhiji woke up at the same time, performed his morning practices, and left his beloved *Sabarmati Ashram* punctually at 6h30.

We're just a few minutes down the road. Jayeshbhai and Anarben live around the corner from the Sabarmati Ashram, in a beautiful house infused by the love of their lives and work. During one small season in their lifetime of service, they spent a year in *Kutch*, helping to rebuild an entire village after the 2002 earthquake. In the years since, many of the artisans from that village have come to Ahmedabad to ply their wares. They often stay at Jayesh and Anar's home, decorating it in appreciation. As such, it is full of thickly carved furniture, traditional mirror- and mud-work on the walls, and brightly colored embroideries. It's the richest home ever to have held me, for a time.

They sat down with me last night to share some of their radiance:

> "Play with the children. The key to parents' hearts is through the children."
> "Sleep is free medicine."
> "Faith. Faith. Faith."
> "Walk slowly."

It is the only advice I have ever received in the Motherland that had something to do with me, relevant to this incarnation and consciousness, and not merely some old man – precious corner of the universe though he may be – wanting to be heard. And they are the only guidelines I have besides the map and list that another friend, Janeshbhai, kindly photocopied for me, arming me with the names of the villages where Gandhi stopped each day, and the distances between them.[2]

The same Janeshbhai also, kindly, called the media. When we arrive at Gandhiji's Sabarmati Ashram at 6h00, we find its ritual peace invaded by camerapeople and politicians. A woman in white speaks to me in languages I don't understand, drapes me in an Indian flag

---

[1] According to the Gregorian calendar, for what it's worth.
[2] See Appendix C

prominent with her party affiliation, and turns me towards the TV camera. I am cleanly shaven and smile.

They seemed to want scripted responses and are satisfied with whatever language they can get. It's a rare thing when anyone less than *old* pays attention to Gandhi and rarer still, perhaps, that the media pays attention to him. It's a rare thing when a foreigner makes a commitment to Gandhiji and rarer still, perhaps, when the foreigner is *not*, exactly, a foreigner.

Jayeshbhai and Anarben have clearly been through all of this before and kindly invite the circus to pray with the lions, a sure method to ensure quiet if not apathy. We sit together on Gandhiji's hallowed *prarthna bhoomi*, speaking the holy words from many religious traditions collected in the *sarva dharma prarthna*[3].

> Om Tat Sat Sri Narayana Thoo,
> Purushotthama Guru Thoo
>
> Siddha Buddha Thoo,
> Skanda Vinaayaka,
> Savitha Paavaka Thoo
>
> Brahma Mazda Thoo,
> Yahva Shakthi Thoo,
> Esu Pitha Prabhu Thoo
>
> Rudhra Vishnu Thoo,
> Ramakrishna Thoo,
> Rahim Tao Thoo
>
> Vasudeva Go
> Viswaroopa Thoo,
> Chidaananda Hari Thoo
>
> Advitheeya Thoo,
> Akaala Nirbhaya
> Aatmalinga Shiva Thoo

A closure, a silence, a signal from Jayeshbhai, and we leave: Anarben, Jayeshbhai, Janeshbhai, his cousin Mayurbhai, Anjali, Lizza, myself, and a group of TV camerapeople with their wires walking backwards. The woman in white, whom I imagine to be Sonia Gandhi

---

[3]see Appendix B for translation

(without knowledge or other justification), implores me not to eat in hotels and always to sit on the ground. All good things.

We leave the last of the morning media at the intersection known only as "Income Tax", where they had set up establishing shots of Gandhiji's statue in preparation for my *darshan* of it. I skip the photo-op, paying my respects while walking. A while later we stop at Kochrab, Gandhiji's first *ashram* site in Ahmedabad. There I absolve myself of the wreaths and flowers I had mysteriously acquired in the morning festivities, offering them to a huge mural of the man himself.

"Did you bring any money?" Lizza asks me as we walk together. Lizza grew up in the Punjab, spent a few years working in the United States, and recently walked out[4] of the American spectacle[5] with her husband, returning to India.

They wish to work with people, take their time, and rethink the way their lives. She has been shaped by the idea of the *gurudwara* – the Sikh temple that welcomes pilgrims at any hour with food and refuge. I see her becoming the gurudwara, herself.

Lizza's parents, of course, are concerned. They want her to have a job and curtains and children. As I steady my gaze the irony shades towards beauty – how so many of our generation, shaped by our parents' courage and values to do something different, find ourselves with neither support nor understanding from those very models. We are just trying to live our inspirations.

Yes, I say. I see myself taking the bus the day before, from my uncles in Nehrunagar to Jayeshbhai[6] in Ranip, finding exactly 312

---

[4]Swapathgami, 'to make your own path and walk it' is also the name of a magazine published by Shikshantar – The Peoples' Institute for Rethinking Development. See http://www.swaraj.org/shikshantar/walkoutsnetwork.htm

[5]I use the 'American spectacle' to refer set of images and relations therein that 'America' conjures up for people across the world, as opposed to a physical territory with humans and governments. The 'American spectacle' thrives all over the planet, and encompasses a set of economic and social relations, but is primarily associated in the popular consciousness with the United States of America.

[6]As mentioned in the introduction, we attach suffixes to the end of a name to show respect. 'Bhai' means brother.

points[7] in my pocket. An auspicious number, so I let the money be, though I had no definite plan to use it on my pilgrimage.

Lizza tells me of a man, Satish Kumar, who planned to walk (for peace, I guess) from India to John F. Kennedy's eternal flame at Arlington National Cemetery. When he went to seek his *guru*'s blessing, the man – great and bearded in my imagination – gave him one piece of advice, a weapon for the non-violent warrior:

"Do not take any money."

By taking money, apparently, he would deny himself the true experience of pilgrimage, and deny those he met along the way the opportunity to take care of him[8].

I am easily convinced, find my 312 *points*, and hand them to Lizza as we walk. She refuses, reminding me I have to come back somehow, and leaves me with 200 *points* I promise to use only for my return.

We reach the irrigation house at Chandola Lake, Gandhiji's stopping point for midday. Serenity. Around 10h30 and four slow hours of walking. Jayeshbhai, Anarben, and Anjali had walked me out of the reporters' range, until we crossed into the old city, and then waved goodbye. Lizza, Mayur, Janesh and I sit together on the quiet lawn and listen to the birds, gentle and part of the quiet. We meditate and Lizza brings some *chickoo*.

It's time to go on alone. I bid farewell to my friends and rejoin the road, already in progress. I walk for over an hour, leaving Chandola Lake for a gauntlet of large trucks, busy intersections, and greasy air. My escorts had left with me with chickoo and goodbyes, and yet I do not, yet, feel alone.

---

[7]'Point' is my term for the currency in any given locale. It signifies rupee in India, dollar in the United States, real in Brazil, etc.

[8]The real story is that there were two men – Satish Kumar and Prabhakar Menon – who, inspired by an act of civil disobedience on the part of Betrand Russell, walked from Gandhi's grave to the four nuclear capitals of the world, in living protest against nuclear proliferation. They found John F. Kennedy dead when they arrived, and ended their pilgrimage at Arlington National cemetary. The guru was Vinoba Bhave. I knew none of this at the time, but it's a great and fascinating story, detailed in books far better than this one.

This is India. The omnipresence is omnipresent. You are always watched. Janeshbhai emphasized as he asked his leave – "Always ask for directions, at every intersection."

Only possible, I think, in India, where at every intersection you will find a group of humans who want to tell you where to go and what to do. Humans who may have walked to the Himalayas and back, or who may never have seen the next village – either way, they know which way to go. Nobody ever minds, nobody is ever bothered, nobody ever feels crowded, nobody ever needs personal space. Except me. It's a fact.

Before we left the lake, Janeshbhai's friend had come from a local newspaper for a final interview. He asked what my message was, what wisdom I was carrying to the people of Gujarat.

I have no message, no placard, and no wisdom I can see. I am not terribly interested in the media.

There is a subtle game to be played, though. I must be okay with the media – it exists. I push myself into the calm, taking advantage of the ephemeral power to promote some positive memes instead of abdicating responsibility:

I tell him the message is LOVE and it doesn't belong to me or to anyone else. All I'm trying to do is carry it on down the line, to walk a few days with such a slippery package without making a mess of everyone involved.

It doesn't even matter so much to me whether it's love for the Mother or love for Gandhiji or love for the Gujarati people or love for the Self. All spectacular flavors in the great candy store of the soul and the point is the flow, the faucet opening itself to the flow.

Soon after noon I want to rest and come to a grove of chickoo along the road. I see no one but an electrician who gives me casual permission to enter. I get the sense property rights don't quite work the same way here. There certainly aren't enough guns to enforce them[9].

I sit down amidst corn and chickoo on hard ground and feel comfortable. Relieved. A little time to practice music or to write. A little peace out of the sun. It occurs to me on the road that all sorts of universe will happen to me. Some 'good' and some 'bad'. If the mystics and *ayurvedic* physicians are right:

1. all these actions have a cause

---

[9] "Financial power too comes from the barrel of a gun" (*Wall Street*, Doug Henwood)

2. that which I find in my life is a microcosm of that which we find
   in the universe[10]

Which means I will meet George Harrison and George Bush on
this epic journey and should be shy with neither. The 'unfortunate' is
diagnosis and homework, the 'fortunate' confirmation and temptation.

Temptation.

The chickoo floats in front of me. Have my sore shoulders earned
me any right to steal fruit? Or just to carry less? The faint perfumes
of Saint Augustine's pear trouble my memories[11]. Did he ever make
it to India? Why should I respect ownership? If Proudhon is right,
Property is Theft[12]. If it's Jesus we're after, then Caesar deserves his
fruit and we our hunger[13]? And the Matrix's Morpheus: none of this
is real and yet 'the body cannot live without the mind[14]'.

At last the errant mind returns to Gandhi: "How can you seek
truth without first controlling your hunger[15]"?

That settles it. I fold my legs and sit. That settles it. I fold my
legs and sit.

---

[10] "Lok purusha samaya" (*Charak Samhita*)
[11] See Book II of *Confessions*, St. Augustine
[12] See *Property is Theft*, Pierre-Joseph Proudhon
[13] See *Matthew* 22:21 in the New Testament scriptures
[14] From the film, *The Matrix* (1999)
[15] See Appendix A

1.2   to Aslali

We get to Aslali fifteen minutes after setting off again. India and myself. On the way into town I receive a call on my portable phone from a reporter who interviewed me yesterday. He offers to notify friends in Surat for my arrival. I get the impression he is collecting information for a follow-up story and my energy chills. I give him short answers and will the conversation to end.

Why? I am walking in the sunshine and singing. Why not be open and loving to a man who is offering me shelter somewhere down the line? He is disturbing my profound journey, my careful solitude, with his questions and generosity! How criminal!

His intention is pure, I know. Then it is me. Am I afraid to be seen with this phone that was pressured upon me? Then leave it! It is both who I am and not who I am. It is my choice and my acceptance. I must understand the distinction – between who I am and what I wear – and then absolve myself from the worry of judgment.

We worry about the judgments of others while we have not yet concluded with putting ourselves on trial.

The town *talav* is on my left and the town unoccupied youth (it is Sunday) is on my right. I throw my phone to neither and tuck it back into my (single) pocket. The highway and trucks fade into the background as I progress down a small paved road, through thick and curious stares, to the *panchayat* office. The youth in front of the office look vaguely threatening and vaguely respectful. Maybe they saw me on television. They tell me the panchayat is closed (it is Sunday) and I should talk to a couple of older men, hanging out in concrete gazebos across the street.

I note – as I turn, more nervous than tired, to talk to the men – that I have not prepared at all for this moment. I have no idea what I will say.

Ten minutes later and in spite of some protest I am on the Mayor's motorbike shooting towards the school where Gandhi spoke seventy-six years ago, today. The Mayor spoke some English and I spoke some Gujarati and the communication predated them both. The Mayor is *Krishna*[16] and like most Krishnas in the *kaliyuga*, he's a little strange.

---

[16] "I reside in the heart of all creatures" as *Krishna* says in *The Bhagavad Gita* 6:31

The Mayor first reads me the plaque on the panchayat hall, where Gandhi had spent the night. Then we ride to the school. One school building dates back to the British era, the others are newer and plastic. After the last earthquake they installed a number of Sintex "lightweight fiber" buildings. As the Mayor explained, when the next earthquake hits, it won't hurt so much when they fall. It's still unclear to me whether Sintex is the name of a material, enterprise, or worldview.

We also see a new (non-plastic) building named Gandhi Hall. There is no need to go inside, I am told. Next on the tour is the shiny *Swaminarayan* temple, some propaganda about how wonderful the *Akshardam* is, and a note that tonight Pramook Swami (the current head of the Swaminarayan sect) will be here in Aslali giving *satsung*. Maybe we'll attend. I meet the mayor's wife and she smiles at me.

When I explained the purpose of my *yatra* to the Mayor, he immediately understood:

> "I will show you where Gandhi stayed, where Gandhi spoke, and you cannot spend the night there now so you will stay with me."

When I suggested we walk the 300 meters (downhill) to the school he countered succinctly,

> "No. You take *bike* now and I bring you back. You walk tomorrow".

His breath smelt somewhere between alcohol and ripe chickoo. I've eaten five chickoo today so I would know – they're very sweet, almost alcohol already.

A little bit about the village, Aslali. It is all *patels*:

> "You won't find a single *Mohammedan* or *darbar* here. Only *patel* and *takkor* and *harijan*."

What does Takkor mean?

> "We have farms but do we work on them? No! The Takkor work on the farms."

The Mayor has three *viga* (some have 100) and a viga might mean 2500 square meters (six tenths of an acre?). At this stage of my Gujarati, it's hard to be sure. He works vaguely in government service – he's not actually the Mayor but he enjoys the title.

How big is the village? 5100 people. By people he means patel, the people of his caste. There must be, then, at least as many workers (Takkor) as people. And God only knows how many of his Harijan. But big enough that there is a medical center behind the panchayat where people from the neighboring villages come for care. Four to five hundred children in the primary school.

It's easy to ask questions and hard to establish context. People will always give you a straight answer for what they know, but anything they are unclear about translates to "never" or "impossible" or some other form of "zero".

I am hot and want a shower so the Mayor takes me on a tour of the different parts of his village. The patel neighborhood has big houses made from reinforced concrete, often two stories tall. The Mayor lives in a three-story house, the tallest in the entire village. You, too, can see it from across town.

The Takkor community sculpts its houses out of mud and cow dung. Draped straw over a wood frame forms the walls, applied with dung on both sides. The designs are beautiful, individual and perfect. Though all the houses are made in the same style with the same materials, each reflects the hand size and attitude of its residents. Each house has two rooms, one for storage (utensils, food) and one for living and sleeping. Everyone sleeps in the same room. A low curved wall protects a porch area from wind and animals, and each porch has a *chula* built-in for cooking.

I take *chai* and talk to the farmers (the ones who work on the land) and ask about the usage of chemical poisons and pesticides. Here they are called "medicines". The parallel is only too true. The Mayor says there are no problems and one of the Takkor gentlemen speaks up to say the older farmers are experiencing strange ailments, problems with their hands, and cancer. They tell me they get to the fields at seven, lunch at one, go back when the heat fades, and come home at seven or eight. They say rice was the major crop and I saw mostly wheat.

I play with the children and one family's mortar and pestle. They seem fascinated that I knew how to use it. I am surrounded by people, left suddenly alone, and surrounded again by people with handfuls of tamarind. Fresh from the tree. Ask and you shall receive. Or, don't ask and you shall also receive.

Back on the bike and to the Harijan part of town. Harijan – the people of God – was Gandhi's neologism for the untouchable castes of

India, who suffer fierce personal and systemic discrimination. On the way to their neighborhood the Mayor offers me whiskey (turns out it wasn't chickoo on his breath after all) and tells me not to drink the water they offer me. I pass. He stopps for *paan* and cigarettes. I pass.

"Anything?"

Fruit?

"Fruit not available but ice cream available".

I pass. The idea in not carrying money is not to make others buy you ice cream, I think. I'm still new to the idea, of course.

A quick spin through the Harijan *vas* shows me run down concrete houses (government built?) and kids who know very little about Gandhi. Not surprising. Everybody seems to know the Mayor, however, in all three parts of town. Maybe he is the Mayor after all. And everybody was playing cricket, in all three parts of town (it is Sunday).

We talked to Harijan and Takkor people who were working outside of *caste*, in government service. The result of strong affirmative action policies post-independence. Perhaps to give me the idea that caste isn't fixed. I did not, however, note any people (*patels*) cleaning toilets.

Finally to the Mayor's residence to put down my backpack. I am shown a terrible scene from *The Bandit Queen*. An eleven year-old girl is sold into marriage. It is violent, I need a shower and am unsure of the point of it all. Finally, the Mayor orders his daughter to bring me chai and goes off to arrange dinner. I take a good shower, rinse my Brazilian sandals, massage my feet, and soak my clothes. I have two pairs of clothes and must wash one each evening, trusting in Krishna and the far-off monsoon.

My back is sore and I'm excited. I feel clean and beautiful, like I'm doing the work I was meant to be doing. It's been a long and wandering path before this long and wandering path and in neither have I seen the sun set on my first day. But there has been no office, no problem set, no essay, no program, no kitchen, and no side of a classroom that has made me feel this content. The only call that comes close is working with the land – farming – but somehow this walking seems to be an even better use of my spacetime. More observation than action. Like I'm finally trying to shut up and listen to the mother.

I'm excited about the pains in my body, about the body it is becoming. I'm excited about the peppery gingery chai I'm drinking as I note the day. I'm excited about having an hour to sit before dinner, and I'm excited about dinner. For years I have wanted to do this walk, to respect Gandhiji in this way, to take this walk around the self. And it's nice to be so taken care of from the start, to feel that people understand – much better than I do – how my steps are connected with their own.

I could imagine so much good coming out of a couple traveling here. They could call a nightly meeting – segregating men and women of course – to ask people about their lives. You would have to speak the language much better than I do, or have some more comfort with theater. But the people are ready – of all castes – to treat you like a star. To listen to you lecture. All they know is that I'm foreigner (which is half true, even), and that I'm following the *Dandi kooch*. And they know that nobody follows the Dandi kooch and for some reason my respect for Gandhiji is to be respected.

All we need is someone who deserves their trust, their excitement, their openness. It's been half a day and already I know it's too soon for me. I'm too young, too ignorant, too proud, too rough. But somebody. There is so much room, so much potential, for somebody to really *be*, here. Someone to take advantage of all the stares and attention instead of getting bothered by them.

Here – in the villages, in the cities, in India, in the Anywhere – you are always watched and always judged. But where are these judgments, where is their hive? In the minds of men – ours and the judge's. Can we feel judged if we think of the judge as merely observing? Or are we party to the judgment? Do we give in? Do we create it? Do we make it possible out of our own weakness, insecurity of purpose?

When my relatives ruthlessly criticize my paths and peregrinations – does my resolve weaken? Do I entertain their suggestions? Must I? When they ask me to find a bride do I discuss the color of the yoke? Why? Can I blame them? Or Anyone?

A few years ago almost every discussion my friends and I had about our paths was singed with comparison, judgment, jealously, regret, and insecurity. Now? I have neither envy nor scorn towards more conventional educations. I'm too busy walking and supporting the walks of my friends. It is and I am originally one, and manifestly (in terms of space and time) other. I have learned not to be free of these desires but to accept them, and to realize them when necessary – I have given up trying to argue against the temptation and turned to the purity and efficiency of becoming it and moving on.

Hunger stirs. Only when I truly feel hungry will he return, so I have time to wash my clothes and to play the flute. Tonight I will have a peaceful dinner, meditate, and sleep long.

When life is a fragrant lake of cold destiny, why do we have burning throats? Why hold on to our desires and judgments of ourselves? What we learned from the bullies and bosses, the friends and lovers, we must now apply to that last mirrored joker, the self. Annihilate it, realize it, understand the whole lake is ours for the drinking and the playing. Desire is the middlehuman and the steel glasses are private cages. Let there be a storm of tickling mus–

Enter the Mayor. My reverie smashed out of lotus and into the synthetic amber honey of the whiskey glass. Krishna wants to get drunk. His friend Anilbhai arrives to give him company since the Dandi *yatri* is sworn to uphold the dogma of the master[17]. Apparently there's another hour before dinner will be ready (where? who? what?) so he turns on the TV to *gerba* at full volume:

Thirty-two. So very India.

He has six speakers for surround sound all pressed together surrounding each other in a cute line on top of the television. We begin to dance but it's not loud enough so he breaks out the *dhol*.

The dhol is a very loud plastic drum. Louder than thirty-two, even. We dance and drum until the consolation of whiskey turns the Mayor and his friend towards the consolation of philosophy. They drink it (the whiskey, not the philosophy) Indian style – a shot of whiskey into a tall glass, and filled with cold water. As they get progressively more involved, the water becomes warmer and lesser.

First, they appreciate Gandhi:

> "Gandhiji was my father and India's father – without Gandhi there can be no India. And Gandhi is a Gujarati like you and me."

Gandhi is from Porbandar, the Mayor says. And then he tells me a story, a sad story that hurts him to tell it (he tells me). He tells me how Gandhi's house in Porbandar is now in control of a Muslim man (minor chord) and this Muslim man (minor chord) uses dear Gandhiji's very room to store *daru*.

---

[17]Gandhi did not drink. See Appendix A

Liquor. The ultimate in disrespect. This to show, I think, that since Gandhiji's death, there's been no respect for Gandhi, to the extent that if I'm running for office, it's best not to mention him. Exhilarating. This is exactly what I'm looking for – or part of it – how Gandhi is seen today by the people.

And furthermore, "If anyone challenges this, you send them to me. Even Sonia Gandhi! You have my address".

I note his address. I sense some dramatic tension between the story and his pungent exhalations, and ask why there is prohibition in Gujarat: It's the only state in India with such a law.

> "Because of Gandhiji! Gandhi didn't want daru and now
> Gujarat drinks the most whiskey of the twenty-six states!"

He points out how you have home delivery in Gujarat (hard to tell whether he's laudatory or critical at this point) and how that facility doesn't exist in other states.

They continue to intoxicate while I continue to hunger. At one point the Mayor confesses he is the master of ceremonies of the town's epic nine-day *Navratri* celebration. He is the lead drummer and spends 15,000 *points* over the ten nights of the ceremony (unclear on what), and plays the drum from 22h00 to 3h00 without a break. Whiskey is his stamina – he will occasionally tell his nephew to bang on the drum for a minute while he sneaks into the bathroom for a quick *pack*.

The Mayor whirls around at this point and wants me to know, "In the 26 days of your journey not a single man will be known to you compared to me."

I have no doubts. We prepare to leave, and will stop by Anilbhai's house. Anilbhai lives, it seems, from his father's pension, who was a freedom fighter. To qualify as a freedom fighter, you must have spent six months in jail under the British *raj* for political agitation. We get onto the bike and ride to see Anilbhai's father's bronze plaque. A man who suffered so that his country might be born. Perhaps the most matronly act a man can perform.

We get on the bikes again to go to dinner. They are both terribly drunk. I am reminded of the journey some friends[18] took through India, "in search of the good". Is that what this is? Have I found the Good, in the Mayor and his friend? It seems I seek not the Good but the Weird. Bottles and blackouts of collegiate karma haunt my fragile

---

[18] Nipun and Guri. See http://nipun.charityfocus.org/about/walk.html

attempts at a *satvic* present. We roll drunkenly to the Takkor section of town and my mother calls.

Timing! Yes, mother! Everything is wonderful. You saw me on TV and Krishna is taking good care of me. I have no money and a place to sleep in the biggest house in town and I'm going to dinner. And I'm not going to lie to you because I'm walking in Gandhiji's footsteps so please don't ask if I'm involved in reckless and drunk driving through a dusty Indian village!

We stop outside a beautiful mud house and stoop to enter the veranda. It's been night for some time now and there are at least two dozen forms squatting in the shadows watching, and a single kerosene light to blind me. No electricity in these parts. It's the house of Kantilalbhai. Anilbhai's mechanic.

There are no women outside the shadows.

The Mayor embarks on a twenty minute prelude seemingly designed to torture a hungry pilgrim. The food is ample and two arms' lengths away. He waxes poetic and wanes gibberish, fumbling between tradition and respect, demanding I say *namaste* to the cook, demanding the cook present herself to be namaste-d, etc. We altercate over the consumption of milk. I have never liked drinking milk. I think I am starving.

My Krishna is quite drunk and has achieved a point beyond fun for a non-drunk, non-enlightened companion. Enlightenment is inhabiting a salt-bath of The Flow and remembering to laugh at everything. I'm hungry and incapable and complain to myself that his actions choke the flow. Except that nothing could possibly choke The Flow – just my image of it.

NOTHING CHOKES THE FLOW, PILGRIM. IT'S YOU.

I ignore the message from Beyond and continue to get annoyed and hungry against the better intentions of my will. I am allowed to eat, finally, and now the Mayor interrupts every moment of the dinner with inane (though memorable) proclamations

"India is best!"
"You must eat the *rotla* like this!"

I must stop eating, look up, and listen each time he speaks. Someone brings out handwo that Anilbhai's wife made.

"You must eat the handwo like this!"
"India is best! Only in India!"

Certainly.

I am forced a second helping rotla and *shak*. The shak excels in quality and quantity. I force Kantilalbhai, our pressed host, to eat with us. He eats half a plate and disappears inside. There is a huge amount of food. Everything is vegetarian of course. How much am I expected to eat? What is the deal with these people? Are they hungry? Have they eaten? Will they eat? Why is the host so unhappy?

"This is my fast friend. This is my house", the Mayor says.

I fight the feeling of imperial shittiness. This is what they mean by the violence being oppressive to the oppressed and the oppressor. No! I am a guest! I have a sacred duty to be thankful! I am flowing. I am chewing meditatively, sending love to Kantilalbhai. He starts to smile more. I say silly things about looking for a diesel scooter to convert to vegetable oil. My language skills aren't quite there yet. Nobody would understand that I'm serious anyhow. My command of the language makes the shadows laugh. I am offered *kitcheree* and forced more shak. I am the guest! I eat it. The energy has changed, I can sense it, we're nearing the end. Anilbhai has arrived with a new bottle of whiskey, but he can change nothing. His friends from the police call, "Yeah I already got it", and they all smoke.

No, thank you. I have a long history of allergy and intolerance of smoking and yet am relieved that Kantilalbhai is smoking. He relaxes and enjoys. Anything for him to relax and to enjoy. Thank the gods for the vices. We go.

I opt to walk with a gang of young men, scared of flowing off the road with the Mayor's drunken bike. They are short and talkative and all have something to do. Chai-*walla*, government service, high school, mechanic, etc. None wants to walk with me tomorrow. Good. The Mayor picks me up along the road and we go home. He stops at the paan shop and a kind old man offers me *ganja*. Apparently all you have to do to get free drugs in this country is start a pilgrimage in honor of Gandhi.

We pass the Mayor's wife on the road and he doesn't pick her up, ignoring my protests. She is coming back from the temple satsung. At home, the sobering Mayor copies my itinerary[19], word for word. I refuse his kind offer for "easy toilet medicine" and opt to sleep outside on the terrace. I thank the waxing moon and the waning Mayor. He is

---

[19]See Appendix C

Krishna. Amazing. I can feel the structure of the trip, the true depth and intensity of reality, reflected in this day's progression. I am in love. I meditate and go to sleep.

Day 2

March 13, 2006

"All I claim for myself is that I am incessantly trying to overcome every one of my weaknesses."

2.1   to Bareja

Past sunrise and mid-*aarti* at the Swaminarayan temple in Jatalpur. Ginger-*chai* and *bataka-poha* for breakfast after yoga and meditation. Everything fed. At the temple I take *tulsi*, *khajur*, and holy water in an attempt to understand. I pray first, in comparative silence within and without, then sit sat to write when the *aarti* begins. A feeling of total dedication floods me – I want to submit, to absolve myself of ego, of this burden I have chosen. I want to learn the rhythm of the ancients. I pray to be a light of compassion, to be love, to everyone in the wide wild Amazon.

Yesterday the man asked me what my message was and all I could think of was LOVE: it's not my message, it's *the* message. To realize our true nature, I float back to the United States, to Washington, to the Olympic Peninsula, to the Farm, to the magnet on Josh's refrigerator reminding us:

> "The only thing to do is to be".

I don't see this "love" as a verb in time, that starts and ends, shines and fades. I see it as the original state of being, outside of the conditions of time and space, an expansive noun we can choose to inhabit, to curl up and wrap ourselves in. So I beg for patience. For gratitude, for humility. Gratitude. Humility.

The Mayor walked me with his nephew to the bypass this morning, then said goodbye and took his nephew to school. Fifteen minutes later he caught up with me on his bike, piece of paper in hand. He rode all the way to the next town just to give me the name of G. S. Patel, a Gandhian in Navagam (tonight's night halt, according to the schedule we now share). How kind! How much gratitude! I can feel the inexorable demand: humility and gratitude. Every moment I am learning. I must learn. Everyone is good, so good, so good to me, even. Everyone is love, such love.

Reserve judgment. Ego expresses itself as learned conversation or good works or watered whiskey. Might it all be the same? We watched a clip from National Geographic TV last night about some explorers lost in the Amazon. Holy Amazon. The Amazon is not the next level. It's the last level.

I don't know quite why I stopped or am still here in this temple. But I like it. The sun rose at 6h55 over a divided highway full of flowers.

Today I feel ready. I want people to talk to me, to ask me what my deal is. I've been hearting out *namaste* like bliss this morning. Wearing a white *dhoti* makes me seem holy, feel holy. I am holy dammit. We are all holy dammit. I should always dress like this. We should always dress like this. I am the *ashram*, always on pilgrimage. The name of god, it seems to me, is the only word there is. Maybe it's the drums and chanting in the background. And maybe there is only one gift of speech, to speak the name of god. Why say anything else? *Bhagawan*. God is Truth. Speak the Truth. God is Love (good news)[1]. Speak in Love.

I eventually leave the temple and walk to Bareja, Gandhi's midday halt. I get there quite early and am unsure of what to do. Everything is a first. I walk on the highway until the intersection and turn towards the town, honing my dangerous smile and distributing *namaste* like party propaganda past beautiful pantless kids. I walk a young tailor into town for the last stretch and he asks what I am doing. I tell him without much fanfare and don't receive much of a response. It is nice.

At the town center, where Gandhiji must have given his speech, I play frisbee and catch with some kids. More come and I get intimidated, sit down, and try to read. What was Jayeshbhai trying to tell me? They wanted me to play the flute. I tell them no. They keep asking. I keep telling them no. It's so dirty.

Why not? I am embarrassed. Afraid. What am I afraid of? That kids will laugh at me? They just want to hear some music. I couldn't provide and tried to talk to them about Gandhi. It feels forced and didactic even to me and they leave to play amongst themselves. Children are really wonderful. Honest. Especially before the systems get to them. The education system. The food system. The chemical system. The fear system. The money system.

I pack up and go to the *panchayat*. There's a plasticky sculpture of Gandhi and nobody would be there for another two hours (until 11h00). Here I am in India, thinking about Gandhi! Is there anybody out there?[2] I decide to walk through the town, turn left and was asked by two men what my deal was.

There is a jerky Gujarati hand signal that means "what's your deal?" or "what are you doing here?" that you get a lot in the villages.

---

[1] According to Henry Miller's *The Air-Conditioned Nightmare*.

[2] "Smile if you can hear me!" ("Comfortably Numb" from Pink Floyd's *The Wall*)

Sometimes it strikes me as conversational and sometimes as incredibly rude. I stop to talk to them with no clear idea of what to say or how to say it. Rather, with no clear idea of what my "deal" actually is.

I'm looking for people who remember Gandhi.

"Everyone."

Gandhi's ideas?

"Nobody."

They bring me *chai* and we started talking. The crowd has been waiting to gather. It's India, you know. They bring me the newspaper with my picture in it, cleanshaven with a typical Bahian thumbs-up. They told me the town was full of devils and one guy who liked to drink wine and talk about Gandhi. Just what I need!

"Not two men in a hundred care about Gandhiji."

That's fine, brothers, show me those two!

"Oh, Ankurbhai, we don't have the hundred here..."

They are terribly sweet. One man gives me the name of a man in Navagam – G. S. Patel – the same name the Mayor rode back to give me. So it's decided. They continue on about how nobody cares about *ahimsa*, just money. They speak without judgment and generally without regret. I can hear lament in one man's voice. They speak as men who are more concerned with money than *ahimsa*, who see themselves as such. They speak of Gandhiji and the days of independence as if it were a different era entirely, as far from the money-grubbing present as the days of *Rama* and *Laxmana*.

We exhaust ourselves and I leave with a copy of the article from yesterday's paper with its large photo and mostly incomprehensible writing. The headline has something to do with "American *NRI* comes back for Gandhi".

Walking out of town I stop to talk with a nice-looking holy man, with shaved head, stubble, and an orange *tikka*. He wears white (he must be holy) and sits next to a shrine (he must be holy). The gesture, "what's your deal?".

I have it figured out – Dandi kooch. Trying to see *satya* and *ahimsa* in men's hearts.

He gets very excited and starts talking to me rapidly about *vedanta*. Who am I? Who is Ankurbhai? Do you recognize him? Where does he reside?[3] *Atman, Brahman, paramatman, jivatman.* He wants to go deep, get into the nuances – *Krishna* and Arjuna talking – do you know who I am, Arjuna? Does Arjuna recognize *Krishna* for who *Krishna* really is?

It becomes hard to follow because his breath smells violently of Big Red and each pungent exhalation launches me into a different world. He keeps getting closer and closer, the smell gets stronger and stronger, and my concentration breaks further and further.

He covets my space. I can't say how much is mental but the whole time I feel like we are fighting a tug of war with serious consequences and I am losing with every second. We are seated so close to each other that I don't understand how he could have been getting or leaning closer than we already were but somehow he was. He wants to kiss me, to grab me, to touch me, and for some reason I am very afraid.

A track in my brain asks to let go and see what will happen and another wants to relax, to breathe, to calm down. Maybe being molested by a holy man on the street wouldn't be so bad. Maybe it would. It would certainly be different. But I can't concentrate on my thoughts or his words because his grip is so strong – both hands on my body at all times, always in motion, a constant reminder. Fingers caressing my forearms, hand gripping my thigh. Big Red like chloroform stronger and stronger. I look to the crowd for hints but it's just one man selling plastic t-shirts from a wooden cart and two kids staring dumbly on. Had they been abused? Had they enjoyed it? What is happening? I must leave. I am twenty-six and I must be stronger than I look. I try to get up. He wouldn't let me. I try to get up. *Namaste*, thank you, I'll think about that soulful *rollo*. We fight. I win. He literally lunges for my shawl. I escape with a nervous smile.

Full belly, afternoon nap, and the healing balm of time restores the balance. The body didn't need the food or rest (only a few kilometers walk in the morning) but everything appreciates it all. Thank you *Krishna*. Wheat *chappati* and rice and *dal* – wheat and rice from

---

[3] *Krishna* says he resides in the heart of all creatures (*Bhagavad Gita* 6:31)

here, this very farm. I connect strongly with the cook, who is also the farmer, and we talk about the life and the land.

He makes 1000 *points* a month plus housing. Not enough for milk even. He sprays the crops with Monsanto, etc. Pesticides and herbicides. I am here to learn and hold my tongue. He loves the land, I can feel it. All the mango trees have been felled, used to build big house. And they get in the way of the pretty fields anyhow. But there are still *jambu* and *nilgiri* and *imli* and the *toran* leaf tree and *bilva* and lots of *neem*. The owning farmers, patel brothers, spend one week in twenty-five here. My new friend takes care of ninety *viga*. I love people who love the land. People who should be farmers and are. I have a feeling there are many more of them than we know. Farming in the name of the lord[4]. It's unfortunate (for me, for him, for all of us) that his technique destroys what he loves, what we all love.

It's Vitalbhai Patel who gives the orders. Vitalbhai Patel who saw me walking on the road and, conscious that I wouldn't accept a ride, merely pointed ahead where his farm lay. When I arrived and he had a cot ready under the *jambu* tree and bade me rest. He brought me a bag of *chickoo* and *imli* from his trees (reward for not having stolen the day before?) and ordered that I have lunch. I survive through his unwarranted kindness.

At three I leave the farm with thankful posture: a slight bow, joined palms, and downcast eyes. Actually saying "thank-you" is considered rude. Vitalkaka sends me off with kind blessings and a bag of fruit besides. I walk slowly and play the flute the four kilometers to the outskirts of Navagam. At the local high school I spy a bust of Gandhi and stop to take *darshan*. As I kneel I notice the officials watching me, and turn to greet them afterwards. They give me water and grab a young teacher as the bell rings to give me a ride to the house of his grand-uncle, the famous G.S. Patel.

---

[4]For the agriculturist Bob Marleys of the world.

2.2   to Navagam

Gordanbhai Shankarbhai Patel is *Krishna* the Statesman. He is 91 years old and wears all *khadi*. He meditates for an hour in the morning and the evening, does *pranayama* ritually, and still sits at his desk writing letters and "taking care of business" until noon each day. He seems to be a model Gandhian in a certain sense of the Gandhian program – impeccably clean, resolutely moral, and imbued with drive and certainty after seven decades of service to his country.

After a warm reception to his house and a quick tour of the *dharamshala* where Gandhi stayed, he gave me a chance to shower, to meditate, and to interview him, all before dinner.

The Statesman is a lifelong civil servant and agriculturist and has traveled all over the world. On his first trip to the USA, in 1965, he toured farms in twelve states, learning green revolution techniques[5]. I, too, am here to learn. He has been the chair of the national government agricultural committee and was a cabinet minister and member of parliament in the *taluka*, district, state, and central governments. He was educated to the 10th *standard* and speaks perfect English. He has total faith in the Indian government and, I think, the idea of government in general.

I asked the Statesman about corporate responsibility and answered that, "companies should not exploit and they are not exploiting", that it was the job of the government to be vigilant, and, furthermore, "I do not think we have not been vigilant". He is not the type of man in front of whom you would casually disrespect the flag.

The Statesman said that, these days, everybody respects Gandhiji, "except for a few damn rascals". He noted that women enjoy much more freedom than ever before and that untouchability is basically dead. The *sarpanch* of Navagam, he cited, is a *harijan* woman. Regarding prohibition, the Statesman is clear that it's the way to go. Gujarat has the best economy of any state and prohibition contributes to that (oh, how true!). Fewer people drink in Gujarat than in all the other states.

However, none of the following Gandhian values are extant: *satya*, *ahimsa*, homemade articles (*swadeshi*), or village self-sufficiency (*gram swaraj*).

---

[5]See Vandana Shiva's *The Violence of the Green Revolution*

For the little I know and much that I respect of Gandhi, those two axes (*satya-ahimsa* and *swadeshi-swaraj*) would seem to be the core. And I am a child.

I ask specifically about *ahimsa*, the value and perseverance of *ahimsa*. The Statesman is immediate and definitive: *ahimsa* cannot be used in every situation. He cites Gandhi's approval of using the army against the tribals in Pakistan and the example of the 1962 war with China. He mentions Cargil infiltrators and terrorists as places where *ahimsa* cannot work.

I decide while listening to note, to summarize, and to attempt to learn what people are thinking, rather than arguing or comparing their statements with some notion of truth. I'm not ready to build a dialogue between the Mayor and the Statesman just yet.

But the Statesman's main passion is, typically and lovingly, to tell me how I should have better planned my *yatra*. I should have called and written to people in each town in advance so they would know when I would be coming and could plan the necessary ceremonies. For his part, between harangues, he writes me letters of introduction and calls ahead to Vasana and Matar, tomorrow's midday and night halts.

I bristle at his kindness. Why do I want to break the chain? This duty of the *khadi*-clad civil servants in each town to house and support is what I'm trying to avoid. I'm searching for ego, for hardship, for the unknown. This trip is not merely about seeing the Gujarati people or their countryside, or paying homage to Gandhi and trying to study his path by walking it, but about developing a dialogue of trust and honesty between me and the universe. About being able to rely on nothing – neither credentials nor introductions nor media nor money – but *ahimsa*, unconditional love, for my survival.

The women of the household serve us dinner. Eggplant-potato curry, *pappadam*, and *bacri*. I refuse the milk (I don't like drinking milk) and sing songs with the children afterwards. There is no question of doing the dishes. As a guest and as a male, it's strictly prohibited. We play with Jiga's magical Casio keyboard and my flute. Jiga, a teenage grandson, sings one of Gandhiji's favorite *bhajans*, "Vaishav Jan To"[6]:

Vaishnav jan to tene kahiye, je peer paraaee jaNe re
Par dukkhe upkar kare toye, man abhiman na aaNe re

---

[6]See Appendix B for translation.

SakaL lok maan sahune vande, nindaa ne kare keni re
Vaach-kaacch-man nischaL raakhe, dhan-dhan janani teni
     re
Sam-drushti ne trishNaa tyaagi, parastree jene maat re
Jihvaa thake, asatya na bole, par-dhan nava jhaale haath
     re
Moh-maayaa vyaape nahin jene, draDh vairagya jena man-
     maa re
Raam-naam shu taaLire laagi, sakaL teerath tena tanmaa
     re
VaNa lobhi ne kapat rahit chhe, kaam krodh nivaarya re
BhaNe Narsaiyyon teno darshan kartaun, kuL ekoter tarya
     re

Stirring. I retire in the Statesman's office as he sits with fellow members of the *dharamshala* trust, eating *buggia* and drafting a letter giving the historic building over to the control of the Central Government.

Day 3

March 14, 2006

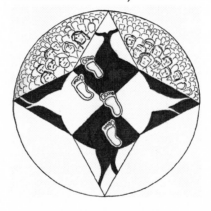

"Non-violence in its dynamic condition means conscious suffering. It does not mean meek submission to the will of the evil-doer, but it means putting of one's whole soul against the will of the tyrant."

3.1 to Vasana

Up at 4h30 to find the Statesman already meditating. I join him for a time, practice yoga *asana* as he pounds together ginger, honey, and lime for his morning tonic, shower, and sit again. One *chickoo*, no bowel movement[1], and the open road.

Fifteen minutes and seventy-six years later than Gandhi, as *kaka* finished my letters of introduction, we left – I can't feel alone here – to a cool morning wanting to be cold, amidst dust and haze wanting to be mist. It's dry Gujarat so those desires remained unfulfilled but it's no matter: India is not attached. A left turn at the *Ambaji* temple and a short *darshan*. Nothing so beautiful as an empty temple in the morning, music playing loudly for nobody but the gods. It's the early mornings when I can really feel the holiness of the temples, the long years of intention and love focused on a particular building or grove of trees.

She sings *"amba, amba"* – a word for both god and mango. As if there were any doubt that we could survive speaking just the name of god. A narrow road, modestly paved and lined with *sou-babul*[2] and cultivated fields on both sides. Beauty and fullness. Slightly cold. I sat down after half an hour to play the flute – full and light consciousnss that I have nothing to do, nowhere to be, no schedule, and no desire for such. No money. No decisions. Total freedom. It makes me laugh. Humans approach (from where?), ask me what I am doing, and seemingly approve (I wasn't asked to leave). I continue walking while playing, aiming lethal smiles at the local farmers who occasionally cycle by.

My mother calls from Ahmedabad and we have a good talk. Everyone is congratulating her for my publicity and success. She says she is proud of me! Elating. Five years of sword-like questions and monsoons of disapproval from the family: why isn't this child in an office or graduate school or marriage or some other confinement? And now? Publicity = Success. The reporters and cameramen whom I scorned and sped by have brought me the affection of my own mother. Which can only mean one thing, hapless wanderer:

---

[1] In ayurveda, it's a very important sign of good health to have a good bowel movement first thing in the morning.

[2] A highly aggressive foreign shrub, perhaps denoting *prosopis juliflora* or *acacia farnesiana*.

Love Everybody Always.

A memory of Allison Gray in the desert[3] floats down, a feather of wisdom from another time and forgotten place[4]. The surest way to fall in love is to do what you love, to devote yourself to what you love. And if you don't meet anyone, at least you're doing what you love.

Focus on the walking. I stop to see the portrait of the wind in the crops and a farmer rides by. He told me it was *bajra* for the humans and *rasmo* for the buffalo. *Chai*? Yes. He rides slowly and fast enough that I have to run along to keep up, less than a kilometer to tiny Bareia. Hidden women served us *chai*. His house was built out of mud: it takes six humans one month to build a beautiful two-room house out of mud mixed with *gober*. A two-room house where six to eight will live. He uses chemical medicines (pesticides) on his rice, but neither on his wheat nor his millet. He does not use herbicides.

Keep on keeping on, playing the flute and walking. Eventually I run into a nice young man who refers to himself as The Killer. He seems gentle enough, had seen my photograph in the paper, and is kind as every other *Krishna*. He explains that if you crossed him he was very dangerous and would 'kill' you. Kill is the only English word he knows, besides 'hello'. As is often the case with Indian English, it may not actually mean 'kill'. 'Hello', for example, is used more to get your attention then as a greeting.

The Killer leaves to take care of some 'business' (errands) and rides back as I sit practicing *bansuri* fifteen minutes later. We talk some more. The Killer says he has a roll of photos from last year's march and even a photo of me. The Killer likes photos. We go to his home in Govindpura, a little down the road, where I am passively shown all his photos of last year's Dandi march and given the newspaper article with my thumbs-up smile.

I hadn't quite realized that just last year, the seventy-fifth anniversary of Gandhi's pilgrimage, the Congress Party had organized a massive march in commemoration. Complete with speeches and film stars and support vehicles and bottled water and the whole modern Indian machine.

The Killer's family roused me to cross the street – it's a small sleepy village, there's only one street – to the house of one Jentibhai, where twenty-five people had crammed into a mud room (meant for six to

---

[3]A talk at Burningman 2003 on "Art, Love, and Sacred Plants"
[4]from *Franklin's Tower* by Robert Hunter and Jerry Garcia

eight, I imagine) to meet me. I drink *chai* and then more *chai* and am offered breakfast (*nasta*) to supplant the lone *chickoo* fermenting under three cups of milk in my proudly resilient stomach. There was the local Indian spicy snack mix and the national pride of Indian *biscuits*: the Parle-G.

A flashback to Lizza on the first day telling me that, according to Nipun and Guri, Parle-G is a pilgrim's best friend. They walked months in India on 50 *points* a day, and often survived on these sweet and inexpensive cookies. As a mostly vegan organic farmer, the combination of refined sugar, refined white flour, and milk is a little hard for me to take. As a starving pilgrim suffocating in the attention and love of a score of unknown smiles, it is just the right thing[5].

We talk about Gandhi. They want me to take them to America. It's not the first time. I asked them why, what's there? Silence. I get the sense these villagers are mostly used to speeches and polemics from strangers: they take my question as rhetorical, the end of the conversation. But I really do want to know what is there. For me and for them. Silence. So I talk about Olympic National Park, how great the national park system is, the hiking and the God-in-Nature everywhere you turn in such a wide and under-populated country.

It's hard to know if anyone was listening or understood but the care is palpable. They share the *biscuits* and *chevro* they gave me, but refuse to help me drink the *chai*. Everyone is so happy to meet me. Part of the honor and respect would have been for any foreigner, but part of it was respect for Gandhiji. I am beginning to understand the hospitality: by welcoming me and sharing with me, they become a part of what I am doing. By walking this path and hearing these stories, I become a part of what Gandhi was doing. It's on the road to answering that question, "why are you doing this?" that so many felt compelled to ask.

Why should I expect to know the answer to that potent question before I had even started? It's only after putting together the puzzle that we understand what it is, what it had been and what it was becoming all along.

Walk with me.

"Yes!"

---

[5]DJ Shadow, from *Private Press*

The men and children from the village walk me out of town, to the local school (1st through 7th grades). I touch the feet of Gandhiji's statue and clean his face of bird-shit. We take our leaves with smiles and *namastes* and I continue on with a dozen or so villagers – The Killer, Jentibhai, two other adults, and eight kids. Jentibhai soon takes his leave and the rest insist on walking me clear to Vasana, my midday halt. The kids run into fields to grab tomatoes and cucumbers for snacks. I empty my pack of tamarind and *chickoo*.

I had never imagined to be walked by one village to another. These people are so full of love, respect, and time. They calm me. The calmer I am, the more love I allow, the more responsible I am with my words. Slowness and thinking through my words are expressions of focus, dedication, love for the moment. Is that true for everyone? Will we all come back to that? It's our natural state, after all – the love and the consideration. I play with the kids, answer questions about American salaries, explain about exchange rates and purchasing power. I learn about farming. It starts getting hot.

Today is the festival of *Holi*. An ancient story celebrating the victory of good over evil, and the end of the cold season.

In Vasana the kids come with me to Kohdbhai's house and then let me go. Kohdbhai is the big man in the town, a local agriculturist who is in some way associated with Gandhiji and myself. I am somehow associated with Gandhiji. He had been notified of my arrival and I give him the Statesman's letter of introduction. Smooth. Kaka suggests I put down my backpack, and walks me to the old *amba* grove where Gandhiji ate and spoke. The grove has since (d)evolved into a single grandfather of a tree, amidst a field of eggplant. Govindpura went back to Govindpura, *kaka* went home to arrange lunch, and I sit down on a conveniently placed blanket. Don't ask and you shall yet receive.

I close my eyes and inhale deeply. Inhale a swirl of perceptions, fruit, consideration, and ego. Exhale peace into nothingness. Inhale gentle perfume of mangos and my mother, the fear of music, the joy of poverty. Exhale peace into nothingness. Inhale sore shoulders and mass media, chemical agriculture and the *caste* system. Exhale peace into nothingness. Inhale the indubitable presence of many companions.

My hour of meditation measures five minutes before I open my eyes to a dozen men sitting around the mango tree in a semi-circle.

"What's your deal?"

My hour of meditation measures ninety minutes of Gandhian chitchat before lunch. I listen to their stories, I will learn from their metaphors. It's the third day on the dry road and without effort the pace has determined itself.

In the beginning I was sure of nothing. I knew for years I wanted to do the Dandi kooch, in homage to Gandhiji. I had no idea about the details – where exactly he went or how long it took him. Or where I might be able to go and how long it might take me.

Four hundred kilometers I could easily do in a week. It was Jayeshbhai who told me to take it slow, that Gandhi could have done it much quicker as well. But he stopped to talk to the people, to learn from the people, wherever he went, and so should I. Freedom. Walking ten kilometers or less in four hours (before it gets hot) leaves plenty of time for roadside flute practice and meditation, too much *chai* in people's houses, for long listenings. It's what I'm here for, in the end. Not for personal discipline or spiritual quest, but to be with people, to listen to people.

And what did these people say?

"How can we help? What service can we do?"

Everyone wants a moment of your time to ask how they can devote their life to yours. And I don't deserve any of it, any of it, as far as I can tell.

A child from Kohdkaka's family comes to fetch me for lunch. I'm hungry and thankful. It's been explained that many people fast on *Holi*, only eating a few dates until the evening. It sounds wonderful. But fasting and hospitality are incompatible, at my level at least.

Instead of a fast, I am presented with a *rajbhog*. Two different potato curries, five *ghee*-d *rotli*, yogurt, *kitcheree*, two *ladoos*, a handful of dates. Kodhkaka talked while I ate, about how life has changed since the days of the freedom struggle

> "Before, we had to walk to Matar [4 km away, across a river] to go to school. Now my child takes a motorbike to piss."
>
> "Before, we lit one oil lamp at night, and all crowded around it to study."
>
> "Now people can't function if the power blinks, and they don't even need the light."

Kodhkaka has many *viga* of land and gets 800-1000 kilograms of grain from each. Wheat sells at 8 *points* per kilogram in the market and his laborers get 50 *points* a day to help them survive[6].

He is very kind and suggests I rest after lunch. I lie down for a few minutes, write for a few minutes, and feel called back to the mango tree. I will rest there and go directly to Matar. Kodhkaka walks me to the door, to the gate, to the road. Somebody told me the host walks you to the road because that when the guest's last, most profound requests might surface, might be satisfied. When the host can be the most helpful.

I lose my balance. It's hard to walk under the weight of such lunch and love. I am the luckiest of pilgrims. The most blessed of pilgrims. And we pilgrims are the most blessed of humans. Why are we so cared for? What *seva* can they do for us? Because we are in Gujarat. Because we are in India. Because we are walking in the most hospitable of lands. Because here the guest is god, *"aditi deo bhavana"*. And aside from all that, because we are doing the Good – whether we feel it or not, they can – walking in the footsteps of Gandhiji.

The wealth of paradox, the paradox of wealth. Because we give up company we are not alone, because we choose nothing we are given everything, because we relinquish control everything is arranged. Because I struggle to be humble, to submit myself to Gandhiji and the gods, I am treated as a king.

I go back to my tree. Soon J.A. Vyas, known here as *Mama*, comes back. He left his shop a few years ago to live in this village and farm. We share an understanding. Earlier, *Mama* talked about Gandhiji as *Bhagawan*. *Bhagawan* is god, god as total knowledge, total understanding. He said India's first misstep was putting Gandhiji's face on all the money. It's true – he's on every denomination of bill I've seen. A vicious irony. Now the children still know enough to say *"rastra pitta"* but in a few years it may just be "Gandhiji! The old man on the money". Or maybe they'll ask me to take them to the spectacle, where they'll make more Gandhis.

Mama looks up at the mango tree that shelters us.

> "Pull one branch. See this tree – pull one branch. Even though it's big enough to build a house, pull one branch and the whole tree shakes. Doesn't it? That high small

---

[6]See Marx's 1847 pamphlet *Wage Labour and Capital* for more on how this works in practice.

branch up there! The big branch going straight up the middle. Can you see it? Do you doubt it?"

I don't. I get up and swing on a big branch to make sure. Many branches move. The ones that don't are at the limit of my vision (I gave up glasses a few months ago). He lets me elaborate the key takeaways on my own:

We are all connected

If you don't see that, you're not looking closely enough

Mama looks up at the tree again. It's loaded with small green sour mangos that we've been eating with salt and chile.

"The tree drops so many small mangos in the spring. Why? It doesn't have enough strength to support them all; The branches would break under the weight of so many ripe mangos. The tree would fall."

How's that for a metaphor in a country with one billion people all watching old televisions and wanting new ones?

I suggest we meditate for a few minutes. They suggest we take *chai* at *Mama's* house. I pay homage to Gandhiji's statue, touching his feet and then my head, and read the plaque:

"Gandhiji stopped here on March 14, 1930".

Yes, yes he did. We take *chai*, I avoid the Parle-G, and hit the road. It's dirt and sand and exactly what I dreamt of when I imagined this pilgrimage: beautiful giving trees, roads no vehicle was ever meant for, idyllic rural life. A field of roses on the left and one companion runs in to grab a few. We walk down to the river and my friends and I wade in to our thighs for the crossing. We pass various ashrams on the other side – *Mama* notes that ashrams and *trusts* are useful for tax evasion – and take the long way to Matar. These men have spent their whole lives in Vasana, are willing to walk their afternoon away with me, and don't quite know the way next door.

3.2   to Matar

We – India and myself – are three nights into this pilgrimage and I'm convinced none of it is real. In what world of real is a pilgrim child welcomed into villages and towns as a national hero? In what world of real do old men touch his feet, old men who have devoted their entire lives to the service of their country? In what world are they waiting for him to arrive, *khadi* garland in hand, *chai* and *biscuits* waiting?

The *biscuits* are as omnipresent as India herself and we sit – with my friends from Vasana, on their first trip to the county seat – under a portrait of the Statesmen himself to take our snack. All care and welcome orchestrated by Natturbhai, *Krishna qua* Trustee.

My friends go back across the river to their village in the fading twilight and Natturbhai takes me around town, pointing out the trusts and organizations that the Statesman runs, that Kodhkaka manages, and those for which he himself serves as the trustee. Natturbhai seems to be the trustee for the entire town. He takes me to Gandhiji's statue and I touch his feet (the statue) and give him the roses we picked earlier.

I walk through the town, watching the preparations for *Holi*. I am, for a moment, a rockstar. Masses stare as we pass by, salute and smile. If I were to offer them the same humble *namaste* that has brought this far, I could never keep up with these old men. So I give the rockstar *namaste* instead, less humble and more confident than the pilgrim's. It feels proud and dangerous, but I have no other options in the dream.

In the dream, in India, everything seems to take shape according to perception. Like the inevitable gesture, "what is your deal", it can be gay or malicious. The key is to understand, at all times, that Everybody Loves You, regardless of how they act or what they say.

Finally Natturbhai takes me to Jayantilal's house. It sits tightly in a crowded colony in the heart of the old city, taller than it is wide, with faded paint on old stone. Inside it is long and damp, firm colors and no decoration. Jayantital H. Bhatt is a lifelong freedom fighter, and I sit at his feet to hear his story. He walks and speaks slowly, with the authority of experience. I take notes and wish I had a strong memory or recording device.

Jayantilal H. Bhatt is 91 when I come through town, which made him fifteen when Gandhi came through. Gandhi walked so fast that Jayantilal and the other kids had to run to keep out of his way. That was seventy-six years ago, today. That evening, Gandhi gave a short talk to the town, maybe five minutes long. Perhaps he was tired or sick.

It was enough. It was enough to change Jayantilal's life forever, to convince him that his true *dharma* in life was *swaraj*, not family.

The background to his story, thick in the cold air of his house and beyond my confidence to communicate, is the family. The most important aspect of life in India – especially seventy-six years ago – is your duty to your family. This duty includes and dictates your school, marriage, choice of work, and children. These concerns are not our own, as individuals, but the family's[7]. To refuse the primacy of the family is to walk out on your *dharma*, your worldview, your fabric of meaning.

Furthermore, the family in India is not a fluorescent nuclear unit but rather an extensive carpet covering the vast majority of your social experience: the *caste* system. Everyone with whom you are allowed to interact is part of your family. You'll generally marry a distant relative, from the same *caste* and often the same surname. To refuse the demands of your family is to turn your back on the greater part of the only society you've known.

Seventy-six years ago today, Jayantilal hears Gandhiji speak on the importance of *swaraj* and *swadeshi* and immediately gets on a train to Ranpur in Saurashtra, now half a state away. He is a fifteen year-old *brahmin* boy with one pair of clothes and just enough money for the train ticket. He goes with two friends to look up Mr. Meghani, who is organizing boycotts of foreign cloth .

Meghani welcomes them into his humble home and shows them where to work. They start the next morning, standing in front of a store all day, blocking customers and teaching about *khadi*, *swaraj*, and *swadeshi*. All day nobody buys any cloth. At the end of the day the frustrated owner (who is Indian) calls the police (who are Indian) and they come down to rough up the kids. But the kids have studied *ahimsa*, listened to Gandhi, and been prepared by Meghani: they know to turn the other cheek.

---

[7]Even now, as I write this in 2008, I am asked by relatives to have the common decency to get married, so my mother would have some company.

At night the boys go home, beaten and abused, and tell Meghani their story. He is elated.

> "Congratulations! You have succeeded in your *ahimsa*. A good lesson."

They wash the only clothes they have, hang them to dry, and sleep in their towels.

I note that the police, judges, and jailors in this story are all Indian.

In morning Jayantilal and his two friends awake to the police. They are taken, in their towels, twenty-five miles away and walked up a hill, up 300 meters of sharp black rock.

At the top, the police bend the boys' legs behind their heads, cross them, and tie them. They laugh and leave.

An endless hour ensues. Some people approach (it's India, right). They fear to free the boys, they fear retaliation. Jayantilal tells them, "Look friends, the cops left an hour ago, they've made it home and are having *chai* and snacks by now! Please untie us!"

A brave onlooker lets Jayantilal loose and he cuts the others free. They massage each other for a few minutes, stretch some yoga, and start walking home. At least twenty-five miles barefoot in towels and a forty degree heat that I can attest to is a goddamn jaguar.

At night the boys reach home and tell Meghani their story. He is elated.

> "Congratulations! You have succeeded in your *ahimsa*. A good lesson."

They wash their towels, hang them to dry, and sleep in their clothes.

The boys go back to work, each night returning to Meghani with stories of the day's events. A few days later the police come back, early in the morning, and take them to an abandoned building. This time they are allowed their clothes. They are locked together in the dark with two jugs nearby, one for water and one for urine. All day and night. At night the three boys huddle together for warmth. They hold their thirst and urine, touching neither jar. The next day somebody comes to unlock their cell and they walk home.

At night the boys reach home and tell Meghani their story. He is elated.

> "Congratulations! You have succeeded in your *ahimsa*. A good lesson."

They wash their clothes, hang them to dry, and sleep in their towels.

After a few more days of work the boys are taken to court. Meghani had warned them this would happen, and had suggested how to act. They have no hope of paying a fine but in jail their food and accommodation would be taken care of. If the police find out where you lived they could enter your parents' house and take everything they had.

The boys give their names incorrectly.

"Where are you coming from?"
"Hindustan," they say.
"Where are you coming from?"
"Mr. Meghani's house."
"Where is your native place?"
'Why, here, sir, in this courthouse."

The judge eventually loses patience and sends them by train to the Sabarmati jail in Ahmedabad. At 2h30 in the middle of their first night in jail they are taken outside, shoved aboard another train, and each handcuffed to different guard. They are sent to a different jail entirely, an abandoned cage in the middle of the jungle with a lock on the door and no hinges. The boys sit there until morning, clean the room and dig themselves a toilet. In the morning they are taken to a 'normal' jail with many other prisoners, other freedom fighters.

Each day they are called to bathe. To shower each man must man heft a large rock onto his head before walking the mile or two to a large dirty pool where he can bathe. He must lay the rock down, bathe, dry himself, and pick up a rock up again, for the journey home. As Jayantilal is the last in line he benefits from the pile's heaviest rock in both directions.

The daily work is milling grain as oxen would, pushing a bar in circles around a heavy shaft. Their hands are bruised and bloody from turning the crank until Ravi Shankar Maharaj, another famous freedom fighter, shows them how to push with their bodies so as not to hurt themselves.

This routine continues for three months: all day pressing oil, milling grain, carrying water.

In jail you can send one letter every twenty days. Jayantilal dutifully writes to his parents. He gets a response from his father after a couple of months, who is mortally ill. When Jayantilal is finally freed, months later, he goes back to the gleeful Meghani and asks permission to go home. Meghani gives him the train fare to see his family and the prodigal son returns home.

After six months away from home and family, the young man knocks on the door to his own home to find he has lost his *caste* and been disowned, for having eaten with the members of other castes, and for having gone to jail. He is not allowed into the house and can hear his mother crying under his father's yelling.

The mother tells the father that if Jayantilal cannot enter than neither would she. India in 1930 is surely no place for a single woman but apparently India in 1930 is no place for a single man; The father eventually relents and allows Jayantilal to stay, but only if he uses a separate set of dishes and does not speak to the rest of the family. Compromise. He and his mother agree and he lives at home but apart, using his own dishes and eating alone. His mother serves him without touching his plate and cries into his bowl. They go on like this for almost a decade years and from his face I doubt she missed a single day of tears.

From sixteen to twenty-six Jayantilal lives banished from his caste, the *brahmin's* son working as a veterinarian's assistant, doing menial work at the mill, and anything else he can to help his family. When his father passes on, after nine years, Jayantilal is free to rejoin the freedom struggle and gives himself fully to the Quit India campaign in 1941. He immediately gets sent back to jail for six months and spends the rest of his seventy years between in public service on both sides of the bars.

He is a strong man and I can feel the tears when he tells the story. I've seldom been blessed to meet people who embody struggle and non-violence so purely. Everyone will give you poetry and propaganda about the flag and nationalism and soliders dying for their country but here is a man who fought for his country with his own suffering as a weapon. I feel Gandhi's words in Jayantilal's life – how it requires so much more power to fight non-violently, to suffer wordlessly, to struggle through the strength of your being, 'to develop the calm courage to die without killing'. Here is a human who deserves to wave the flag.

We get up for dinner. I don't want to get up for dinner. I want to – I need to – get more of this grandfather's stories. But I am a guest, I have no choice.

Jayantilal's daughter-in-law serves us with love. A dinner for break- ing the fast I didn't keep. *Vatana shak* and *puri*, *dal* and rice. Two *ladoos*. Infinite love. What more can you ask for? What more can I ask for than nothing? After days of potato curries I asked, to no one in particular, for some green vegetables. And there they were. It seems that *Krishna* is no one in particular, and he's granting all my wishes.

After dinner Jayantilal's son takes me to the *Holi* fire in the center of town. *Holi* celebrates the victory of Good over Evil. Nobody explains the particulars to me and I'm too embarrassed to admit I don't already know. I do know that each town lights a bonfire and everyone walks around it in remembrance. The women walk devoutly around the fire and the girls are dressed in their festival finery. The boys dance and leer at the girls. Many of the men look drunk. I can smell a sexual aggression in the air, repressed and fighting to surface. I think of Jayantilalbhai sitting quietly in his dark house. I can smell plastic burning in the piles of debris. I want him to be on television or to be plastered on the money. I can see Good and Evil in the shadowy faces around. He is the gold I've been searching for, and I left his side for this.

Day 4

March 15, 2006

"Let me tell you too that I do not regard
England or America as free countries.
They are free after their own fashion, free
to hold in bondage coloured races of the
earth."

4.1   to Dabhan

The morning light. It's now clear to me that eating and sleep are both proportional to each other and unnecessary. There is a deeper energy that swirls around us, that keeps us moving and focused. And it seems the more I eat the less I avail myself of it, and the more I eat the more I need to sleep. Last night, for example, I was so nurtured by this subtle food that I awoke many times throughout the night, feeling alive and impatient, reluctantly taking sleep I didn't need[1].

I awake at the Swaminarayan temple in Matar, with a group of kids traveling to see their Swami and play *Holi* with him. He will squirt them with chemical colors, even squirt the gods. Everybody is very excited.

I finish my morning practices, shower, and sit outside listening to the gorgeous music that pervades India. Flutes and sitars and womens' voices. No wonder their films are so garish and commercial – there's no need for subtlety or artistry because India itself, rural and sublime, is its own daily art film, abundant with twists and symbols, imagery and soundtracks, tribulations and modernity.

The farmers have to buy *urea* because they don't have enough cow dung to fertilize their large holdings. Concentration of land and commercialization of dairies. The puja begins inside. They drag me in to do *darshan*, garland me with flowers, and feed me sweets. I want to leave while the earth is still cold and romantic but they organize a special *aarti* in my honor, take special pictures, seek special sweets.

"What is your message?"

I know how to answer that one. These men last night – in India so many of the men are kids for so long – were so high on their religion, their morals, their *guru*. High on Pramook Swami's magical powers and how large their temple is in Dehli, how many more people visit their *Akshardam* than the Taj Mahal. How much the temple cost to build, and how many statues of pure gold you could find inside. How they don't drink or smoke or chew *paan*.

I'm confident more people visit Disneyland than their *Akshardam*, and more people visit certain pornographic websites than Disneyland. I

---

[1]Consider Gandhiji's explanation of *asteya* in Appendix A, and Marx's oft-quoted line, "From each according to his ability, to each according to his need" (from *The Critique of the Gotha Program*).

want to ask how many South Africans min(e/o)rs died for those golden statues. Whether they abstained from both liquor and its judgement. I want to ask which numbers make you holy and which numbers make you profane.

Who is it in me who would harass other children?

Gandhiji had two important points for us – among many –

1. The importance of doing your own dishes. In doing our own dishes we eliminate the illusion of difference in temperament and capacity. Those doctors and engineers (so hallowed in India) who clean toilets soon understand that those who clean toilets might also like to be doctors and engineers. Through working in all castes, we eliminate our implicit support of the *caste* system[2].

2. The distinction between a man and his actions. When we can criticize the actions and not the actor, we stop threatening the ego, and allow the ego to change. The actor can evolve his actions without feeling attacked, without feeling he has to lose himself in the process.

There was a thought which came yesterday under the tree – we are merely channels, conduits. For the good love of the world. And the more we relax our valves, the bigger we open our hearts, the more of the One fruit flows through us. Enlightenment is this flow. The degree to which we expand our concept of self, the less we see as other, is the extent to which we widen our piping and let the free love flow.

I'm called away from the silence and cold to play the flute. I don't play like the CD and at this stage I prefer the produced version. Another *mitai* and I'm allowed to hit the road to Dabhan.

Dabhan.

> "The English were great. We were better off under the English rule. There was no poverty. Freedom came too early, a mistake. What we need is one-child law, like China. Rule by the gun. Fire and Shoot."

---

[2]See Appendix A for Gandhiji's take in 1915.

The *sarpanch* of Dabhan motions appropriately. How did I get here?

> "Dictatorship! One man is central. The English were good at planning. Like the U.S.A.: They think about the future. They need oil and gas so they plan for 20-25 years to start all the wars. Bush is king – I don't care what people say – he's taking care of his country, making sure that his people have what they need."

The road is ever-changing. I walked this morning a few kilometers away from Matar on a small paved road, turn down kind offers of bicycle rides and stare at fields of grain. An hour later I reached National Highway 8, whose thick asphalt carried me fifteen kilometers to Dabhan. The bigger the road, the smaller the love.

I arrive to Dabhan sweating and exhausted, praying for hot food and cold water. In Matar they told me, of course, to go to the Swaminarayan *ashram*. I do, though reluctant as always to follow advice, and find a fat *swami* who welcomes me, equally reluctantly, to shower and lunch. Though the swami is lukewarm, the water is cold and the food is hot, just as I had asked for. Their official vibe and insular culture guide me to meditate outside under a convenient banyan tree.

These are all the same, players in a feedback loop: rejection, hurt, sourness, ugliness, anger, distraction, unholiness. They do not make a peaceful pilgrim. I can already feel the subtle energy of my last interaction seeping inside me.

I walk to the *panchayat* office (closed) and someone gives me a ride to the *sarpanch's* house. He speaks his mind and blesses me with sweet lemon juice, before a servant to show me the town.

Every dictator knows he's benign. The *sarpanch* has a big stomach, grandfather[3] shirt, and *dhoti*. He shifts the conversation away from Gandhi at his earliest convenience. No respect, no question of a '*ji*'. I think he might hate me, and have a hard time seeing the *Krishna* in him. It's been months since I'm worn my glasses though. I feel uncomfortable, unwanted, under attack. How do I deserve this?

Every minute I am with him is discomfort. We play the game of obligations: it is only his notion of culture, I think, that keeps him from throwing me out immediately.

---

[3]In the US these thin white sleeveless shirts are called 'wife-beaters'.

Salim – the servant – takes me to the lake where Gandhi gave his speech, and points out the *harijan vas* where Gandhiji had famously bathed. Bathed? If Jayantilal lost *caste* merely by eating with others, how strong an earthquake was it that India's national hero *bathed* in the untouchable neighborhood? Seventy-six years later and I'm still told not to drink the water in "those people's" homes.

The side of the lake is dotted with banyan trees that serve as public toilets. I thank Salim (by posture), and retreat to some fields to seek a sliver of shade from the high sun. The whole town had seemed hostile. Fat swami, angry mayor, and disinterested servant. Remember pilgrims: no matter how much you may be tempted, it's the earth that is your true home.

It requires more faith and effort perhaps but everything you get in the city is a mediocre facsimile of the beauty and abundance of the mother. The pure welcome and goodness of green grass and cold shade. What else is the *ashram* – the ashrams that have so kindly housed me – but an attempt to recreate the oasis? At the oasis everyone is fed and watered, the lions and the camels alike may drink deeply. I'm surrounded by butterflies graced with the occasional breeze.

Dabhan is no Matar, no Govindpura. Nothing is other than what it is. I can see myself wanting the yesterday for today, when it's no longer appropriate. Pilgrim! Shut up and listen to the Is, to your new suite of asphalt *Krishnas*. In four days you have never felt hunger, thirst, fatigue, boredom, sadness, danger, or doubt. You must know you will feel them all[4]. Listen!

Last night an idea came as I was asking Narayan (Nattukaka's son) why people treated me with such respect. He said it's because they want to do what I am doing, but don't have the power to go. Don't have the power? It's their kindness and respect that allows me to go, that gives *me* the power to make it there. Especially considering this walking that might seem so difficult is really the most natural course for me, and the idea of, say, holding down a job seems terribly difficult to me.

I thought we could all share in the journey by having some tangible symbol of their presence on my walk, more than their love in my eyes and food in my belly. So I offered my extra *dhoti* – they could write their names on it and thus walk where I walked, through the fields and counties and districts and finally to Dandi and the great ocean

---

[4]See *Ecclesiastes 3:1-8*

and whatever lies beyond. I could wash the *dhoti* in the ocean and their *yatra* would be fulfilled alongside my own. It's a strange idea and needs perhaps more courage and eloquence than I've developed, but the underlying connection is already there.

At 15h30 I leave my resting spot with echoes of the flute and Gandhi's words, and walk the last four kilometers to Nadiad. I ask *Krishna* for fruit. The grass has healed me some, but I still walk with a bitter aftertaste. I play *Holi* (I am slapped and squirted with various colors) with some kids, but am more annoyed than joyed. I play games of my own, smiling at passerby and keeping statistics by age and gender: Young men and old women have the highest rates of return. Indices are generally low: there's no hiding a sour attitude in the intensity of India.

After walking twenty-odd kilometers on the first day of summer, I ask for water. Water is considered a public right in India so I should have no fear in asking for it. Restaurants to shopkeepers to service stations to houses all participate in the culture of public water. Eventually, I must ask them all.

I stop at a tailor's small shop to ask, and the man catches wind of my truer purpose. He sits me down, orders me *chai*, fixes the torn shirt on my back, and fills up my water bottle. I want to cry as I sit there, shaded, while he reinforces all the stitches on my shirt. Such silent goodness in the world. As he hands me back the shirt, the tailor tells me how much deep happiness I have brought him. Merely by ambling by? Again, it's not possible.

I leave convinced, once again, that I'll never understand the depths of emotion and generosity of these people, convinced that I don't deserve anything – be it fat *swami* or kind tailor – the road serves my way.

4.2   to Nadiad

After the tailor's stitching, we walk (in a city you are certainly never alone) just a couple kilometers more to the Santaram *Mandir*, a large and popular *ashram* where Gandhi spent the night in 1930. I wander the holy grounds and wait in line with pilgrims and young mothers, seeking blessings for their sons. A freakish cast of saints and *saddhus*, *brahmachariyas* and *sanyassis*, wander along the highway of diamonds[5]. Finally the manager speaks to me, recognizes my picture from the paper and my mission from the history books, and assigns me a room. Mukeshananda[6], in charge of the rooms, gives me the key and settles me in.

Mukeshananada looks like child. He is thirty-five, and has been here for the last fifteen years. His job consists of smiling, meditating, and helping guests into their rooms. He is very accomplished at all three tasks.

His room, next door to mine, is a veritable shrine to a Tamil mystic named Ramana Maharshi. Mukesh gives me the saint's bio, trading card[7], and a small book. He is Love as Patience and speaks to me kindly in a slow sweet Gujarati about meditation, peace, and other aspects of the "God is Love" paradigm. My spiritual vocabulary is, apparently, not very well developed. I ask if we can meditate together and he is elated to show me his practice.

I sit on the floor in his room on a thick red blanket. Mukesh sits on his bed, directly across from me. He instructs me that, normally, I would have to focus my thinking away from my thoughts, and consciously listen to my heart. However, just for today, he would take care of my thoughts, leaving me to focus on listening to my heart. I am too surprised to be skeptical, and we begin.

Half an hour later I emerge in a state of pulsing bliss. I had felt him, *literally*, enter into my mind and stop my thoughts. Like any gate-keeper, there was no perfection, but the vast majority of my thoughts simply *were not*. My entire body vibrates with my increased awareness. I sit speechlessly ruminating for a time.

---

[5] See Bob Dylan's *A Hard Rain's A-Gonna Fall*

[6] The name means "the eternal bliss of being a liberated being" as far as I can tell.

[7] There are these little pictures of all the gods and great gurus on floating around on cardstock. You couldn't possibly collect them all.

When I'm ready to enter *samsara* again, Mukesh wordlessly takes me where I want to go. The only part of the *ashram* that has not been remodeled is the balcony from which Gandhi gave his speech. The plaque, now familiar, proclaims Gandhi stayed here on March 15, 1930. Seventy-six years ago. Mukesh makes the connection and smiles.

We go back to his room and sit together again for a time, and afterwards he leads me down to the dining room. I feel no desire to eat, only to continue meditating with my new teacher.

On the way to the dining hall, where they cook for over 1000 people every day (free), one of the elderly *swamis* overhears my story, feels responsible, and tells me I cannot continue to live like this, that I must get a job. The words seem so irrelevant, leftover from another age. The head holy *swami* blesses me impartially (it must be part of Enlightenment, the impartiality) and I am allowed to continue with Mukesh. *Krishna* had sent *bindi shak*, *vatana shak*, *kitcheree*, and *curdy*. After eating, Mukeshananda sits in meditation with me one more time before I retire to my room.

It's too good. I have a room with a fan, three beds, and space for yoga. A hot meal. I have not thought once about money in four days. My new friend sleeps but a few hours a night, and passes most of his time meditating. He brings me the fruit I had asked *Krishna* for, as well as *prasad* from the temple. On the first day I was scared and excited to have to humble myself and ask for food. But somehow I've decided that it's fitting only to ask the gods, and to spend my times with the humans in thanks.

Except for water.

Everything I needed arrived within 24 hours – green vegetables for fiber, fruits, shade, phone calls, company, solitude. A little time seems to be all *Krishna* needs.

Day 5

March 16, 2006

"And so I am not pleading for India to practise non-violence because she is weak. I want her to practise non-violence being conscious of her strength and power."

5.1 to Boriavi

What I'm learning in everyday life is what I'm learning in meditation.

We wake up – *Krishna*, India, and myself – shortly after 4h30, and successfully execute morning yoga, movement, shower, and meditation. I don't want to leave. I eat the fruit Mukeshananda got for me and have an apple, banana, and orange for the afternoon. Mukesh doesn't want me to leave either, but we both know it's important I keep the schedule. I leave the kind embrace of the *ashram* at 6h45, wishing I could spend more time with my friend, and walk out of Nadiad town to the village of Boriavi.

I am hounded by wild dogs on the edge of town. They are everywhere on the margins here, millions of them, sick, pregrant, mangy, abused.

> "Peace between men and dogs.
> "Peace between men and dogs.
> "Peace between men and dogs."

I develop a phrase to repeat, to deal with the wild dogs without fear or aggression, the flute at the ready as weapon of calm or submission, depending on my mood.

A twelve kilometer walk with a few stops for the flute, a *neem*-covered two-lane road and a gentle atmosphere. By 9h30 I arrive in a village painted grey with age: Boriavi. Idle thoughts along the way, I remember with amazement how my pulse and sense of time slowed so dramatically while meditating with Mukesh, and wonder what to make of yesterday's fascist-sympathizing *sarpanch*. Nothing to make of anything, I'm sure. Just observe.

At Boriavi the *panchayat* is still closed so I sit at the *dharamshala*. The *dharamshala*, where Gandhiji stayed, is beautifully run-down, a perimeter of rooms surrounding an open courtyard. A man in an office hands out faded medicines and a mustached Rajasthani fellow sits, bored, in the corner. Nice moustache. I borrow a broom and sweep a square big enough to lay my blanket down. I meditate. The gallery arrives a few minutes later to discuss my invasion of their village. Attention is a common enough occurrence when a foreign visitor is an uncommon enough one. There are usually many people (men) silently observing any given interaction, not trying to speak or understand in any verbal sense, but tangibly present nonetheless.

One man, who works as a lawyer, is especially happy to meet me, and eager to get me *chai*. He is so adamant and vocal in his commitment to serve me that he won't waver enough to actually order the *chai*. We talk rapidly instead, for the better part of an hour, in poor English, as was his style. I talk to the people in general about Gandhi and the notion of "God is one".

My faithful servant, as the lawyer insisted on being called, asks what god I worship. I think the sense of worship is more important than the God.

"Yes, very true. Do you speak the name of *Rama*?"

I speak all the names that I know.

"Yes, but you are not American. You are Indian."

Well, actually

"All religions are Good, but *Rama* is best!"

I try to bring us back to the One Love, while he insists on stretching us out to *Rama*. Everyone is together in agreement (with what, I don't know) and nodding their heads – I motion broadly and mention the importance of worshipping the sun and the trees and *Allah* and *Krishna la fois* and my servant-lawyer says:

"Yes, but you're a Vaishnav, you must worship *Rama*. Speak the name of *Rama*. *Rama* is the best. You know that Gandhiji did."

And I do know that Gandhiji lived and died with the name of Ram on his lips but I am now *quite* sure I am not Gandhiji. And my commitment to the One Love which means I must speak all the names: I'm not Indian, I'm from some garish green land of post-modernity. But he isn't in the mood to understand my future and I am not in the mood to understand my past.

The town eventually returns to its business and leaves me to talk with the Moustache for a while. He's not very vocal but I learn he's the personal assistant of a group of *Jain* priests and pilgrims who are following a bus *yatra* to a special temple. They're not tuned-in to the Gandhian anarchist do-it-yourself stream of the religious experience, and their servant is decidedly not tuned-in to the religious and templar aspect of his job. I am distracted from our conversation by his prodigious moustache. It's the kind of moustache that makes you want your camera. I now know that, had I brought a camera, I could have had a lot of fun.

I meditate instead of waiting. Words and birds float around me, as I catch snatches of conversations from the street -

"Dandi kooch"
"America thi aiva"

Listening hard, trying to make sense of it all, my mind can only process it in the limited vocabulary I know: words about me. Sweet delusions of grandeur. They're probably not even speaking Gujarati, but some other language from some other region I've stumbled into. I return to the breath.

When the *panchayat* opens they call me to sit in the office with the bureaucrats. The bureaucrats in Boriavi are blessed with a clever bell under their desk to keep their servants occupied. During the fifteen minutes I sat there, in the presence of the mighty, they must have rung it twenty-five times.

Shortly before I decide to return to the peace of the *dharamshala*, a man comes in to the office to invite me to eat.

Yes, of course. His name is Jetibhai, and appears just as I am getting worried. We go outside together and check out Gandhi's statue in the center of town. He buys me a *limbupani* and some horrible red *sherbet*, both full of sugar and against my will. You can't explain "refined sugar is white poison" to pure *Krishna* hospitality, certainly not at my level of Gujarati. He's an SUV driver for local tourists. We lean against his car as his wife finishes making our lunch, then walk to his house.

Jetibhai's house is cool, dark, and half underground. It's hard to tell a man's wealth in such circumstances but I think he could afford the extra vegetables. We watch the Japan-Bahrain football match as his hidden wife prepares to serve us. It would be divine to eat with somebody, even once. He watches me eat, claiming a lack of hunger, and immediately sits down to eat when I finish. *Kitcheree*, potato curry, astringent *chass*, and the *siesta*-inducing *ladoo*. I watch him and write of his generosity and rigid hospitality as he eats. After lunch his son arrives from school, says hello, and sits next to Jetibhai on the bed.

Parents here are so close to their children. Literally. A child who enters the room will sit nowhere but touching his parents. There is the palpable power of the human form, the aura.

This morning, on three different occasions, people got off of their motorcycles to salute me, to welcome me, to offer me rides. They had recognized me from television or the newspaper and each time showed they had no understanding or recollection of what I was attempting. But the picture and the illusion of fame had stuck. It must be the aura again, the power of being near to the physical presence. They didn't want to talk to me or learn verbally from my experience – they wanted to be next to me, to be part of me, to, literally once again, mingle.

I try to write a little in the cool refuge of their house, but the Bahrain-Japan game ends, allowing the household to refocus on my handwriting. Jetibhai is, now, a huge fan of my upside-down left-handed scrawl (which many people think is Urdu) and takes me around town to display it. I take advantage of the opportunity to thank him for his generosity and his contribution to my physical perseverance on the planet. I am free to leave.

Mukeshbhai had recommended an *ashram* on the way from Bori-avi to Anand as a nice place to meditate and relax in the afternoon. The grounds are small, green, and clean. I find the community sleeping and rest in the silence of the meditation hall until people awake. When I come out the (large) *swamiji* is sitting near the kitchen, in a plush chair, surrounded by disciples. He listens to my introduction without recognizing Mukeshananda's name, and gives me a thorough inspection.

"Why don't you wear *khadi*?"

I have two pairs of *khadi* pants (that I designed myself, mind you) and usually wear one of them or a *dhoti*. I have two thin plastic shirts given to me by friends. I respond on two levels:

1. I would prefer buying *khadi* over buying other fabrics. But I have clothes already and would prefer not buying over buying.

2. I don't want to portray myself as purer than I am, to have the outside belie the inside. The truth is, I'm still very plastic.

He looks somewhere deeper than my words. He is not wearing *khadi* either. It's delicate. I always seem to place myself beyond my

limits, positively and ambitiously claiming to pray more than I do, to
have faith more than I do. I know doing so has a concrete effect on
my mind and the world, on our growth. I wear *khadi* to show where
I am vis-a-vis global imperialism and local economies, and maintain
my old clothes to honor my past, my comforts, my doubts, and my
complications.

"Half *khadi* is no good."

A pause. I give him the gift of *prasad* from the Santaram *Mandir*.
Flow. We sit for a few minutes in silence and he says I should stay. I
tell him Gandhiji's night halt is in Anand, but tomorrow will be a rest
day and I could come back to sit here. He repeats many times that I
should stay, that if things don't work out in Anand I should come and
stay with him.

Conditional affection?

I keep walking, alone. Immune to judgment. I have begun to feel
like a child in more ways than one. Like the child of the future. If
Spectacular America is the future many in this country desire – "take
me to America / get me more money" – then I am the child of their
future. I am the present of that spectacle and the future of India.
In which case it might be wise for the uncles and *swamis* to suspend
judgment and watch their living future in torn *khadi*, a week away
from the barber shop. That's a scary channel for social classes which
just want more money and more watches and hot *rotli* for dinner.
Because prosperity and culture are not "separate but equal". The
future is halter-tops and inter-racial marriage and inter-racial divorce
and organic frozen dinners. The future is the dissolution of the family
that I represent, an only child walking alone in India while his single
mother works ceaselessly in a faraway land. That reality, whenever I
present it, seriously disturbs them.

5.2   to Anand

I continue to Anand with Mukesh's words, "No money, no problem," and it seems strange that I have ever lived another way. That I have ever had money to spend or worry about, that I have ever cooked my own food or worried about how something tasted or what I wanted. The *yatra* is submission – there is no room for worry because there is no hope of control. I am beginning to see it as the ultimate cure for the suite of modern diseases: for stress, worry, anger, desire, insomnia, obesity, and diabetes. In the *Charak Samhita*, you might recall, pilgrimage is recommended as the poor man's cure for diabetes.

In Anand I work my way through town to the Godhi railway station, where I have an appointment with Bhagavan Das. Bhagavan Das – the servant of God – is the uncle of a friend, and only too eager to take care of this wandering pilgrim. On the way to his happy home a hungry begging girl gives me the opportunity to release all my accumulated fruit and *biscuits*. The lighter you try to travel, the more people want to give you.

I pass the school where Gandhiji stayed and spoke, seventy-six years ago. The gates are locked and posted with armed guards. Terrorism?

Exam-time. They fear the cheating during more than the suicides after, as I understand it.

Bhagavan Das meets me in the afternoon light under the banyan tree. A smiling, wiry, 71 year-old, bald, Indian man. As beautiful as all my other grandfathers. A natural teacher of Indian culture and behavior. I want to describe our conversation in detail not because of its originality but because it is here in Anand that I took another small step towards coming to terms with India, and thus myself.

First, there was no option. He had been given my number and called me only to ask when, not whether, I would come. Part of my idea for the *yatra* is to be independent of commitment and connection, to let each experience flower on its own, to provide myself with no safety and no nets. As such, I wanted to say no. But there was no option, "you go to Godhi station and call me."

Yes, okay.

When Bhagavan Das comes to meets me, in the afternoon light, I am playing my flute under the banyan tree. He stops himself from speaking, and looks around.

"I thought you would have five to eight friends! But you

are alone. It's not fun to go alone!"

Actually, I'm quite happy to walk alone.

"No. It's no fun. With a friend you talk, you pass the
time."

Actually, I'm meditating on Gandhiji and India and silence. I've
spent my whole life talking.

"Yes, yes, but *no*! No fun alone. Now with friends, you
can really pass the time, otherwise this walking takes very
long."

Actually, uncleji, I'm trying to feel the time, to know the time. You
know? The walking is a meditation. I don't want to pass the time, I
want to feel each and every minute of it.

I try to say it's my goal but I don't know the word for goal. We
cross the tracks and walk to his house. Bhagavan Das has worked his
life as a bureaucrat in the Western Railway, and lives in a nice colony
of houses by the train station, all built for bureaucrats in the Western
Railway.

"Now you wash your hands and feet and then we can take
chai and *biscuits*."

Wonderful. I want to take a quick shower and wash away the day's
eighteen kilometers.

"No, no. You just wash your hands and feet now, go ahead
and take your time. We will take *chai* and *biscuits* and
then we can go for a walk."

A walk?

"Then you come back and shower and then you will eat
dinner."

Okay. He's really too kind. I have no idea who he is, how I got
here, and why he's running the show. Unless it's to show me that I
was never running the show to begin with. Bhagavan Uncle gives me
the soap and the towel – both of which I travel with, I tell him (futile)

– and teaches me how to lather. He makes sure I wash my hands after touching the soap for the last time. He's too attentive to fool. Too kind.

I get clean, my hands and feet. He takes out a map. I have it already and have no heart to tell him that.

"This is a list of the towns where you must walk".

We read it slowly, from the beginning, reading each town name two or three times.

"March 12th. Sabarmati Ashram. Mid-day halt at Chandola lake. Night-halt at Aslali. Aslali. Aslali. March 13th. Monday. From Aslali to Bareja for mid-day halt. Mid-day halt in Bareja. Then, night-halt at Navagam. Navagam."

I am getting hungry. My feet hurt. He will make a copy for himself and give me the original list. No, uncle, please, I actually have this list. It's been very useful. We negotiate and he accepts keeping the original and giving me the copy. *Chai*. Parle-G.

I can say nothing against the damn things at this point. Cookies. Biscuits. I love them. Repressed memories emerge from childhood, from forgotten trips to India. I ate them on trains and wanted more. They were good.

"Now we will walk. I will show you the dairy."

He forces me to wear his slippers (I have sandals of my own) and to comb my hair with coconut oil. I have lived this before.

This is exactly what I feared. This is exactly what I created. It's okay. Do I really need personal space? Sugarcane juice? To be listened to? No? Why? Because it's now clear to me that I've been given everything I need. And if the *Krishna* conspiracy of spirits and uncles hasn't seen it fit to give me sugarcane juice or understanding, it's because I don't really need such luxuries.

Indubitably, now: I need water and love, much like a plant. That's enough and it's been flooding me since Jayeshbhai and Anarben sat me down five nights ago with their blessings and advice. Who am I to choose or to judge or to *anyverb* but accept the flow of love, however alcoholic or overbearing it may be.

We walk the ten minutes to the Amul Dairy Cooperative in about thirty minutes, down the railroad tracks. Why not? I walked all day, what's another hour or so? I came for Gandhiji. For *ahimsa*. Bhagavan Uncle takes me to the milk cooperative. Thanks for listening, India. Please note that the two – *ahimsa* and dairy – don't even rhyme. He talks about the factory:

> "You could see it but the trees are in the way. The smell and sound can be noticed all around the town. The factory runs day and night."

What is a co-operative? Though I carry no money, Istill read the billboards: Amul is the #1 in Asia. "There is a man who lives in Madras. He is the king of the co-operative. All the milk comes here from all over and gets boiled and distributed." Throughout Asia, presumably. I wonder if the profits get distributed to the farmers.

> "You know, Ankur, if you had come earlier there was at a tour. Daily 4pm tour. We could have had fun. It would have been really fun. If you had come earlier. But you came so late – what fun can we have?"

We successfully glimpse the factory through the trees and, being too late for a tour, walk back along the road. The city is crowded and filthy with pollution for each of the senses. I miss the countryside and the roads. We photocopy the map – I wish I could convince him not to do it, I wish I had a coin to pay – and return home.

At home I am allowed to shower and made to comb my hair with coconut oil. I assert myself enough to refuse a shave. As the wife and daughters finish preparing dinner I sit to write. After fifteen minutes the tension is palpable. Personal time is a crime, an American rudeness. I apologize and talk with Auntie, attempt to learn something in the kitchen. It is not my place, not here.

Dinner is excellent, all of us eating together (eventually) in front of the television. Thank you *Krishna*! Just as I asked for: to be able to eat with the human who cooked my food. *Tindura shak*, okra *shak*, puffy soft *rotli*, sweet mango *athanu*, *dal*, rice, and some sickly sweet vermicelli. The Indians have destroyed vermicelli by boiling it in milk and sugar until it turns nasty and congealed.

After dinner we all must drink water with lemon and salt (I would have enjoyed it before) and walk for twenty minutes. I sit in *vajrasana* as uncle paces indoors for the allotted time. I did enough walking today.

"Do you have a camera?"

No, uncle.

"A camera is nice. You should bring a camera. A camera is nice because when you are in a nice place you can take a picture. And later you can remember where you were, looking at your picture. You can also show your friends and share with them where you went. And after your trip you can have pictures of your trip."

I'm learning valuable lessons.

"No after-dinner walking?"

No, uncle, I feel like I've walked enough.

"That is because you were alone! With four to five people you could have had fun! But to you it seems far, because you walked alone."

He paces into the dining/television room to tell the women, "Imagine. This kid going all the way to the ocean, to Dandi, alone. Maybe with four or five people, together, they could have had fun. But alone? What fun can he have?"

No protest. Back to a life of no privacy and no control, a life of people opening your flute case and reading your journal when you go to the bathroom. With a beautiful roof terrace and moonlit night above, we all must sleep downstairs, in the same room. They have taken me into their hearts like their own child, accepted me in the deepest confines of their generosity and expectations, and tapped into my deepest annoyances and fears, my visceral need for independence.

Above all, below all, it is Love. I've put myself in a position – the guest – where all I ask for and desire is love and I should expect nothing more than that flavor of the Everything. I rest amazed at how in five days, every wish I've imagined has been answered. Except for the sugarcane juice. Thank You, angels and *Krishnas*. You are too plural and too kind. I am your ignorant, tired, child.

Day 6

March 17, 2006

"If one has pride and egoism, there is no non-violence. Non-violence is impossible without humility."

6.1 Rest Day: Anand

Time spent together has magically erase prejudice, opening deep and honest affection. I stayed up until late night talking with the beautiful Bhagavan Das.

Sleep is free medicine and today I plan to take a nap.

If there's one thing I like to smell burning, it's a brazier. Bhagavan Uncle's *puja* is long and strong – four incense sticks, half an hour meditation with me (he does *japa*), and now waving a smoky brazier all over this gentle home. After waking up at 4h30, I practice my yoga on the roof, and shower by 5h15. We sit together until 5h45 and I go upstairs to practice the *bansuri*. I have the sniffles.

As Gandhi was accustomed to taking each Monday in silence, these days became rest days for the Dandi yatris. For me, these days of rest fall on Fridays, and today is the first. Feeling I wouldn't have much in the way of silence or rest in Uncle Bhagavan's grace and presence, I tell him I will spend the day meditating at the Omkar *Ashram*, a few kilometers back in Lambvel. To my surprise, he agrees to let me go. My mom once told me that three days was enough for any guest. With this oppressive level of hospitality I can see how that might easily be the case.

Bhagavan Das even allows me to skip breakfast – I may decide to fast – and walks with me from 6h30 to 7h00 through awakening Anand. I continue another thirty minutes on my own back to Lambvel. I don't know much about Anand for the traveler. There's always the dairy, but if you miss the tour at 16h00, there's not much fun to be had.

At the Omkar *Ashram*, I am welcomed by the portly *swami* with more warmth than I expected and shown to my room. Most *ashrams* and hotels in India are identical. Concrete, clean, bereft of decoration, with three cots and one bathroom in each room. Cold water, bars on the windows, and a functioning fan. It is at once the bare minimum and the height of luxury. I am always thrilled.

Swamiji looked a little sick yesterday and is feeling worse today. I try to send him some magic cosmic energy in case he is running low. Can *swamis* run low on cosmic energy? I don't know. I want to ask him all about it. He's fat, wears orange, smiles, and has an *ashram*. Does that mean he's enlightened? What is enlightenment? Is it oneness with the divine all the time? Or just once, for a moment? Does he have magic powers? Does he know I want to ask him these questions? How do you become fat and wear orange? How do you start an *ashram*?

Can I tell him I didn't call last night because I assumed he would know I decided to stay in Anand and would call in the morning? Is all of this very presumptuous? Sinful, even? But as an enlightened, fat, and orange being, would he not already have forgiven all my sins and presumption?

I sit in further silence. My concept of enlightenment arose, stretched, refined itself in the *swamiji's* ailing energy. The enlightened know what a person needs and know how to help them get it. The enlightened understand that everything is Love, and can translate that understanding into the vocabulary of action. In this conception, somehow, self-important, fat, idle, and sick people are excluded. I have no idea how I developed such illusions; I am merely unearthing my own prejudices. Hopefully as a prelude to dismissing them.

It hasn't yet been a week and I feel this trip has gone on forever. The memories of that other dream have been erased. I learn so much from every interaction with every person and still rest contentedly in the wide expanses of my ignorance. It's a wonderful world. Today is my rest day. I will practice the *bansuri* softly, sit frequently, heal myself, and read. I will try to fast from food and words as much as it makes sense to do so. I need a nap.

By the early afternoon the *swami* has convinced me to eat. He has very good apples. Apples are generally terrible in India, but not at the Omkar *Ashram*. He's winning me over. He tells me to shampoo while his disciples tell me about Gandhiji's *ashram* in Sevagram, in Maharastra. I must go one day. When Gandhi left Ahmedabad to walk to Dandi, seventy-six years ago, he promised he wouldn't return until India was free. After the walk and civil disobedience movement, he had to settle somewhere else. Will India ever be free?

I spend the morning sitting in my room and in the meditation hall. In the hall, underground, other *sadhaks* hyperventilate around me. It must be a special technique. Another woman sits in what sounds like carnal bliss, murmuring the sacred *Om* with various inflections of satisfaction and desire, submission and prowess. Another man reads pacifically.

I think I prefer silent group meditation, *la* Goenkaji[1]. During my

---

[1] See www.dhamma.org for details. I cannot recommend the experience highly enough.

second sit a mysterious voice speaks to me and asked me a question, in a language I haven't yet learned. I don't understand and don't answer.

By sunset, I'm tired of resting. The stillness is a different teaching than the walking, a teaching I haven't yet learned. I feel lazy and bored for the first time. I nap to prevent the threatening cold: "Sleep is free medicine". I feel hungry and slightly weak. I am excited for dinner.

Swamiji gives me an audience, but when I face him I have no courage to ask my presumptuous questions. He confirms my suspicions:

> "God is one."
> "God is nowhere outside but inside everywhere."
> "All rivers lead to the same ocean."

These are good things to hear. He is missing some teeth and has a crooked beauty to his smile.

He asks what meditation I practice, what doctrine I follow. There is nothing to say. I learn what little I can in my travels. I am always experimenting.

> "You are like thirsty a man seeking water. You know you must dig a well. But instead of digging one well, you are digging many wells, and you have found water in none of them.

I squirm.

> "To find water, you must choose a single well and dig deeply. It doesn't matter which one, but you must choose *one.*"

Later, on the stairs up from the evening prayer, a man stops me to talk. I open the door for him and regard him coolly, jealous of the peace I have earned. He knows I took no lunch and asks me in Hindi, "You will eat, won't you?"

Like a slap – such care and concern in the face of pride and suspicion. I feel sick – I don't deserve any of their affections, their smiles, their concerns. What am I holding on to? What have I to lose by talking? Everything true is immaterial, infinite.

Dinner is tomato-potato-pea *shak* and *bacri*. Big, tasty, satisfying *bacri*. *Swamiji* has been very kind to me. Earlier one his devotees was telling me that *swamiji* is both *shastri* and *pathak*. *Shastri* means he's read the scriptures and understands them. *Pathak* means he can recite them at will. Both are rare talents.

Not only that, *swamiji* has done the Narmada Parikrama. The what? The Narmada Parikrama is a pilgrimage around the entire holy Narmada river[2] that takes a couple of years. People seem to think I should do it next, as if this walk was merely training for larger and larger *yatras*.

Well, maybe it is.

Humility is a major battle for me – I want the respect I won't give myself. I want to say nothing of my credentials, be judged apart from my clothing, and be understood as an accomplished seeker when I come to these places. Roadside *ashrams*. Why? Why do I want to be judged at all? Why do I want anyone to hold any opinion about me? And why would I balk at introducing myself? I don't know. I'm wed to a level of respect I know I don't deserve, from years of being the only child, participating in the charade of intelligence, and studying at an elite university. I have been given so many gifts by this world, and I know I will never do anything to deserve them.

I walk around the grounds after dinner and play frisbee with the kids and the mosquitoes. "Play with the children." There is a post-prandial prayer session with mantra repetition. Ignorant of the details, I try to shut up and focus on the Is, already in progress.

Back in the room, exhausted from rest, I breathe in the smoke of the neighbors' cooking fire. The ashram's hired help live next door[3]. What time will the moon rise? I will awaken early tomorrow because I'm five kilometers behind in the spacetime schedule. Excited to be on the road agian, playing the *namaste* game, no plans or friends or quotas. I have a dream of crossing a huge river on a narrow broken bridge. Maybe it won't come to that. In my mind it is huge, a broad swath of valley cut from Gujarat's non-existent mountains.

I fall asleep reading Gandhiji. A 61 year-old man marched this way and convinced a whole country to do it with him, to break the law, and to risk their lives. There can be no force more powerful than his

---

[2]Currently being damned in various ways, see Arundhati Roy's article "The Greater Common Good"

[3]See "swadeshi" in Appendix A

strength of character, his *ahimsa.*

> "Non-violence is not a cover for cowardice, but it is the
> supreme virtue of the brave. Exercise of non-violence re-
> quires far greater bravery than that of swordsmanship. Cow-
> ardice is wholly inconsistent with non-violence. Translation
> from swordsmanship to non-violence is possible, and, at
> times, even an easy stage. Non-violence, therefore, presup-
> poses ability to strike. It is a conscious, deliberate restraint
> put upon one's desire for vengeance. But vengeance is any
> day superior to passive submission. Forgiveness is higher
> still. Vengeance too is weakness. The desire for vengeance
> comes out of fear of harm, imaginary or real. A dog barks
> and bites when he fears. A man who fears no one on earth
> would consider it too troublesome even to summon up anger
> against one who is vainly trying to injure him. The sun does
> not wreak vengeance upon little children who throw dust
> at him. They only harm themselves in the act."

from *Young India,* 12-8-1926

There seem to be two options. Either the commodity spectacle will
wreck itself or check itself. For the latter proposition we must have
more than peace: we need harmony. Not as goal but as process – not
just in the fields and skies but in the hearts of men and women. This is
what Gandhiji calls *ahimsa,* not a negation of violence but a dynamic
transcendence of it. His non-violent resistance is as powerful as the
resistors' awareness of their ability to be violent, to be *violence.* It is
of the strong. For Gandhiji, this strength, this *ahimsa,* is only possible
when we are willing to be killed, willing to relinquish the physical
body, to die. When we understand that the force of our energy is
much greater than what the body can hope to contain. Only when we
confront the spectacle of death for what it really is, mere theater, can
we truly reach the foundation of our power.

How then to this nascent harmony? Not merely within ourselves
but with the other species in the vast *Amazon* as well? Love. And
what is this love premised upon? Death. We must unhinge these
concepts from their spectacular contexts and make them into realities,
immediacies, in our everyday lives. How then to come to terms with
this death that Gandhiji wants us to experience?[4] We must understand

---

[4] As Rumi says, "Die before you die"

that we are not our bodies – feel the expansion of the self, the unity with other. At every stage we are moving forward, transcending. This acceptance of death is not that of the suicidal teenager, but that of a human in the prime of her humanity, alive and in love. How does this happen? Meditation? Walking? Dance?

Day 7

March 18, 2006

"A few thousand years are but a speck in
the vast time circle. Someone has to make
a beginning with a faith that will not
flinch."

7.1 to Napa

What do I feel? What can I learn? I feel crushed by *Krishna's* gifts, drowning in his beauties. They want to balance my ego, let the two – *ahamkar* and *prana* – become one. The balance has shifted for this week and this voyage, and now the people are fooled into believing I am a sort of saint. I try to refuse and release but it keeps coming back. The love and inertia are again at play – when you're up, up things happen, and when you're down, down things do. So it is – one man sends me to the next, and each time I try to escape, to get back to some primordial neutral. I want each act of generosity to come of its own accord. Why? To further test myself and the universe (the two become one[1]), and our faith in each other.

I leave the *ashram* at 6h00 in the morning with two (good) apples in hand and no plans for the future. No plans, no worries. No money, no problems. Having started a few kilometers behind, I caught up to Gandhiji at 6h40, at the sign to Borsad (18 kilometers of future ahead), and left the smoggy development of the city for a treed two-lane highway. *Imli* and *neem* trees grace the skies and the sun rays through the clouds (I'm walking southwards) arrest my pilgrimage. I stop to 'whoa' and to play the flute.

This universe is beyond. Though I feel like a capable young man, if a little on the skinny side, I know that the slightest bit of this design is beyond me. Not just my comprehension or my intellect or my faith or my appreciation, but beyond any notion that could arise out of me. I'm just here trying to stay myself, trying to hold on to my ego, being mercifully crushed by the beauty and blessing of it all. Drowned. Squeezed.

Three kilometers out of Anand and two men on two bikes stop and extend their hands silently. They have flattering trimmed moustaches over the corners of their lips and teach social studies at the local school. They know who I am, what I'm doing, and even a little of why (as much as I do). They offer me everything – to contact the *sarpanch* of Napa, water, *chai*, or sugarcane juice. I have learned the habit of polite refusal and perform my duty flawlessly before realizing today might be my only opportunity for the sacred sugarcane juice. It's gone. Ask and you shall receive, if you're ready.

---

[1]See the apocryphal *Gospel of Thomas*, Chapter 22

Everyone beams love and excitement. They tell me they can't express how happy they are to meet me. I don't understand it. It couldn't be me, they must be waiting for someone else. I continue walking with the *sarpanch's* good favor ensured and thoughts to write an essay, "How to believe in everything in 26 days". Or six for that matter. Including a simple cure for diabetes.

The pilgrimage is to positivity. We don't have to know or to believe why we are going because we will eventually experience it. Experience obviates the need for belief. We determine the causes in advance, to be revealed in the future. Cause and effect? Simple. A bell rings, we eat. Which is the cause? Did we not organize the ringing of the bell to satisfy our hunger? Mediated but true. We find the true reasons for our pilgrimage as we walk. Nothing is ever other than what it is. Time is fractal[2]. The true *yatra* is an infinite moment, like the true moment of mindfulness or the unity of sex. We are lost, waiting in the foyer of the conditional realm[3].

Jayeshbhai's words come back to me, "Faith, faith, faith."

A blissful shock: the moment I received the faith to start, I had already arrived.

By 9h30 I arrive in Napa. It comes sooner than expected and I walk right past the town arch, continue a few minutes, feel a nagging insecurity, and turn around to head back into the bowels of the town. A child leads me to the *sarpanch*, Babubhai's, house. It seems nobody had warned him of my arrival after all, or at least nobody had warned him to care. Is this what I was hoping for? He barely greets me and goes inside to take a shower. By this time of day the Statesmen would have written a dozen letters.

I sit at the request of his wife.

> Oh! His wife! Oh! Round Gujarati matron, your body lost in colorful swirls of silk, how I love you! May I wear thin the stones at your feet! I can never hope to honor your girth and greatness!
> You, *Mataji*, are pure love and kindness! He who owns may bathe noiselessly behind but all my focus stays with you.

---

[2]Patterns demonstrate self-similarity at every level of detail.

[3]I'm trying to evoke the Kantian distinction between the noumenal and the phenomenal without the weight of vocabulary. See his 1783 *Prolegomena to Any Future Metaphysics*

> You bring me into your house! You bring me sweet and
> milky *chai*! You bring me sticks of batter fried in sweet
> coconut oil, mixed with peanuts, raisins, and cashews.
> You bring a grace and love that no balaji[4] or *mitai-
> walla* could hold pretense to! You bring me white bread
> caringly saved from its disgusting buddha-nature by a
> bizarre *vagar* of salt, sugar, *mirchi*, and *curry patra*.
> You bring me bright red *masala* popcorn left over from the
> gods!

She sits with me and tells me of her daughters, three of them in
Philadelphia, studying abroad. She tells me how hard they work and
how one of them was killed last year, at the age of 22, in her American
college.

What? Retreat to silence.

What more to say, to ask, in broken Gujarati? Condolences? Questions about the *masala* popcorn? I don't know. Does the tragedy make
her so giving? Her husband so closed? Did she always dream a wandering son? Who knows? I eat, he showers, she loves. She lights a
lamp, smiles, goes to the plants. My breakfast finished and the master
clean, I make to leave. She insists to us both that I leave my bag here
and return for lunch. We're both hesistant men: it's clear he views
me as pure botheration. But she is the woman of the house and we
bend our heads to submit. As the scriptures say, there is no force as
powerful as a chaste woman.

Babubhai walks me through the town, pointing out where Gandhi
ate lunch, where he gave a talk, where he relaxed. Now there are a few
older men there, making and drinking tea, standing sand squatting.
The locals question -

> "Where is he from?"
> "To whom does he belong"?

The sour uncle replies, "He is ours, Gujarati". I inflate with pride.
Why? This is what I want from everyone, what everyone should say.
Whose are we? We are ours.

In Gujarati there is a strong linguistic distinction between the ins
and outs, the "ours" versus the loose general public. It is this rigid
wall, I think, that allows for such passionate and intense hospitality

---

[4] A name for Hanuman; Also a snack food company.

to thrive in a culture crowded with indifference. Many people who wouldn't smile at me on the street are ready to share their each and every possession after a good introduction.

Uncle brings me to the *dharamshala* were Gandhi's troupe rested. He wants to go home, to be free of me. I want to be here, to be free of him. It's a beautiful place, a broke-down palace[5] devoted to *Mataji*. I've seen so many fancy new *mandirs* and so many decaying old monuments. Why not spread the love and *trust* funds a little bit?

The trees have remained however, stronger than the walls. The birds and the insects are comfortable here. What more do we want, really? They recognize its holiness.

The *pujari*, the old man who takes care of this place, approaches. He has no hair and a huge carcinomas nose. He is the priest and the watchman, day and night, the master and the servant of the temple. I missed the *aarti* and he doesn't offer to do another one. I want to come back one day and take his picture. Bhagavan Das was right: I need the Moustache of Dabhan and the Nose of Napa.

I am able to write and rest before the eight kilometers left to Borsad – this morning's walk was so simple and easy in the clouded skies. The clouds save us. The sun saves us. Everything saves us.

There's a wall here too. A wall in India is always something. *So something.* Not just a wall but something more. Its four colors – brick, mortar, white wash, and green wash, are all tinged with dirt. The dirt rains in from above, the green rectangle is not quite true, extending out from the door like an aura. Neither green nor white reaches the bottom. Or perhaps someone is eating it from below. And the final element, a ladder hung horizontally across the tapestry at eye level. The ladder, too, is something, *so very something.* It has five rungs, each with its own angle, some roped on, some nailed. The light will be perfect, soon. It is perfectly Indian already. Incense and *hingu* and always *chai* in the air, the ever-buzzing flies behind me.

I love how people here – and everywhere – have little concept of my life, of a life so different from their own. I remember Bhagwan Das telling me about the electric trains they have here, electric trains just

---

[5] "Fare you well, fare you well \ I love you more than words can tell," from Robert Hunter's *Broke-down Palace*

like the electric trains in America. He has no idea that most people in United States have never ridden or cared about a train. He was so terribly worried for my needs and comforts and yet had no idea that jumping down three feet to cross the train tracks would give pause to most westerners. He would have forced me to take the over-bridge in a second if he had any idea how many times I've heard and read "Do not cross the tracks". He might have cancelled the dairy visit entirely if I had told him walking through a slum, or fields of human feces littered like land mines, was something unusual for me.

I ask for a bathroom and the *pujari* points to the field next door, overgrown with weeds and monkeys: "Take some water".

No idea that *"America, America"*[6] mourns his statement with a multi-billion dollar toilet paper industry. And thank God. I scowl to imagine the roadside scene if a billion Indian people with no littering aversion were to start using toilet paper.

Eventually I walk back to the temple near Babubhai's house to write some more. He appears and sits with me to criticize my writing. I am left-handed, write upside-down, and perpendicular to the kindly provided lines. A fountain of consternation to those who obsess over my movements. After half an hour I've had enough and change the conversation to his health.

"Not good" he says. It shows. It hurts nowhere and everywhere and he's 74, in pain from aging. We soften towards each other. It's hard to focus because the crowd has gathered and everybody is staring but I'm starting to realize his anger and harshness are just symptoms of his pain. Is this always the case? Is the shortness and meanness and selfishness we find everywhere, within and without ourselves, a result of our pain? Isn't that beautiful? That we could look at every war-mongering politician, abusive policeman, and snide remark as an expression of pain, worthy not of criticism nor reaction but simple compassion?

A group of children appear. He breaks my gaze and goes inside to check on lunch, leaving me with a gang of young jackals, incensed by the bloody smell of my handwriting. They tear through my diary (no permission necessary, welcome to India, pilgrim) and asked me for free rides to America. Suddenly I've forgotten all silence and shyness and am trying to incite non-violent anarchist land reform in pathetic Gujarati.

---

[6]In reference to a music video directed by K.P. Sasi. You can watch it online.

My command of which language has improved with necessity in the last week but not, alas, to the level of a good tirades. Especially not to these brothers, who openly and gleefully aver they pray to Money because you can buy anything with Money, even love. I ask directly, "Even love?"

"Even love."

They clearly have never heard the Beatles. Which might be a better place to start than the Anarchists.

I'm seeing over and over on this trip how these people, my people, are covetous of money. We Gujaratis have transcended being known for business to reach a monomaniacal obsession with Gandhi's face on the bill without much more than lip-respect to any of his ideas. Except, of course, prohibition. I back myself into the silly position of arguing that we don't need money, we need what money provides: now the luxuries in first-world economies: hand-made clothing, organic food, sculpted mud houses. I'm sitting on a bench in a tiny Indian village, trying to tell people what they need. But it's clear that this money is functioning on a much more spiritual level, far beyond blankets and rice: it's providing pride, security, and peace of mind.

The lunch bell rings and the kids disperse. I eat *rotli*, *gobi shak*, *cuchumber*, *dal*, *bath*, *mugus*, and *shiro*. Not a word to the uncle, silent and angry again, and I play the flute for *masiji* afterwards. We share a powerful moment and, through our silence, it becomes clear to me that meeting her was the reason I bothered with Napa in the first place. Besides the whole historical-Gandhian element of this pilgrimage, of course.

We say our goodbyes and I walk out of town, pass the town's *dharamshala* and monsoon lake, and clear out of town. Farmland. I sit at the side of a field, enjoy my siesta, and give away my pains.

7.2   to Borsad

Saturday evening in Borsad. A loud room after a great shower in the
Surya Narayan Ashram. Soft yoga outside in the fading light of the
seventh day. I feel compelled to share that all I've learned is that
there's only One Love, waiting to be felt. Anything else is nothing at
all.

I took my siesta next to a small field, and, Indian-style, the farmer
eventually came out to meet me. Usman grows wheat and tobacco
to feed his extended family of 24. He's the first Muslim I've really
connected with on this pilgrimage, which makes me wonder how this
route was chosen, and how I am choosing my hosts.

I leave Napa's run-down old-India feel, the sadness of peeling paint
and skin, for a quiet road and *babul* forest. On the outskirts of Borsad,
which seems more major than I care to experience, there is a broad
open *Jalaram Mandir*, full of stone benches. It would be good place
to play for a couple of friends or troupe of artists with frisbees and
drums. One brother told me the *Surya Mandir* was nearby, and in the
fading light I choose it over the other building the Statesman, back in
Aslali, had told me to see – the *Satyagraha Chaavani*. I am tired and
eager to rest, to gain a brief reprieve from Mother India's incessant
sensation and stimuli.

A wistful passage by sugarcane and watermelon vendors who likely
would have shared their bounty had they only known what I was doing.
People have suggested I carry a flag for publicity, or some other sort of
advertising. But part of my faith, our test, is in letting the happenings
flow naturally. And I have no business lusting after luxuries like sugarcane juice anyhow. Fruit is different – I have prayed (ask gods, not
humans) for fruit and vegetables and received them both. As always, I
am fenced by my own limitations: I don't pray for them enough. Ask
and we shall receive.

Statistics are hard to keep but generally *Krishna* has a twelve hour
lag-time, or at least his agents do. I haven't seen him personally, yet. I
was, however, stopped by two scootered gentlemen – one I believe the
mayor of some other village – and offered *chai* at his mother-in-law's
house. I accepted, provided I could walk there, and a few kilometers
later, in Dedara, I walked up from the road through buffalo pens to
sweet *chai* with fresh milk and no *masala*. *Chevro* to go with it and
quite a lot of water. They let me practice the same conversation -

"Where you are from?"
"What's your deal?"
"You are alone?"
"Sardar Patel is better than Gandhi."

He asked how I got the idea to walk, and why I am doing it (some people guess 'PhD thesis?') and I have come to like that question the best. I can be honest and say something real, to the extent my language faculty provides.

At this point I say I've been planning it for four years, Gandhiji is my *guru*, and I am meditating on his life and message.

But really, I want to farm. I want to build my house and to farm. Usman was one of the happiest people I've met so far.

The supposed mayor eventually let me back onto the cooling road and I made it to the *Surya Mandir* for *darshan* and a security check. The guard searched my bags and checked my intentions before allowing me to stay.

The *ashram* itself is empty, so I play the flute until the manager, Bharatbhai, arrives. He unlocks a room and shows me where I can shower. I do so, wash and hang my clothes, and retire to room 17.

No lock required, one high power fan, two beds, and four nice blankets. Pure luxury. I'm still amazed India has this subculture where any pilgrim going any direction for any purpose can stay and eat for free at a huge network of *ashrams*. It's almost the way the world should be.

At seven I can hear *aarti* starting so I descend to see the beautiful people dressed up for the gods, to stare into the sacred fire.

The ritual is out of control. I focus on the central fire like a Zen meditation, my eyes watering from the strain. Blinking Christmas lights, acrid smoke, incense, and braziers surround me. All senses are under assault. Altars and Gods peer down at me from all sides. Gongs, huge drums, recorded singing and flutes, and deep live chanting approach from all sides. A man waves fire, a chariot of *ghee* lamps moving in unison. The ritual is alive, overwhelming, Indian.

I am crushed by the weight of sensation – smell, sight, and sound – and lost in its expanse. It's too loud and gaudy for analysis: submit to the steamroller over your senses, or leave. Annihilation as realization.

Afterwards somebody appears to lead me to dinner, outside on the floor with the guards. I must be the only guest. We are each given three thick *bacris* (soft) and potato *shak*. The curry is red from chile, not tomatoes.

It's been a nice cocktail of personal interaction and alone time, days of cursory meditation and nights of profound entrancement. When I need the space, *Krishna* provides. The evening is free for *bansuri* and meditation. Tomorrow starts another day, another week, another in an infinite series of beginnings.

Day 8

March 19, 2006

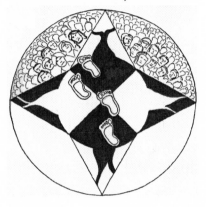

"To practise non-violence in mundane
matters is to know its true value. It is to
bring heaven upon earth. There is no such
thing as the other world. All worlds are
one. There is no 'here' and no 'there'."

8.1   to Ras

There's no awakening without sleep. I must have done something wrong out there, somewhere, beyond the wall of swarming mosquitoes. They know no mercy and ignore the fan. It's too hot to cover myself with blankets, too painful not to move. Before any hint of dawn, I go outside to the concrete balcony to try my luck, too harassed to sleep, meditate, read, write, or practice music. All my toys are broken.

Outside is little better. My mind races within the grip of a rabid insanity, thoughts breeding and collapsing in angry crowds. Each thought loops back to me in an echoing cascade: I get nowhere. I can't imagine a more effective torture than denying a man sleep. Jayeshbhai: "Sleep is free medicine".

And insomnia?

By two-thirty, still outside, the swarm subsides; I rest until five-thirty, ignoring Gandhiji's alarm. Yoga and prayers notwithstanding, my insect escorts return after dawn, forcing me to retreat to the cold comfort of the shower, a stream of water cold and hard as a metal pipe on tender morning limbs. I pack and pray, take *darshan* at each of the technicolor gods in the *mandir's* pantheon, and take my leave.

Borsad waxes grey and dirty and none too kind to our faded hero. I am set on finding the *Satyagraha Chaavani* – where Gandhi probably gave his speech – instead of heading directly to Ras. I ask my way through body-shops and *chai* stalls, people and cows who look as tired as I do. Nobody seems to know. Of course, I get a much lower return on investment with polysyllabic words in general: every phoneme carries with it another opportunity to mispronounce, to say a different word entirely. Maybe *Satyagraha Chaavani* is just too much.

But I'm following the trail. There must be a reason why.

And there is. The place – I finally arrive at 7h45 in the morning – is beautiful. It's now a school for 200 boys and 200 girls, based on Gandhian principles of swadeshi, bread-labor, and sustainability. The kids do their own dishes, wash their own clothes, chop wood for the school kitchen, and help out on the school farm. The rector gives me water and has me wait for the principal, Jashwantsinh.

Jashwantsinh is a hell of a fellow and knows how to treat a pilgrim right – *chai*, the infamous Parle-G (I am now past resignation and have begun to enjoy them), fresh hot *buggia* and fried *mirchi* from the vendor across the street. He gives me water, water, and more water. He tells me the history – there was a home here for *satyagrahis* during the early days of the independence movement, and the British eventually destroyed it. In 1931, someone donated the land and they built this *chaavani* in service of the revolution: a convention center for revolutionary activity. One of the primary actors was Jaswantsinh's father – who will be coming any minute to meet me, I am assured.

Now the farm cultivates wheat for its own consumption, and the grounds are peppered with mango, *chickoo*, and lemon trees. A well-tended field of eggplant occupies the central plaza, where you might normally find a well-manicured lawn not meant for walking. It's a nice change. The trees and history keep the morning peaceful and cool.

I can feel the trail again.

He says I should have come and stayed the night before. He is, of course, right. It was only my fear and laziness that kept me from walking the extra hour last night. My fear of having to meet more stares and answer more questions. Too lazy to walk a few more miles. Only my fear that kept me miserably awake all night, far from the Path. Could that be right? Might there actually be a Path that lights up when we walk upon it, an airplane in distress? That rewards us with coincidence and chocolate when we make the right turn, and throws us into calamity and mosquitoes when we do not?

Our friend Denali once hiked to the end of the world, through the islands of Tierra del Fuego, across a forest that knew no trail. He told us the only way through the thicket was to feel it, that as long as he was listening and paying attention to the forest (whatever that might entail) he could walk. Beyond mere attention, he told us, each time he broke his stride to think – to engage the mind – he would get stuck, be unable to progress, lose the thread.

Pure parable.

Jaswantsinh also recommends I send postcards ahead to the heads of all the villages, to prepare them for my arrival. A good recommendation if I wanted to be appreciated, expected, and treated well. But somehow I'm still not interested in that – even after last night – I'm not interested in helping them help me. It might take away the challenge, the virtue, or the fun. I ask him about Gandhi then and Gandhi today, about the children in his school. In *lieu* of a response he chuckles and runs his hands over the old photographs of *bapuji* that cover his desk.

He raises his eyes and draws a circle in the air, from here to America, "People there want what's here and people here want what's there."

Perhaps.

I wait for his father, hyper from the *chai* and impatient to get going. He comes with a car and driver, dressed all in white *khadi* and a simple cane, like my own grandfather. I touch his feet in reverence, amazed at my luck to be so close to the breath and life of those who gave everything to serve. I listen to some stories of his incarcerations for resisting the land tax, and can barely understand his dialect. I am honored to meet him regardless; I have learned from the village people to feel the boon of proximity and leave the fascination of comprehension aside.

I go on my way, alone.

The road from the school to Ras is a wonderful 12 kilometers long, shaded with broad trees – *amba*, *babul*, *imli*, *amla*. The countryside looks so perfect and peaceful that over and over I am tempted to stop and lay in the fields of wheat and millet. The pavement too attracts me, it is old and narrow enough that it looks made for walking. The people here are pleasant, happy, and interested. Many stop to stare, or to ask me questions -

"What are you doing?"
"What's your deal?"
"Did I see you on TV?"

Along the way I see a man riding a bike in place, sharpening knives. We learn customs as quickly as language: I stop to stare and to pester him with questions. He has attached a narrow, metal, spoke-less rim to his normal back wheel and a grinding axle to the cycle's frame. A simple rubber belt connects the two. The traditional Indian kickstand holds the back tire entirely off the ground, so the grinder spins as the uncle pedals, fast enough to make a living.

I've often dreamt about attaching a food processor in a similar fashion and am suitably impressed. The family of clientele, proud to have sharp knives and an itinerant foreigner at the same time, plied me with water, *chai*, and conversation. There is no end to the smiling here.

A couple of people along the road, after hearing my story, had told me to seek Gordhanbhai in Ras. Gordhanbhai, it seems, will take care of my everything. Armed with that sole piece of information, I enter the town. The now-familiar interaction of the underemployed village men (it is Sunday) giving me quizzical stares and the rapid wrist twitch, palm ending upwards, that can mean anything from "What the hell are you doing here?" to "How can I help you, *bhai*?" depending on the attitudes involved.

Sanjay, who describes himself as a 'school *peon*', takes me to Gordhanbhai, who was deep enough into his siesta or prayers that he wanted nothing to do with me. Another man eventually leads me between the buffalo and wooden buildings to an older part of the village, where Kiritbhai, the school accountant, lives.

Kiritbhai has a passion for history and gives me a powerful introductory lecture to Ras's powerful history in the independence movement. Ras claims the most *satyagrahis* of any town in the struggle – 101 villagers who left their normal lives to dedicate themselves to civil disobedience. Maybe they're all like Jayantilalbhai back in Matar? It's all apparently written in a book in the school, which is closed today (it is Sunday).

"You must stay until tomorrow.."

No, I need to follow Gandhi's schedule.

"Gandhi himself stayed the night here on his way to Dandi."

A moment of terror. What if my information is wrong, and the map is not the territory[1] after all?

The confusion continues without my involvement, leading to a brief town-wide discussion. Typically, people appear out of nowhere to voice their opinions. Finally, they resolve the issue: "No, no, you must go." Oh, thank you.

Since the commemorative march last year, many people are aware that Gandhi once came this way. The memorial statues had been dusted off, for a time.

Kiritbhai offers to show me the *dharamshala* by the lake and I think of yesterday's decaying treasure in Napa and am romanced. But yesterday's warehouses are tomorrow's condominiums and the old stone and wood affair had been demolished and re-poured in naked concrete. We return to his house and I ask gingerly if there be some place for travelers to get food (it is Sunday).

---

[1] *pace* Alfred Korzybski

I'm toeing the line, but the line was my own. So far, without a doubt, *Krishna* has been overwhelmingly generous. And yet, a doubt – my lack of faith – inspires me to ask. . .

"Why not here?" he says. I agree, at ease, accepting my third *chai* of the day. I don't normally consume caffeine, milk, or sugar. But it is be social suicide to refuse *chai* on such a journey. Be aware.

The family has already eaten so I eat slowly and peacefully, under the careful watch of five pairs of eyes, squatting all around me. I am getting better at listening to the language of bodies and auras – I can sense care from father and fear from grandma, curiosity from the children and apathy from mom. We (I) eat *bindi shak* and too many *rotli*, then *kitcheree* and terribly astringent *curdy*, with a sweet *keri athanu* and *pappadam*. By the end of it, chewing slowly and intentionally, we feel at ease with each other. The alchemy of food. I feel pride of eating the *curdy* and winning over the household after an initially lukewarm reception.

After lunch they let me walk alone to the renovated *dharamshala*, which I pass over for a large *vad* tree at the edge of the town *talav*. I write for a while, the lucky object of intent stares from various bystanders, who have not yet chosen to address me. It's a different culture, that's all. There's nothing rude about it. There's no reason to get shy or angry. I suppose I should see it as loving. Loving stares. Stares of Love.

I work hard to resist the 'none of your goddamn business' side of me itching to come out. And the side that thinks writing is more important than being with humans, whereas Jayeshbhai clearly told me:

"Talk to the people."

Jayeshbhai. Jayeshbhai goes for long walks through the mess and metropolis of Ahmedabad, smiling at the men and taking cigarettes out of their very mouths, gently admonishing them with, "If you're my brother and you're killing yourself isn't it my duty to stop you?".

And instead of scowling or hitting him they smile in shame and hand him the rest of their cigarettes! That's Jayeshbhai's idea of a walk in the park. If there's anybody to listen to, it's Jayeshbhai. Men continue to gather, smoking, and hover over me. They talk amongst themselves, watching me write. It's all very good-natured and, yet, something tells me I need a break. Or, more likely, could use a break from the very 'I' that needs a break. To return to that place where it's all love even when the *bidi* bodies crowd out the noonday sun with energetic claws into my short

shanti
shanti
shanti.

8.2   to Kankapura

Is there anything more than making an old woman happy?

The road from Ras to Kankapura is slight and fielded, through tobacco, wheat, and cotton. So many gnarled trees and villagers, who have shared their entire lives with this land. I stop under a shaded stand to play the flute and can see my grandmother enjoying the tune while carrying her firewood, spindly and weathered though she may be.

I want salad.

A scant kilometer later, a man blazes past me on his motorcycle, turns around, and offers me his home. He, Bharatbhai, seems to know what I am doing, and tells me he will be waiting for me in Kankapura. The road is so small, apparently, because it's the end of the line: no more villages between here and the delta of the mighty Mahisagar river. No more large temples or *ashrams*.

The humans never fail to offer when I need it, and don't bother when I don't. As he got back on his bike Bhartbhai said to me, "you've given me *ananda* in meeting you". *Ananda* is incomparable with happiness – it is the baseline bliss behind the tumult of the emotional rollercoaster, it is a deep and steady joy. In my mind, unlike happiness, once *ananda* is shared it can never be spent.

So sweet and generous a term.

What can I do for these people? With them? Gandhiji gave me a clue – written large upon the walls of his Sabarmati Ashram:

> "I will give you a talisman. Whenever you are in doubt, or when the self becomes too much with you, apply the following test. Recall the face of the poorest and the weakest man whom you may have seen, and ask yourself, if the step you contemplate is going to be of any use to him. Will he gain anything by it? Will it restore him to a control over his own life and destiny? In other words, will it lead to *swaraj* for the hungry and spiritually starving millions?
> Then you will find your doubts and your self melt away."

So much lies in the smile, the depth of the gaze. Could merely sharing our peace and our love be enough? There is nothing mere about Being.

I've also been reflecting on the staring and intrusion I 'suffered', both this morning and throughout this week. We hold the power of interpretation – I can choose to interpret the staring as rude and invasive, or I can choose to see it as a form of devotion, albeit perverted. In that context, people watching me write should give me strength, not sap it. Even if we don't know to what extent we are in control, pragmatically speaking, it behooves us to act as if we did.

That's what Rorty told us, anyhow[2].

As for the talking and the questions? I remember that golden rule of human interaction: people give what they want to receive. Should I not then ask silly and personal questions to everyone I meet? This is the Kingdom of Heaven on Earth, the meditative consciousness in everyday life. Instead of seeking thoughtlessness, I can drill into focus, focus my attention and love on whoever is talking at me, regardless of dialect or comprehension.

This morning, under the sun and the monkeys in the banyan tree, a fat man interrupted my meditation to ask me harshly -

"Who are you? What's your deal? Are you alone?"

. I tried to be cool, to explain briefly, to gather my wits. It was like being shaken out of bed.

"Have you eaten yet?"

I know he cares. Yes, I have eaten. Thank you.

"What is written on this paper?"

He reaches for the scrap of paper folded in my pocket. My peace and tone snap, together, angrily –

"Why all the questions?"

Why can't I have a measly piece of paper in my pocket without it becoming a village issue? Am I really public property? Are those the terms?

But biting back really turns people off. The man physically backed up a few steps. I felt bad and began to question him: "What's your name, what do you do?" He said he was a buffalo herder, but he had

---

[2]In a class at Stanford entitled "From Religion through Philosophy to Literature". See his *Contingency, Irony, Solidarity* for more.

only two buffalo. Two isn't very many buffalo, I was still mad, and I wanted to tease him, "I know men with more wives than you have buffalo, *fatty*."

But actually, I didn't *really* want to tease him, the grammar would have been too hard, and that's not why I'm here anyways, now is it?

I'm walking a dangerous line and am trying to stay aware. I am the blessed recipient of so much love and so many good deeds, straight from *Krishna*. When I wonder where I will stay, a man rides by and offers me his house, before I can even check the name of the village I'm headed towards. Why? It's their *dharma*, just like walking is my *dharma*. We're on the *dharma*, together. And I know, I just know, that if I get off the *dharma*, I lose everything. All I have to do is follow the rules, to be devoted to the truth. So far, so good. I have the sense if a drop of *daru* or chicken passes my lips, or I lie or want to use someone for sex or insult someone or give in to my darkness I will be struck down with a thunderbolt. A literal thunderbolt from beyond. And that's an experience I can do without, the fall from this high holy precipice to which I have wandered.

At Kankapura, I reach the frontier. The road leads to Bharatbhai's house and no further. Tomorrow there is a river to cross (I have no idea how). I am given *chai* and water at Bharatbhai's house and told to bathe. I obey. I shower in a large, musty, bathroom in a large, musty house. It is bare concrete, either new or unfinished, and nobody seems to mind. Bharatbhai tells me, "All we have here is love!"

An astrologer arrives for a consultation and I climb onto the roof in my *dhoti* for evening meditations and prayers. The cows are golden in the sunset and it's almost dark when I come down.

We sit talking with Bharatbhai in a chair and his wife on the ground. It's progress – most of the women have been hidden thus far. He has a daughter who even smiles occasionally, though Bharatbhai does not. He is not friendly and open and welcoming like he was on the road. Something has happened. I piece it together from fragments in conversation: He is worried about his daughter's marriage, the astrologer upset him, and now he needs to go to the temple.

First, one of Bharatbhai's friends comes over and we walk together, the three of us, through bare arid canyon-side to the bluffs overlooking the river. The land is dry and cracked, with small thorny shrubs for decoration. I learn about my new friends: Bharatbhai teaches primary school and *Maharaj* labors on a farm. Bharatbhai seems very devoted, and is kind with his wife. *Maharaj* is jovial from the start and only as the evening wears on can I feel the weight of his sadness.

The river is very large. The Mahisagar. In the pink twilight, I cannot see across it. Could it be two miles? For the original Dandi *yatra* there was a raft to take the *yatris* across the long delta of the Mahisagar. For me there is no such effort. My new friends think I should go around. The river is very large. We stare at it through the twilight dark.

'Around,' Bharat and *Maharaj* explain, means at least 15 kilometers back inland to the bridge, crossing the bridge, and coming those 15 kilometers back West to the coast, to my next stop, Kareli. It's longer than a hot day's walk on foot, so Bharatbhai suggests I take a jeep.

Another one of those moments when I feel nobody really understands the parameters of what I'm doing. No, I can't have a glass of whiskey. No, I can't stay an extra night. No, I can't travel in a vehicle, and I don't even have money to hire one if I could. Thank you.

We stand at the banks of Mother Mahisagar and lose our discussion in the darkness. I have faith in their knowledge, yet I cannot break my rules. They want to help me and are more concerned about my safety than I have ever learned to be. I just want to know when the tide will be low, so I can cross the delta on my own. They don't know or won't tell me. *They* would never do such a thing, so I shouldn't either. Never mind that *they* never would have come all the way here to begin with, never would have walked through the villages to be welcomed into their own homes by people as generous as they are.

I ask about the fisherman – shouldn't there be fisherman who live near the river? Bharatbhai tells me they won't help me without money: that's how they are. What do I know? I remember on my last family visit to India, two years ago, walking barefoot across the street. My mother, shocked and distressed, told me that "nobody does that, nobody walks without shoes".

Millions upon millions of nobody walk the streets and fields of India without shoes. Maybe millions of fisherman would help me without money?

Maharaj and I walk back to Bharatbhai's house, while he goes on to the temple. At home we find, his absence notwithstanding, a sort of party in progress. An old bearded man and an excited schoolteacher stand in animated conversation. Assorted relatives persist. The nerdy older teacher is on a rampage, assaulting me with phrases in Hindi and English. At one point he recites the entire preamble to the U.S. Constitution in rapid-fire Indian English, wagging his finger in front of my face. I refuse to hit him and push the finger away.

> We the people of the United States, in order to form a more perfect union, establish justice, insure domestic tranquility, provide for the common defense, promote the general welfare, and secure the blessings of liberty to ourselves and our posterity, do ordain and establish this Constitution for the United States of America.

Maharaj claims to be a musician, to sing and to play flute and *tabla* and *harmonium*. In the end he does none of these things but asks me to take him with me to the United States. He's not interested in farming anymore. I recognize his sadness as desire and inform him, gently, that I'm on the outs with government, I work on a farm myself, and I can't get him either kind of visa card.

The women bring the bearded old man and me inside the concrete bunker to serve us dinner under glaring lights. I want to wait for Bharatbhai, still at the temple, but am not allowed. We eat obscene quantities of *kitcheree*, a spicy red potato *shak*, and a carrot salad.

Salad.

The carrot salad, despite its name, is quite cooked. Apparently, if we are to engage in preferences, we must specify them explicitly. I am given a tall glass of buffalo milk to drink with the *kitcheree*, to my chagrin.

Bharatbhai arrives as I prepare to sleep. He looks tired and we talk about the Mahisagar with futility. It is decided through ignorance and apathy that I am on my own, to my relief. That is, five hours into the game, I have overshot my welcome. Such is the nature of Indian hospitality – they want to take care of everything, manage everything, control everything, solve everything. And when they can't it's because they've tried everything they never should have worried about in the first place, and have failed in the magical role of the host. At which point you have to get along as friends, which is what I've been going for all along. I ask *Krishna* for some people who will just let me be.

An occupational hazard, perhaps: one of the risks of traveling with nothing but a toothbrush and a few cosmic trading cards.

Day 9

March 20, 2006

"A non-violent man can do nothing save
by the power and grace of God. Without
it he won't have the courage to die without
anger, without fear, and without
retaliation."

9.1 across the Mahisagar

A dream.

> The pilgrim reaches New York City in a tattered white *dhoti* and frisbee shirt, long hair, clean shaven, and accepting eyes. He takes the subway, uptown on the Lexington Avenue local, and a misty New York Woman sits across from him and then next to him. Broadway-Lafayette. The car rattles the entire dream, even during the stops. She flings the hair away from her face with dr(e)amatic flair. One asks the Other – the scripts are muddled – "are you celibate?". The other explains through the rumbles and screeches of Union Square, that life is not object but relation, that relation evolves through a spiral. The background of the subway car changes from red and blue ads of black people holding cheap beer to a dynamic tapestry of shimmering helices. No one on the car of any color looks up. 33rd Street. One guides the Other through relations' climbing path from friendship to lovership to divinity. The flat view knows only a celibate binary. 48th Street. What is next?

A breakfast of garlic, *triphala*, *haldi*, and *saunf* from my *ayurvedic* medical kit. I need almost everything I have. I awake naturally at four, heeding the river before the alarm. A short yoga and reiki session help ward off the approaching sickness. I know it's coming. Too much *chai*. Too much food. Morning prayers, meditations, and movement.

At six Bharatbhai wakes up and I bid him goodbye (literally, 'come again'). I hit the road with total faith, pure positivity, openess to all options, and no goddamn clue where I am going. I have to cross the river. I am not a strong swimmer. There was no bridge last night. Maybe the morning will be different. I walk through the town with a vaguest sense of direction. I walk by a man brushing his teeth with a short stick.

"Walking?"

Yes.

"Mahisagar?"

Yes.

"You go to Dehavar – they will know."

Okay.

A land of angels awaits me. How could he know?

I walk to the next town, perhaps two kilometers back the way I came. Last night everyone could only say how difficult it would be and how it couldn't be done. Part of the Indian 'I will take care of everything for you' culture is that if they can't take care of it, they are sure it cannot be done.

Something to watch out for.

Dehavar is a small sleeping village, and I enter, following the sole flagstone path to its end. The path meets a fence. I jump it and head through fields and canyons, past the rotting carcass of a buffalo to the edge of a bluff, one hundred feet over the riverbank. I make it to the river: Now what?

It is huge beyond my twilit reckoning. Huge. Wide. It looks both low and in motion – I can see both a lot of bottom and a lot of water. It's really quite big. I don't see another bank and nothing but faiths leads me to believe in its existence.

I wait.

For once there are no humans.

Below and to the left, perhaps a kilometer away, there is the temple to *Mataji* that Bharatbhai spoke of. A large grey stone building built into the cliff-side. It must be underwater for half the day and, during the months of the monsoon season, all the time. I walk eastwards and see a house in the distance, further east across the canyon. I must re-cross the canyon, walking carefully up the far slope. The spikes from the *babul* tree pierce my worn Brazilian sandals every time I break concentration. They give me no room to worry.

Within twenty minutes I make it out of the canyon scrub and come to a house. The sun is well-risen and an old woman is working, carrying a bucket of earth on her head. I greet her with reverence, hyper-conscious of my predicament.

Namaste. Is there a man around?

It just takes a week to learn to treat only men as people.

"You want to cross the Mahisagar?"

I can only nod.

"Come with me."

Thank God.

She throws her load of dirt to the ground and leads me through thickets of dry trees to the village. She is as old as her dirt: dark, small, and frail. She has sent herself to help me. We walk quickly past men squatting and brushing their teeth. She answers their unvoiced questions with an economy of words. She takes me past a small village center to a trail, steeply descending south to – presumably – the temple.

"You go down."

Okay, thanks. I have been instructed to pray.

I go down, down to the huge stone temple, and take *darshan*. Reverently, carefully, sincerely. I am conscious that my fate lies not in my hands but in theirs – the river, the tides, the moon, the fishermen. I need their help, they are my gods. The resident *saddhu* is nowhere to be seen. Who will be intercede on my behalf? Where have the holy men gone? How many rivers are there left to cross?[1]

I wander to the sandy floodplain, slowly, confused and shaken by my lack of fortune. There is sand and stream and dark grey mud and a tentacled ground cover everywhere. I don't know whether I can cross, or whether I should. I can feel the tide coming back in. I've never had to go backwards before.

I see a figure in the distance before I can attempt a decision or begin to think. I don't even know where my glasses are. It's either a man carrying a javelin or a horse. It moves north, leaves the mud and reaches an island of sand. I shout "brother!" and run towards my only hope. I do not want it to get away. I'm up to my knees in mud and am running so fast I have no idea where my next step will be. But I get there, to him, sandals in hand and white *dhoti* caked with grey mud. It's a boy or a man – I can never tell – carrying a long bamboo pole, each end weighted with a net full of fish. Not a horse.

I tell him my plight, slowly, reverently, praying my language skills pull through. I know I must look crazed.

He understands.

"No tension. There's a line of footsteps through the mud.
Follow them through to the other side."

---

[1]See the Jimmy Cliff movie *The Harder They Come*

He has just crossed the river. It can still be done. He thinks I can do it too.

Will you show me where they start?

"Yes, of course."

We walk to the edge of the mud-bank. He lays down his gear and I store my sandals, shawl, and *dhoti* in my backpack. The sun is already strong. We climb down the bank and he sets me on the path. He points to the footsteps. I walk. Walking on water is not like walking on land. No matter, I keep walking.

I turn to thank him but we have disappeared from each other. His trail goes in and out of mud, sand, and water. The ground beneath the water is slippery and difficult to find: slow going. I hallucinate whatever sound signifies the tide coming in. I can see neither river nor solid ground on any side. I hear intermittent shouts and calls from the village behind me, the day's work getting started. At one point I stop and look west towards the ocean, towards America, towards home. Am I ready to become this river? Am I that wise?

If I come to a point I cannot cross, it is likely that I will neither be able to go backwards. If I retreat upstream, I will only encounter more water. At that point the only options would be to ...

A nervous laugh and I keep going, make it down to what might be the middle of the Mahisagar. As if I have any idea. I walk across the sandy bottom of the ocean, conveniently adjourned, for the better part of an hour. As I get back to muddier pastures I can hear shouts behind me. I ignore them for a few minutes – I have to beat the tide – before realizing they are for me.

The fisherboy has come back with a friend. They tell me it will be too deep, that I've already missed my chance. It's too deep now.

"What happens if you get lost in the river? You will drink water and then what? Then what? We must take you across. You have no choice but to let us take you across."

Okay. I humbly and politely accept, to the best of my ability. I am ignorant and perhaps incapable of demonstrating my thanks. The thank-you posture seems grossly insufficient.

Why did they come back?

We walk quickly. They explain it will soon be too deep even for the boat with its fifteen foot pole. We reach a spongier zone and cross it to a small boat moored ten feet outside of the solid. He bails it out while I unmoor it, and my savior grabs a long pole to push us off. In half an hour, he's pushed me to the other side and turns the boat around. I have to cross a few hundred meters of river shallows to reach the land. He points to a colony of feeding herons by way of goodbye.

"There will be many fish there."

I get out and say goodbye ('I'm coming'), walk through the quicksand a few steps, and fall. I continue walking with no idea of the soundings or surety of the sand, changing direction whimsically to avoid sinkholes in the river of brown. I remember Denali walking to the end of the world. Closer to the bank it's clearer and the impressions of the waves are mesmerizing. I don't let myself think about the river.

Eventually I make it to the other side and lay down my pack. I bathe, wash my clothes, and hang them to dry on a jagged *sou-babul* bush (even here). It's quiet, natural, and hot. This is where Gandhi's group apparently had lunch. There's no trace, thankfully. I watch the ocean return. Soon there is no trace of me, either: my mud, footsteps, passing, and arrogance are all swept out to see. Those kids saved my life. I still don't understand. Fish jump everywhere. It's so vast out there: no wonder rivers are considered gods. They can kill you. Perhaps a god is anything that can kill you.

9.2   to Kareli

Almost out of water and I've no idea where Kareli is, but I'll get there. It can't be across another river.

Bharatbhai told me that Kareli was full of bad people. During last year's mammoth memorial excursion, somebody's cell phone was stolen there. Back to property and theft. Or what it means to own a cell phone when millions can't afford rice. Not that they could eat the cell phone either. But were I to indulge my time in complaining about injustice, stolen luxuries might be pretty low on the list[2].

So far, Bharatbhai has been wrong. About the river, the fishermen, and Kareli. Less than two kilometers of walking from my beachhead, I see a man walking towards me, down the sandy path, with a radio in hand. I had passed one house – empty – and had begun to see beautiful fields of millet, wheat, and onions. Smiling men with radios make for good conversation, so I stop to chat. Before I could ask for water – that which I permit myself – he asks if I would come to his farm. Certainly. So he turns around and we walk together a few hundred meters more, until reaching a little turnoff through the sand. We leave the road and join the path, walk towards the river, around a line of trees and into his *sasro's* house.

The farmhouse includes one room built out of reeds, a large covered area to its side, a high grass bed, and a well-shaded fire pit. The roof is palm fronds and the floor is dirt; There's no concrete to be seen. It turns out Gulab, the *sasro*, is a veritable rockstar: in less than fifteen minutes we are set for life. Father and son are both into *Bhagawan* – they have a very happy-go-lucky conception of the divine – and Gandhiji, and have good memories from last year's march. They are the happiest, most relaxed, easy-going, under-bearing Indian people I have ever encountered. Just what I asked for. Gulab has a *guru* somewhere who preaches the virtues of *seva*, so apparently it's his personal mission to be hospitable to random people and not just family in the typical inside\outside way.

Real progress and the way forward for all of us, I know.

We drink lots of water and a hidden woman prepares me thick country rotlas and *shak*, the first food I had eaten all day. After we drink the unavoidable *chai* Gulab smokes a *bidi* and goes to pick some dry orange leaves from the field.

---

[2]The author's laptop was stolen during the editing process. He got over it.

"*Nasila.*"

Tobacco, apparently. I've been talking about tobacco recently, with various farmers around Ras, but these leaves look a little different to me. And isn't tobacco dried, fermented, and roasted before smoking anyhow? Father and son grind it up in a mortar and pestle and try to explain –

"You know, *nasila. Tamaco. Ganja.*"

Ganja! And they don't mean the river. I spend the next hour watching them smoke the *chillum* and listening to them talking about meditation and seeing God. The *ganja* is apparently pretty common for them and might be for me on another sort of pilgrimage. Instead I content myself with sharing recipes for infused oils and vinegars they might want to investigate. Pretty soon it's time for a dip in the river.

We walk through Gulab's ten *viga* of crops – onions, wheat, millet, and garlic – to my old friend the Mahisagar. They know I crossed it this morning but I can't explain any of the details. The fear. The proximity of death. We dive in with some of his naked children (there are five), swim and soap and laugh in the current and on the bank. There's no reason to leave.

In the afternoon I must dress for the typical cultural theater. My friends in Kankapura told me they would call the *sarpanch* of Kareli to advertise my arrival. Whenever someone says *sarpanch*, they signal the power and importance of the job with a balled fist in the air. *Sarpanch*! Almost as if they are punching the air . . .

Summer is here. Everyday gets hotter and hotter. Gulab and I walk the three searing kilometers to Kareli proper, where he has a typical concrete house with none of the paradisiacal joy of his farm shanty.

Luckily, the mayor is 'out of station' so Gulab and I are free to wander around, to drink *chai* and water at our leisure. An old man listens to my story and treats me with simple respect. I am reminded how rare and uncomfortable all of this is, how little I deserve it, how maybe I could never deserve it, how the only things left to me are giving thanks and begging for water.

There is something scarier about the reverence in his face than the rising of that river.

Everyone we meet talks about how important *seva* is, how great Gulab is, and how the road through town is in such a terrible state. It starts where I found it untangling from the wilderness along the river bank, and runs to Kareli and south towards my future. They call it 'Gandhi Road' which is cute; Gulab says if there's one thing I can do for him, it's fix the road. I look down. It's a normal dirt road, like most others I've walked. Because it's not paved or wide, cars do not pass. I like it. But I owe these people everything, so if I ever meet somebody who wants to build five kilometers of road for the Indian peasantry, I can tell her where to go.

Gulab runs an errand while I investigate the *khadi ashram* at the edge of town. During the heyday of the *khadi* movement, many towns had their own village-industry centers to weave their own clothing. Now it stands in disrepair, while the farmers send their cotton away to the big mills. *Swadeshi?* I sit under the *vad* tree and have a great meditation. I open my eyes to play frisbee with the kids for a while and then sit to practice the flute. It feels ridiculous to maintain my practices under strict observation, but I keep trying. The kids want me to see Laxmansahib, a teacher, when Gulab shows up. For a moment I'm not sure what to do. He prods me towards his house to drink lemon sherbert and I remember that it was never up to me. There's a big crowd there to make small talk, and I am suddenly very hungry and thirsty and tired and crowded.

I am not able to tell if people are actually excited to meet me and talk to me – like the old man in the street – or just excited to have something to do, to be attached to something they think is famous. What a mess it must have been last year, with the whole political machinery of the Congress Party, by virtue of its existence so far adrift from Gandhi's ideas, giving speeches and buying votes. Film stars and sound systems and *peons* and sycophants. I bet *they* weren't eating on the ground.

It's been over a week in India, I didn't die before lunch, and now I hunger for food and space. I need fruits and vegetables. Gulab has something to do and lets me walk the forty minutes home alone. Thank you *Krishna*. The sun is a black jaguar, fierce and relentless.

Along the way, thirty women pop out of nowhere, excited as gopis for *Kanaiya* at my mission. They are all ages and sizes, have long dark braided hair, and want me to stay with them. Hell, I want to stay with them. I had even been asking *Krishna* for more female interaction but now I feel I can't connect with anyone until I get back and eat. A man shows up -

"What's the deal?" (with accompanying hand gesture)

A woman answers, "We need to take care of this pilgrim."

"What's it to us?"

Which, I think even he would agree, was the wrong answer. They turn to at yell him, vicious and concerted as a pack of wild animals. I enjoy both the display of power and the distraction it affords. They allow me to beg off until tomorrow and I head back to Gulab's farmhouse sanctuary.

I pass the afternoon swimming, eating, and fluting with his five kids: Hetal, Raju, Dilip, Suraj, and Toral. It's familial and soft and pretty. We touch each other and smile enough that I don't feel the need to be alone. We eat lots of green mango salsa and have a fresh bean *shak* instead of potato. Ask *Krishna* and you shall receive. It's a beautiful life, a bountiful life. After dinner the whole family sits in *vajrasana* with me and we talk about the importance of eating properly and giving proper thanks to everyone involved.

I am talking and laughing with mom, mom and dad are talking and laughing with each other, and all the kids are happy. I walk back to the riverbank to watch the sunset and to write. I'll play with the kids some more and then meditate before sleeping. I will sleep on the grass bed outside and the seven of them will sleep on the mats inside. That's how they want it.

Day 10

March 21, 2006

"I do not conceive the average individual's soul force as distinguished and existing apart from the political form of government. In other words, self-government can only come through self-effort."

10.1   to Gajera

Notes from meditating under a banyan tree.

1. Gandhiji is god. *Ahimsa* is love. Pure Jesus *Bhagawan.* Amazing.

2. People stare. Trial of your stillness.

3. The *panchayat* is a means, no expectation of the end.

Now, after lunch.

Indian families are so beautiful. Maybe it's just families in general. He wants his daughter to be educated and she doesn't seem to want anything. Or anything she'll tell me about, at least. I'm with Sureshbhai now, after one of the best lunches I've had the fortune to enjoy:

> raw *keri athanu*
> *mori mirchi shak*
> *bataka shak*
> *dungri shak*
> (that's three vegetable curries with no vegetables, mind you)
> something between *chass* and *curdy*
> *kitcheree*
> *shiro*

The girl reminds me of my cousin Nipa, reminds me that I am already family here, that whether or not anybody in this room cares about Gandhi we still share the same blood and skin and hair and noses. Which is new, relatively.

I walked here through wheat and cotton – mainly cotton – by 9h45 in the morning. I passed the post office with a tinge of desire – there's so little so far that I've wanted to buy, but stamps really hit the spot – and found the *panchayat.* Closed. A boy led me through town to a temple where I prayed for a few minutes, then meditated under a mango tree. I walked around the *talav* and through the town, small but bustling by eleven in the morning, and back to the *panchayat.* The notion of a town lake, a town grove of mangos, a town grove of banyan trees, strikes me as so civilized, so refined. Peaceful and communal and advanced. High technology.

The *sarpanch* (a takkor) was in the office and sent his servant to get us *chai* and *kaman*. I drank four glasses of water before the *sarpanch* tired of me, and sent me with Sombhai (his *peon*) to the giant banyan tree where Gandhi gave his speech. Everytime I meet the fist-in-the-air they ask me what they can do for me and all I can really think of is to see the place where Gandhi gave his speech. Most of them aren't too interested in anything but the media side (if I show them the news article, my Golden Passport) but I wonder if some future, more constructive pilgrim could get them to do something for the village – build more latrines or start co-operatives or treat their *peons* kindly.

Sombhai took me to the plaque where I sat in meditation and eventually drew a crowd. Gandhiji was here, drawing a different sort of crowd, seventy-six years ago today.

Yesterday, Gulab's kids sang for me, immortalizing Gandhiji alongside Vishnu's two most famous avatars:

> Sri Ram had Sitaji,
> Sri *Krishna* had Radha,
> *Bapuji* had Kasturba,

> Ram killed Ravana
> *Krishna* killed Narkasura
> Gandhi killed the British

So beautiful and appropriate to today's conversation – how everyone has forgotten Gandhian philosophy, that ethereal Truth to which he was pointing. They only remember his face from bird-shat statues and, of course, the money. The fact that Gandhi's face adorns not one but *all* the bills never ceases to amaze me. A perfect irony. Many people here in Gajera don't know even what the *namak satyagraha* was, along its very path. And here I am fantasizing about giving away Gandhian books in Palestine. Let's start with Gujarat – no translation necessary.

A man exploded today about how the march last year, to commemorate the 75th anniversary of the Salt March, was a sham. They spent 850 million *points* of public funds, drank bottled water all along the way, and made the pilgrimage in limousines and jeeps. He vented for twenty minutes and still looked feverish. Obviously, it was a political show that had nothing to do with Gandhi behind the marketing and kickbacks.

So? Here I am, tired and hot and still glowing, having walked ten days to get here. Why complain to me about how cheap and lazy and crooked the Indian people are?

I see and do this all the time – on this pilgrimage and on the travels that led me here. We are so ready to dismiss our culture and compatriots, our brothers and sisters, as stupid, cowardly, wasteful, and selfish. And the conclusion always rationalizes an injust reality:

> "And that's why the American political system is so messed up."
> "And that's why India is such a poor country."
> "And that's why the occupation must be."

Why? What's really going on? I have limited language proficiency wherever I am and I certainly don't know this *Krishna's* past but it seems the more unhappy someone is with the situation she sees, the more she feels she should be doing something more. And the more she feels she's not doing enough, the more harshly she looks at everybody else's actions. And the more negatively she sees the actions of others, the more depressed she gets in general. Which depression, I think, does not help anybody Do the Right Thing[1].

Incense overcame humility and I gave a short speech on positivity and the importance of setting an example *for ourselves*, how the vices and virtues we see around us are reflections of our own process. Discussion calmed into staring and the grove taught us the virtues of stillness:

1. People only stare if you pay attention to them staring.

2. The more intently your focus on your Thing – whatever it may be – the less people will stare. They will join you or leave.

I have a hard time concentrating on the Truth because of all the conversation. Solitude is the ultimate luxury on this *yatra*. My balance has been out of whack for a couple of days now and I can feel and fear the writing getting thin, the meditations shorter. I must learn to see chatter as elegy, walking as meditation.

---

[1]You've seen the Spike Lee movie, I trust.

When I opened my eyes Sureshbhai kindly approached and asked me to come to his house for lunch. It was 13h00 and I was hungry, though not yet afraid. I accepted, took a cold shower in the dungeons of his *bungalow*, and sat with the family for lunch.

Now Komal, Sureshbhai's daughter, speaks up and asks again what I'm doing here. I tell her what little I know. I am trying to study the philosophy of Gandhiji, and since his philosophy was lived and walked, I am trying to live it and walk it. She tells me Gandhi was okay and everything – a national hero, father of the country – but his ideas were dead wrong.

> "He put Hindus and Muslims together and now the Muslims all get together and kill us."

Well. Do I tell her about Godhra?[2] What do you say to a child? What does a child say to a child? Is it my role to correct her? To defend the dead? Or just to be a good student, to love her, to accept all these sweets and gifts and smiles without letting them exhaust me?

I tell her that it was a Hindu who killed Gandhi and a Sikh who killed Indira. She had thought the assassins were both British. I tell her the Gujarati word for glass ('galas') comes from English. She doesn't believe me. We all lie down for the *siesta* and the mind drifts back to the morning ...

The sunrise is long and orange as I walk through Kareli. I awoke late, bathed in the river, and abbreviated my yoga. I walk with the kids to school until Banaben – the head of the women I met the day before – stops me to take *chai* at her house. She offers me a second when I finish and – unprecedented – I accept, hoping I can convince the matron to walk with me. She is strong fire and if any woman could do that to her husband – serve him his lunch late, I mean – it is Banaben.

No luck, though, and I keep walking, pass the town, and meet some laborers on the road. They tell me they make 40 *points* a day picking cotton, 50 doing farmwork, and 60 building roads. They are building roads, and we smiled at their fortune.

---

[2] See the Human Rights Watch report at
http://www.hrw.org/legacy/reports/2002/india/

60 *points* is more than a US dollar.

One and a half kilometers of reddish cotton fields out of Kareli, Gulabsinh catches up to me with a cool 100-point note for the road. *Bapuji's* blue face looks up at me from Gulabsinh's calloused brown hand. I speak the truth:

> "If I take this from you then I can ask from *Krishna* no
> longer.
> And *Krishna* gives me so much more than what 100 *points*
> could buy.
> So, selfishly, I have to say no."

My friend hugs me and rides his *cycle* home.

10.2   to Ankhi

15h30 and the sun is demonic. I've walked ten minutes and it's over,
I'm totally exhausted. An intense 40-degree heat descends from the
jaguar in the sky. A field of dry cotton soaks it up, and the sparse
trees provide sparse shade. I note a slight breeze and, somehow, a
headful of mucus, in this land of buffalo milk and cane sugar. At least,
overheated and exhausted, I am alone to meditate and play some scales
as the world cools.

Back in Gajera, the buzzing of the flies and the mind cut my *siesta*
short, and I asked Sureshbhai to show me out. He walked me to the
Gandhi *Mandir*, the official town remembrance of Gandhi. Sureshbhai clearly has a deep love and respect for Gandhi, like many men of
his generation, but with little deep knowledge of what the man was
about. There is some beauty there: admiration without the conceit of
understanding.

It's quite different of course, than the elders who dedicated decades
to experimenting with life along Gandhian lines. And different, also,
from the kids who have no idea his ideas are even to be respected.
With Sureshbhai's generation, at least the feeling perseveres.

The memorial sits in the *harijan* neighborhood: closed, disused,
and without demonstration of respect. Nobody paying homage or selling peace. Instead of playing this flute I could be cleaning these holy
places. Why doesn't someone? Why don't I? Because I don't want to
preach, to intervene, to get involved: I'm just walking by.

Sureshbhai gave me two road options as we stood in the scalding
sun – the long and the short – and somehow I chose the long one. I
think I didn't quite understand, and I couldn't figure out which was
the original road.

Future pilgrims beware: take the short road.

At five I leave my resting spot at the cotton's edge, and begin again.
The small road quickly turns westward into The Big Road – the cotton
fields harden into ceramic, brick, and glass factories, all flattening into
a large black commercial highway. From agriculture to industry to
commerce. The highway is full of trucks, exhaust, the collected rumble
and heat of the day. Nobody stops or talks or ask you anything. It's

just like home. The spectacle.

I am lucky I know about progress. After living everywhere comes enjoying everything, with enjoying everything comes missing everything else that you've enjoyed, and sometime after that must come this delicate acceptance, this balance of relish and *saudade*. I know it's out there and today on the American road I am ready; I don't want people to ask my name or *caste* or what my deal is. I want them to whiz by and pelt me with rocks and a hot breeze of exhaust as they do.

That is: it's cool both ways.

After a few kilometers on the royal highway I turn South again to a scraggly path through grass and trees. I meet a man at the crossroads, Ashok, who gives me water and good directions – a pilgrim's only true loves. We walk together a spell towards Ankhi, the next town. The path wanders in and out of delightful mango groves rich with young fruit and then, finally, into the town.

In today's walking, along sandy paths and national highways, I find finally the groove of walking as meditation, not just endless hours to think in circles.

I leave my reverie only when I cross the threshold of a new town, Ankhi. Normally I rest a few minutes outside the gates, to give myself time to adjust from the solitude of the road to the density of population, from my internal language to the local dialect, from the self comfort I am developing to having to prove myself time and again. But today I forget, or am hurried by the coming dusk. Today I do not prepare.

The town opens. A gang of kids take me to the mayor's house (she is not home) and then to the *panchayat* office (closed) where I stand outside in the plaza feeling late and weak and silly. I don't always want to meet the mayor, you know. I like random humans not affiliated with the power structure. Nobody appears. What if you threw a pilgrimage and nobody came? In times of doubt, I wondering again what exactly I am supposed to be doing here.

Tired and frazzled, I fend off questions rather than embrace them. They are the same questions. Yes, I am walking alone. My language and loving-kindness skills are sub-par in the twilight and I begin to worry. There's a critical moment when you first enter a new community when the pendulum is in the air as to whether you're holy or profane, an honored guest or a corrupter of the youth. I don't want to end up like Socrates, not yet.

My command of Gujarati has gotten good enough that they think I am an uneducated lout rather than a foreigner, and when they ask me if I have been to school I snap into pride and arrogance: "Of course I've been to school! Hell, I went to a university! In *America*!"

It's kind of violent. Hospitality by gunpoint is not usually my style and I should have just walked out if they were welcoming degreed pilgrims only, but instead I show them the Golden Passport and everything calms down.

They could read in perfect newspaper Gujarati how strange and exceptional I am – I still have no idea what the article says – and all of a sudden they fetch me hot water and a mattress and everything is set up to sleep in the mayor's office, to write away the evening at a big desk under a big *tubelight* and portrait of a powerful man.

My newly eager hosts leave in a hurry, leaving me to wash my hands, feet, and clothes before going to the *sarpanch's* house for dinner. It is a large old concrete affair with stylish tile inside and a painted wooden swing. Swings are very important in Gujarati culture. The mayor is actually a woman, a beautiful woman with Arabian features, yet it was her husband, back in the office, who took control. Division of labor? She had cooked or overseen or perhaps had nothing to do with the feast of a dinner – okra *shak*, potato-eggplant *shak*, *athanu*, *mirchi*, great *dal*, *bath*, *ladoo*, and *jalebi*. Everything so good and rich and I would have been happy with the peasant's serving of just *dal* and *bath*. I must remember to ask *Krishna* for some green vegetables.

They talk a little bit about last year's march and how so many people participated for political reasons. More media filming than walking, etc. Nobody seemed to mention that in the first towns, but it's been a major theme since crossing the Mahisagar. Both mayor and husband (or mayor and wife, if you will) understand I have a totally different agenda, though I sense they approve more of the former. They both regard me somewhat coldly. I notice that though she doesn't exactly eat with us, the rightful mayor starts eating before we finish. Small steps towards liberation.

I return to my home-office, no longer surprised at how everything works out. We must be a careful Midas, of course. Earlier today, as requested, I walked with a woman for a few minutes. No words and no fears. Just walking in step, for a time. I have meditated under mango and banyan trees, as per my dreams. I even walked along railroad tracks, as imagined. After three nights in the houses of good people I need the expanse and privacy of an *ashram* and tonight I'm staying alone in the *sarpanch's* (fist!) office. The fulfillment is so exact and immediate – so harmonious – that I wonder whether those desires were ever mine to begin with it. Can we end our suffering, merely by learning to desire in the name of the universe instead of our own, by desiring what the universe desires, and thus save everybody some work?

Day 11

March 22, 2006

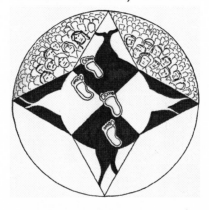

"You cannot divide social, economic, political, and purely religious work. I do not know any religion apart from human activity."

11.1   to Jambusar

I wake up to something different. Like the thread that has carried me so far is losing me, or fraying, somehow. Last night, though a needed solitude, was the most makeshift and least welcoming place I've stayed: there were no people.

Today I am late and have a runny nose. My morning yoga is interrupted in *shivasana* by Prakash Ambalal, the mayor's husband, who barges in announcing, "that's it, time for shower". They brusquely and briskly provide me with hot water, to take my first warm shower in recent memory, enjoying but not relishing it. The mayor gives me *chai* in their living room while they watch TV. The husband walks me – after initial threats of a motorcycle – fifty meters outside town to the Gandhi memorial room, where I should have stayed, had it been properly equipped. I found it dirty and cobwebbed, in fitting disarray. They would not let me clean it – that other oppression of servitude – for the guest is not allowed to work. I am left to meditate alone with the buffalo under a grand cathedral of a *vad* for a few minutes before finding the road.

I walk out of town through an impressive *ambavadi*, heavy with luscious young fruit, on a path specifically bulldozed for last year's Dandi *yatra*. I can see why the people in this area are so concerned with the march being a sham; The government never comes to town, and when it finally does, bulldozing a path for its own publicity stunt is the extent of the public works. I follow a narrow irrigation canal for an hour or so until coming to a major road. My mom calls, we chat briefly, and she gives me tips on surviving (beating is unimaginable) the heat:

> shredded green mango with onion
> lime juice with salt and sugar
> a hat

At this point the pilgrim has three choices for the last half hour to Jambusar – along the highway (past the gas station, et al.), the railroad track (Tolstoy and Flaubert exchange a glance), and through the farms (under the power lines and over the thorns). For the sake of research, I did all three. The railroad track seems most rhythmic and appropriate to the dry morning heat, stretching inexorably in front of me. It is, however, occasionally in use.

Jambusar itself is loveable in that polluted third-world city sort of way. Walking through the enviable progress of its suburban outskirts, I see service stations, pre-A\C office buildings, and appliance stores. And eventually, inexorably, I walk into the twisting maze of the old city. Of course the *panchayat* is closed until 11h00 and I'm not clear why I even try going there in the first place – it's just what the old men say to do.

Well, if I had been listening to my elders all along I surely wouldn't have ended up walking penniless through India.

But India is India, and thickly so, and the old city is full of sensation. Temples and mosques and plastic sirens and frying oil and frying *buggia* and frying *jalebi* and cows and cows' dung and natural dyes and chemical dyes and huge sacks of rice and ginger and sugarcane and everything else India should and shouldn't be and is.

The people tell me where the tree was (it's usually still around) that Gandhi spoke under and I found it reliably accessible. They are building some sort of museum next to it but nobody has come to work today. So I'm free to sit between the plaque (Gandhi was here on March 22, 1930) and a *neem* tree, with only an old smoking man and his old smoking wife across the grounds.

Maybe they live here. Maybe they live nowhere. Maybe they are following Gandhi's footsteps back from Dandi.

It can hard sometimes, when you're lost in the passion and distress of the moment, to realize that everything is an expression of this rosier One. It's the walking that makes it clear. This morning, I felt I was physically walking not to Jambusar, but to the One Love. In walking I learn that everything is an expression of love – that very word contains more than my entire imagination. I think back to Ankhi: the *sarpanch* was so beautiful, her very coldness was beautiful – and though I may not have realized it right away, it still Is. So we are left nothing but to treat people accordingly – to treat others as if we understand that they are showering us with limitless affection and care.

I sit to meditate, navigating past imaginary catechisms, images of Thoreau, Gandhi, and Martin Luther King, to silence. I am silent, for a moment.

. . .

I open my eyes to the greeting approach of Abbas Hassan Haji Patel. AHHP is a Vohra Patel, meaning he used to be *brahmin* (250 years ago). He tells me the story:

> "At some point, many years ago, a Muslim Akbar from Vadodara came to power over this area. He gave the local *brahmins* a generous offer – I'll cut off your holy string or your head. A *brahmin's* string is his spiritual identity in material form: the ruler's message was 'Convert or Die'."

AHHP's family has been Muslim ever since, a family of dharmic cowards or the avant-garde of Hindu-Muslim unity, depending on your perspective.

The 'Haji' after Hassan means Abbas' father, Hassan, has completed his pilgrimage to Mecca. Abbas, who shares his father's dream, will one day (*enshallah*) then be Abbas Haji Hassan Haji Patel when he completes his own pilgrimage. AHHHP, that is.

For now, AHHP and I spend a few hours together, in answer of my prayer to connect with more Muslims. Thank you *Krishna* or Allah or whomever. AHHP wears a button-down shirt and pot belly, and has four brothers, all of whom are educated to the degree level, though his father is (only, he says) a primary school teacher. AHHP thanks God for this repeatedly. AHHP does everything repeatedly. AHHP is interested enough in my comprehension that he says everything three times, in Hindi. I don't understand Hindi very well, but AHHP is not tuned in enough to my comprehension to speak in Gujarati, his native language. More powerful than my protests is the notion that since I'm kind-of a foreigner, I should kind-of speak Hindi.

Like everything else, it evens out in the end. AHHP is a terrible listener, has five kids (the youngest a daughter), and is the construction supervisor for this site.

We are sitting in the soon-to-be Gandhiji *Swaraj Bhavan*, whose ground was broken a year ago (in concert with the big march) and should be finished in a couple of months. It will house a museum, library, and exhibition halls in an L-shaped building with concrete beams, designed to replicate the aesthetic of the traditional wooden beams of the time. The floors are *terra cotta* and the walls will be covered in a concrete plaster, colored and shaped to resemble a natural earthen plaster. It's called the 'mud look'. Outdoor reading pavilions and a concrete replica of Gandhi's hut await general admiration. An auditorium, performance space, and two podiums await long-winded speakers.

The workers left for *Holi* festivities, back to Rajasthan, some weeks ago. They aren't expected back until their household grain supply runs out. AHHP is very accepting of the situation: That's how the workers are, you know.

While we sit and talk I note the relative peace of this oasis in the city. Frenetic trucks rumble by and the perfume of burning trash still thrives, but the trees do wonders for peace. We wander over to a large banyan tree enshrined in a smooth concrete ring, which has already begun to crack.

AHHP tells me the land was donated by some forgotten uncle of mine, Bogilal Shah, who has a cotton jin next door and another one in Ahmedabad. I think of the decaying *Khadi Bhavan* in Kareli: Cotton grown in every field, processed in the industrial centers, and sold back to the villagers. Factories that make good returns for business and ease of access for consumers. A different idea of *swaraj*.

Two laborers come to speak of freedom and fashion. They ask about my look: a thin white cotton shirt my friend Chanoor has given me, my grandfather's *dhoti*, long hair pulled back and ten days of beard. No, it's neither Indian style nor their (1980's) conception of American style. It's the true style of freedom: In the untelevised American West, you can do what you want and wear what you want and nobody stares at you or asks you anything. Or cares. That's what I tell them at least, to make a point. I call it freedom and AHHP nods in solemn agreement,

"Very bad."

He starts in on the skanky clothing Americans wear (on TV) and their loose morality. Which may be true – stereotypes generally are – and gives me a chance to preach the connection between male desire and female style. In fact, my dear AHHP, the only way you know what these skanky foreigners are not wearing is by watching your beloved skanky TV channel. While, I assume, you only permit your wife to leave the house in a *salwar-kameez*? He nods in agreement. Isn't it silly to blame the women for obeying the pressure you are creating, when you prize obedience as a virtue?

He, thoughtfully, confirms my assumptions.

I turn to the laborers, who are still unimpressed with my attire (as it should be). How much are you paid?

"100 *points*, daily wage."

It's not a rude question here. Really. I get asked it every day. If AHHP paid you 1000 *points*, daily wage, to work with your shirt off, would you do it?

They shake their heads 'yes' without conferral. Everybody seems to get the point, and for the first time on this trip, and one of the first times in India, I feel I actually communicated something. They look at me expectantly and I can only laugh at the pressure.

We keep talking. AHHP is Muslim and thinks (knows?) God is One and Everywhere. He'll even take me to the mosque later. I'm not supposed to ask anyone for lunch but I give him That Look. No response. I'm unsure if that counts as breaking my rules or not. Again, I'm not so much hungry as afraid I will, at some point, get hungry. Which is often the case with humans.

I return to my meditation as AHHP wanders off. No matter. Any small suffering on my part adds to my respect for Gandhiji. I don't quite get the math, but it's what I'm told and I happily accept it.

11.2   to Amod

My ears open my eyes, below the banyan tree and above the concrete, to behold AHHP approaching with a small child and a *thali*. The child laborer unpacks my lunch: my first commercial meal of the trip. The lady politician in white comes back to my mind, hurrying to bescarf me with her party colors, warning me against eating in *hotels*. I apologize, sitting under Gandhiji's tree, quite surprised and content. I eat in peace. Too many *rotli*, too sweet *dal*, two potato curries, and rice. It feels great to be served, to be surprised.

Hafiz says we have a choice –

> You carry
> All the ingredients
> To turn your life into a nightmare-
> Don't mix them!

> You have all the genius
> To build a swing in your backyard
> For God.
> That sounds
> Like a hell of a lot moe fun.

> Let's start laughing, drawing blueprints,
> Gathering our talented friends.
> I will help you.
> With me divine lyre and drum.

> Hafiz
> Will sing a thousand words,
> You can take into your hands,
> Like golden saws,
> Sliver hammers,
> Polished teakwood,
> Strong silk rope.

> You carry all the ingredients
> To turn your existence into joy,
> Mix them
> Mix them!

It's the first time I'm not eating from someone's kitchen, but if the chef didn't love me then the messenger did[1]. Somewhere along the line, everybody wins. Or, more precisely, is my happiness constrained by the logical "and" or relaxed by the logical "or"?

Can something be my everything?

I move through the food to an afternoon full of meditation and *Krishna bhakti*. *Sans* conversation. Just me and the banyan tree in various poses of meditation, relaxation, and *mantra*. I can feel myself getting somewhere with meditation as I relax into it. We have been getting more complete together. Focusing on the heart and breath combo, keeping Mukeshananda from Nadiad present and alive inside me. I am beginning to understand what it is to remember someone, to carry them with you, to be present within absence.

It's 16h00, AHHP still hasn't come back, and the weather is cool enough to head for Amod. I want to wait and go to the mosque with him – I feel it might be my only chance – but I must continue the walk.

I stop to get directions and confirm what an old man had told me this morning: that from the main highway, Amod lay in direction and Jambusar in the other. Which means I need to backtrack a couple of kilometers to get to the next town. It's a strange way to lay out a pilgrimage. I wonder immediately if I've done something wrong. Paranoia.

I walk back to the highway through a crowded Jambusar, get a good liter of chlorinated water from a local mechanic, admit to being on television, and roll out of town. By 16h30 I'm back to the same gas station and have another ten kilometers to Amod. The fast walking is hard on the mind and feet. I'm hurried and anxious to arrive before dark, though I can't say why. Maybe smiles don't work as well after dark. And I'm certainly thankful for each bridge over each river. I stop each time to wonder what it would be like to cross alone.

The countryside is dry and poor and covered with cotton, save next to the rivers where the rich grow sugarcane. Or, perhaps, the sugarcane makes you rich. At ten minutes a kilometer I make it to Amod at 18h30 with almost no interactions. Only one scooter stopped to flip the familiar hand and "What's your deal?"

---

[1] "If the thunder doesn't get you then the lightning will" from *The Wheel* by Robert Hunter

Turns out he is the heat (*'police-walla'*) and recommends I don't stop in town, but go straight through to the *Gurukul* near Nahiyer instead. It's an extra 'two' kilometers down the road. There is a vague power play behind the suggestion, which I interpret as the force of *Krishna*, so I listen, passing quickly through Amod. The town is full of smiling Muslim students who love the thumbs up, rotting carcasses and animal skeletons on the side of the road, and a large *Masjid* and *Madrasa* pair. Nobody notices me in the twilight and I continue through tree-lined roads to my destination, which, in accordance with the 'two kilometer' rule – is four or five kilometers outside of town. They got me yesterday as well – from Gajera to Ankhi – an old woman on the street, a sculpture chiseled from sun-sharpened bone, gave me 'two kilometers' of hope to my destination.

Most distance answers are one kilometer off, up or down, but here 'two kilometers' means, empirically, "Pilgrim, I've never been there".

The trees alternately thicken and fade in the orange glow. I stop to drink some water and suddenly I know: I will be speaking English tonight: American English.

I continue.

A giant pink building emerges from a forest on the left; I reach it by sunset. Only a religious *trust* has enough money to build big buildings and save the holy trees. The *Gurukul*, a temple school, is run by the Swaminarayan sect, who receive me kindly as I finish the last of my water at their gate.

A monk leads me to the steps of the giant temple, replete with baby blue statues of *Krishna* and friends. I leave my weight behind and enter to give thanks, for making it, for the feeding and the listening and the walking and the sunlight. For my mom and AHHP and the Swaminarayans and everyone who is helping me out all the time. For being able to receive gifts and to offer thanks.

I come down to a waiting gentleman in orange robes, Mr. D.K. Swami. He speaks to me in English:

"Your country?"

We chat. He has a California accent, a result of having lived the last few years in San Diego, officiating ceremonies for rich devotees. He loves the United States and gets me a room and a shower. Since the guest room is otherwise occupied – I should have called in advance – they house me in the rector's room and the rector, all smiles, goes to sleep with the boys. Everything is possible and nobody is ever hassled, it seems.

D.K. takes me to the monks' quarters for a special dinner. The two of us sit alone at a table. I eat slowly and drink lots of water, speak English as foretold, and listen to his stories. The *curdy* is too astringent to enjoy and he slyly waters it down, making it palatable. A good trick. He chews *paan* and lives no contradiction, half of his time here and half in the other world. He is truly holy in that he likes everything.

After dinner he leaves me to the kids' questions and I field them with discomfort. With large crowds I still can't step out of my inadequacy, my ego. I take *darshan* of the head honcho and answer his questions as well. It's hard to tell whether he approves of my journey. I note a deep prejudice and arrogance within me that sees these priests as Pharisees, and doesn't care what they think anyhow. It's rooted enough that I can accept his blessing without worries and meet my merry sleep.

Day 12

March 23, 2006

"I hold that non-violence is not merely a personal virtue. It is also a social virtue to be cultivated like the other virtues."

12.1 to Buva

India is so full of it (everything).
Full of lessons a young *Krishna* must learn.
There's so much of it (everything).
Scarcity, like coincidence, is Not.

I might need to fast, just to prove it to myself, but I'm pretty sure it's true.

I leave the *Gurukul* with my faithful guide, D.K. Swami, on time at 6h30 this morning, after some morning fruit, *chai*, and *chevro*. The most beautiful thing about temples, for the fruity pilgrim, is that fruits are especially cherished offerings to the gods, so there's generally a lot to go around. D.K. walks me down the road for a few minutes and then returns to his *Gurukul*. I turn down the small path he had indicated, and walk alone. The road is small and the vegetation sparse, I see nobody and speak only to Mukeshananda, who calls me. His love is inescapable. I am happy to answer the phone, and know I must return to visit him.

After the short phone interlude, I practice walking while playing *bansuri* the rest of the way to Buva. It's a long road. It's been a dozen daylong eternities since Jayeshbhai wished me well. I can feel the road go on forever, I can't conceive of an end. I am sad and honored to think of the saints who send their love with me – Jayeshbhai and Anarben, Jayantilalbhai in Matar, Mukeshananda – their care is a reponsibility I must honor. It's not about me now, and maybe it never was.

I walk slowly into town and stop playing, to prepare myself for civilization. A villager gives me the standard greeting and I the standard response. Raised eyebrows and pointing to the *sarpanch's* house with the standard closed fist indicating power. It's always different and always the same.

The house is under construction and the owner not around, and I am happy to sit at the edge of the *talav* for a while. As I turn to leave, a young man on a bike roars up. The firstborn son.

"What are you doing here?"

I'm following Gandhiji's path to the sea, to my respects to the past and understand the present.

I make a noticeable mistake in my speech – maybe a gender error – and he laughs at my grammar. I can't even correct myself and he laughs more, a mean pointed laugh whispering 'uneducated, unworthy, unclean'.

Twelve days walking and reading Gandhiji and I can feel the anger going to my fists. The love is gone and I can do nothing but leave. I walk up the hill to a tree and sit to breathe. Breathe.

The town lake is empty.

Meditate.

It works like a magic lamp. I open my eyes some time later to find a man crouched intently in front of me. He smiles in greeting and we chat. Raoji is a worker. He gets 30-50 *points* a day taking care of the grounds of a local landowner. Behind the high fences, just across the path, there are fruit trees, beautiful flowers, and green grass. He does good work and goes back to the *vadi* to prove it to me, bringing back a few *chickoo*. He's had no house since the floods last monsoon season, and can't build one out of mud because the water here is wrong – too hard or too salty for the adobe to stick together. So we're homeless together.

Here in Buva there is a wealth of dryness and a paucity of water. I ask him how long the town reservoir has been dry – they're supposed to last from monsoon to monsoon, September to July.

He says, "From the beginning."

We eat *chickoo* together; They're very good. His father died a few years ago, and his mother soon after. They both had stomach pain for fifteen days and then left their bodies. I don't ask about doctors or hospitals. I ask why he has no kids and cannot quite understand his answer. Images of Indira Gandhi, the Emergency, and forced sterilization come to mind[1].

We sit in comfort and silence together until the men on motorcycles find us. It's the official welcoming committee, headed by the mayor's firstborn son.

"What are you studying?"

Twelve days and innumerable kindnesses behind me and my initial reaction is still 'Why do you care' or 'None of your business'.

---

[1]Events described in Rohinton Mistry's book, *A Fine Balance*.

It's not the question but the presumption with which they ask – they don't care about the answer but they have the right to know. I tell them I study Computer Science and Gandhi, and threaten to read aloud.

> "... I would say that merely to refuse military service is not enough. To refuse to render military service when the particular time arrives is to do the thing after all the time for combating the evil is practically gone. Military service is only a symptom of the disease which is deeper. I suggest to you that those who are not on the register of military service are equally participating in the crime if they support the State..."

Maybe they have the right to know because I have taken the barge into their world? I explain myself, to the best of my ability. How can I explain my self? But it's their village. One has to try.

"Any business?"

It means, I have learned, "How can we be of service?" No, no business.

They won't leave until I give them something to do. It's that love, again.

I ask, "Is there an old man here who remembers Gandhiji?"

"Chandukaka."

The head biker – the mayor's son – orders another biker to take me over. We are both relieved to have done our duty, accomplished our mission. When he leaves I turn to my appointed guide for directions. But no, we must take the bike. Raoji is gone.

Chandukaka is my grandfather. He remembers Gandhi's work and talks at me while I drink water, then *chai*. His wife has made one hundred thousand of cups of *chai* and she does so perfectly.

"None of this would exist without Gandhiji."

He waves his hand. The buses, roads, the growth of the trains. Chandukaka loves transport. He was eight years old when Gandhiji came through town in 1930, and doesn't remember much. There's not much more to tell: like my grandfather, he's old and tired. They give me their blessings to carry with me.

My guide gone, I am lost amidst the old brick and adobe houses. Buva is a small village, great for wandering. There are old men sitting on the street, waiting for me. They dress in perfectly starched white cotton, and sit together on the ground. Toothless and wrinkled. They ask something I can't understand, but I answer anyways, attentively and politely. Respected, they desist and wave me on.

Permission granted, I wander to the *mandir*. Sculptures of *Rama*, *Laxmana*, and *Sita* surround me, with color photographs of Lord *Krishna*. I meditate, then speak the name of Rama, because Gandhiji used to. Like the lawyer in Dabhan told me to do.

The priest comes to closes the curtain, isolating me from the divine. It's lunchtime. Ruffled, I leave. I'm beginning to feel quite parched in this town. But I only need to think of Raoji to remember fruit and the presence of the divine. India is full of love, full of angels. You are always taken care of eventually. I remember my life before this faith: harder and more complicated. I had to think more, to worry about my future, to make decisions. And now I'm giving away some of that agency, trading it for an understanding that it's all been planned out. For every misstep I make, somebody creates a new path. A dynamic algorithm.

It wasn't until that leap of faith, until I started walking, that the proof started pouring in, replacing my belief with experience. Rationality to faith to experience.

Kicked out of the temple, I head back to my tree. There's nowhere else to go. It's too early and too hot to continue walking. Each day, each hour, it gets hotter and drier and browner. I haven't seen wheat for days – only cotton and tobacco.

Walking along the (dry) lake, I come to an elderly uncle sitting by a tree in silence. I stand next to him and smile.

"What's your deal?"

But interested, I can tell by the hand motion. I don't feel bothered. He stares curiously, not out of boredom.

Dandi kooch.

"Oh! Gotcha."

He gives me directions to the next town. I share that I won't be leaving for a few hours. He introduces himself as Shivbhai and suggests we go to lunch. I am elated at the prospect and ask if we can postpone our meal a couple of hours, that it is still early for me. It's no problem. He was here for Gandhiji's visit. March 23, 1930. That's today. *Really.*

I ask then, "Why do things seem so different now – where is the *ahimsa?*"

The core of India, according to the vedic sages and the moderns ones, is *ahimsa*. *Ahimsa* is love. I can see that now. Non-violence merely describes the actions of a soul fully embracing love.

Shivbhai answers my question about *ahimsa* by talking about *seva*: service. How the politicians of that era truly cared about serving their country, submitting to it. Shivbhai tells me how Nehru, India's first prime minister, came from such a rich family that his father sent their clothes to France by steamer to be laundered. How Nehru's father would send a Rolls Royce to pick his son up from school every day. And how in eighteen years of government service, Pandit Jawaharlal Nehru never took a penny. But with Indira, he says, everything changed.

A millionaire refusing a salary doesn't sound terribly strange to me.

It seems, too, that anybody who understands service would refuse a salary. True service taps us in to the supra-terranean wealth flow. *Krishna's* wealth is infinitely greater than Rockefeller's. There is no scarcity. How could there be? Here I am worrying over attention and lunch and *Krishna* was here waiting for me, sitting in a tree disguised as Shivbhai. Don't worry, pilgrim: there is always more. Accept everything, accept the wait.

I have so much to learn. It's not about loving but Being the Love, with everyone. Not the verb but the noun, independent of space and time. It's the only game in town.

I go back to my tree to practice, repeating *Rama* for twenty minutes with no appreciable results. Maybe it's not my kind of meditation. Maybe it takes more than twenty minutes.

At Shivbhai's for lunch, I sit alone in a chair, facing the entire family. They sit, all together, on a swing: two uncles, two aunties, and three grandchildren. The room, like most Gujarati houses I visit, is concrete, dimly lit, and barely furnished. There is a bed in the corner, a few pictures of gods and deceased elders on one wall.

I am instructed with care to wash my hands, to wash my feet, to have my lunch. Spinach *shak* (green!) and *rotli, kitcheree* and *curdy* (finally, it wasn't *katash!*).

After the eating and staring, I am instructed to wash my hands and to be seated. We talk. We talk more about India, how politics and profiteering entered during the age of Indira Gandhi, how the British inflamed antagonisms between Hindus and Muslims. We talk about Indira starting problems with Pakistan. I note that from Jambusar onwards it has been a more Muslim area; Buva itself is mostly patel, the family tells me, with forty or fifty Muslim houses. Shivbhai tells me –

> "In Buva, there is no problem, we are friends. We sit in each other's houses."

I ask about land reform. What? Shivbhai is patel, a member of the land-owning class. What could I mean by land reform?

> "They've never owned land. That's how it is. How could it work?"

I try to explain the theory of the co-operative, of group decision-making, of inclusion and alienation. My vocabulary is impressively poor.

> "Listen. I have a factory and 100 workers. Now imagine if those 100 workers each opened a factory. How could it work?"

Hamstrung by vocabulary, I conclude it is not my role to argue. I was just curious to see what he thought.

> "Furthermore, these people are totally uneducated. The government gives free milk" – milk is very important in India – "and free school but they don't even send their kids to school – they prefer to have their children *come* to work."

Come, not go, he says. It is he who pays their children to work instead of study.

"They spend whatever little they have and come to work only when they need more – if they have 20 kilos of rice in the house they will eat it all and then come to work. And they drink wine all day – if they take 100 *points* home, they will spend 50 on wine. That's how they are: uneducated."

The case against land reform:

"That's how they are."

And us? Are we, too, they? Is there a 'how they are' for us, too? Or can we grow into our future, become what is asked of us?

The family disappears, leaving me to meditate on the swing and then take a *siesta*. I wake up at three and think to show Shivbhai my Golden Passport, given to me so days ago by the kind people of tiny Govindpura. He lights up with pride: "Such a man, like Gandhi!".

I blush at the error[2].

He has no idea what's really going on inside. But Shivbhai is really proud of me, like no one in my family has ever been, and it feels wonderful. The article, Kublai Kahn's Golden Passport, is like a new credit card. I am filled with gratitude for the author and the humans who gave it to me, yet I try to use it as little and as late as possible. I want people to feel the love in their own breast before being told what lies the media kindly presents on my behalf, before they're told that I'm holy or famous. I want to give them the opportunity to apprehend directly, to open like a *Gulab*.

I leave having figured out the *shanti* way to a village visit – forget the mayor, find the tree, and the village will come to you. Trust in *Krishna*, sharp eyes, and word of mouth. The world may yet be our home.

---

[2] "He makes full confession of the misdeeds of his youth, but in fact there is not much to confess. As a frontispiece to the book there is a photograph of Gandhi's possessions at the time of his death. The whole outfit could be purchased for about 5 pounds, and Gandhi's sins, at least his fleshly sins, would make the same sort of appearance if placed all in one heap. A few cigarettes, a few mouthfuls of meat, a few annas pilfered in childhood from the maidservant, two visits to a brothel (on each occasion he got away without 'doing anything'), one narrowly escaped lapse with his landlady in Plymouth, one outburst of temper – that is about the whole collection." (from George Orwell's *Reflections On Gandhi*)

12.2   to Samni

Tomorrow is the 26th anniversary of Archbishop Romero's assassination in El Salvador and the 30th anniversary of the coup in Argentina. Two years ago walking up the stairs in that latter land a woman I barely knew bade me pull a tarot card: The Wanderer.

I remain, blessed.

All my prayers come true. Somehow. Why should it be so? I'm tempted to credit the praying but I know I was blessed long before all that started. I walk and think back to distant worlds, to my militantly atheist days in college. Hunting missionaries with Holland McTyiere, looking to break faith with reason. Has anything changed? I can't repent. I am still searching for the Truth and the Party[3].

On the road today, I see more and more cotton. Mainly Muslim territory and, coincidentally, there are no planned stops on the official itinerary I'm following. I also encounter long afternoon treks and confusing roads. Ever since Ankhi the paths less direct. And it seems like a long way to Samni. I wonder if these are same roads Gandhi took, or just the itinerary designed by the Congress Party last year. But the plaques and dusty statues couldn't be faked, could they?

Before reaching Samni I encounter various villages. Karavada is tiny and full of traditional potters: old men sitting outside on the earth, each with a long pole to spin his wheel. They give a few strong spins, then drop their poles to shape their pots. A craft much older than electricity or pedals. They seem content in their yoga and are happy to bring me water, to fill my bottle. From Karavada I take the dirt road through a neighborhood filmed in sepia, past a large Muslim cemetery. The green cloths draped over the tombs are the only dustless elements in the whole panorama.

I twist through towns on the heels of old singing men and emerge into fields of cotton and millet. The fields are hot and endless; I marvel at and pity the plants. The cotton is ready and I pick some. The fibers of independence and oppression, à la fois.

We are in the nowhere of Gujarati hinterland. Tiny villages innocent of electricity, plumbing, or powdered milk. Between two villages' nowheres, I meet a man backing a bullock cart into a dairy. He offers me water and the village children besides, to take with me to Dandi.

---

[3]As Trotsky said: "In the end, the Party is always right"

"Maybe you could teach them something!"

There are fewer than ten of them and they don't go to school. They're very cute, but I decline, tempting as they are. I pass the lake and reach another largely Muslim village where I am not instructed to stop. The men are threshing grain in the field and I stand in the dust of their chaff. It's the closest I get to 'work'. The road hardens into pavement and twists through the dry beauty of dry-season trees – no green in sight – all the way to Samni. It's easily a three hour commute, even without the flute.

Samni proves unreceptive to this wanderer. There are so many closed *dharamshalas* and memorial halls on this trek. So much wasted energy, time, and space. Nobody seems to care about Gandhi or *aditi deo bhavana*, the guest being God. No pilgrims and no hosts. Why else would the *dharamshalas* be closed? We are spitting on the most beautiful Indian tradition – the culture that supports wandering holy people as a fundamental part of social wisdom and fabric. All over India, for thousands of years, the renunciants have not only been accepted as part of society, but also mandated by social norms. I believe the four stages are as follows:

1. Education (0-25 years)

2. Work, marriage, family (25-50)

3. Retire, advise larger community (51-75)

4. Renounce, dedication to spiritual pursuits (76-100)

Which is why every town, big or small, tends to have an ashram or *dharamshala* to feed pilgrims and saints. And now, they are modernizing.

The paunchy men sitting outside the *panchayat* office don't seem to be concerned with their new guest and I learned enough from lunch not to bother with the Golden Passport. There is no scarcity. I see a nice looking temple across the lake and away I go. I arrive to find one *Maharaj* (with family) and two gentlemen who like to hang out. Needed financial support comes from an *NRI* whose medical degree is from Zambia and lives in Leicester, U.K. So say the plaques.

I stare into the dust and stones of red and grey and can't imagine two places further away. There are garish statues of Gandhiji and Kasturba, and shrines to all the gods. I take *darshan* and explain myself, wash my hands and feet, take the sweet, blessed, coconut *prasad*, and talk with the two gentlemen.

After a few minutes of introduction and interest, one of the men, Rajendrabhai, asks for a 'write-up'. I show him the Golden Passport. He is impressed and asks for my journal to write the names of his friends whom I must visit.

> "These men are pure Gandhian! In thinking and in living, and I think you must be meeting them!"

He's a sharp fellow with 'powerful' English, though we continue to converse in the native tongue. After he leaves me, I take a shower and sit down to play music with *Maharaj* after the evening *puja*. *Maharaj* takes me to the inner sanctum of the temple and shows me the temple heirlooms: a drum machine and some *Krishna* dolls. The drum machine is a mechanical contraption the size of a CT machine: it includes several large drums within it, its large beaters powered electrically by the flip of a switch. I touch everything with reverence and play the flute for my new family.

Auntie – the caretaker's wife – tells me how blessed they feel to be here, that it is a lucky place for all who come. Tomorrow is my rest day so I am doubly blessed. I am fed fruit and given the opportunity to play my music for a *Krishna* idol.

Today at lunch and here at dinner my hosts were proud of me, for my suffering. I haven't felt much suffering, yet. I haven't much wanted things to be different. Isn't that what suffering is, desire? Ice cream and sugarcane juice are the extent of my unmet desires. And sleep. I notice there is neither fan nor wind nor net, and I fear for my sleep. The classic conundrum of heat versus mosquitoes returns: too hot to cover your body, and too itchy not to.

For dinner I am caringly served thick rotlas with carrot and chile *athanu* (with a wasabi edge from crushed mustard seeds) and a very good *vagar kitcheree*. The loving auntie gives me horrible *chass* that I first try to water down (thanks to D.K. Swami for the hint) and finally end up throwing over the railing, to water the sacred plants. This place, like so many other temples, is so green. Ramji *Mandir*. Without the religions' – Hinduism and Islam alike – obsession with trees, India might be totally deforested.

After dinner I am given *sopari* under the name of fennel. Betel-nut: a digestive aid, they say. Only after it's too late do I realize *sopari* is a stimulant, a drug, the kind they put in *paan*, and the kind that could keep me up all night.

Survival here is based on the opposite of 'rugged individualism' – in India the struggle is submission to the intensity around you. Even the insects here are intense. Huge families of huge cockroaches gawk as I take my shower outside the well. They own the walls. I lay on the floor of the temple, in front of the gods, across from the night watchman. He's already asleep.

Between the drugs and the bugs, I know I may not sleep tonight. I am the blessed wanderer writing in the dark, surrounded by flying insects. They cover my clothes and my skin and they, too, want it all.

Day 13

March 24, 2006

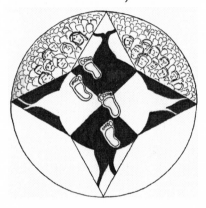

"It is not enough to love [your enemies] by remembering their virtues. You must be able to love them in spite of all their misdeeds."

13.1   Rest Day: Samni

I am very tired. I wake up at 5h00 after sleeping from 3h30 to 4h00. Failed attempts at yoga, meditation, and sleep. Once again, the mosquitoes broke my toys. I should have brought a net.

Auntie brings me a bucket of hot water to bathe and cup of sweet strong *chai* to welcome the day. I practice scales and melodies on my flute and revisit my attempts to sleep and to meditate. Two aunties with two nephews come for prayer and leave me five *points* each. They think I am *sanyassi*. I tell myself I will sit in meditation until I can no longer hear them chatter, but they outlast me. So much to learn.

I am too tired to notice it is a rest day, but somewhere I must be happy not to be walking. I am served lunch – I am ever served and never serving at these places – at 11h00 and eat more than my usual, even though I've done nothing to be hungry. It is same meal as last night. There is a school next door, where the bathrooms are, and I talk with the rector before napping.

These were silent days for Gandhiji.

I've noticed during this second leg of the trip – since crossing the Mahisagar – fewer people show interest in Gandhiji's walk or my own. There is still always someone to guide me[1] but until we find each other, fear is my companion. Maybe the media coverage is wearing off. Maybe the Gandhian cult never took hold here. Maybe I need to shave.

Nothing about the gods or what I am doing has changed. If anything I am more convinced of this lifestyle, this purity. I must maintain that confidence, that faith, that high – without expectation of accolades or worldly support. Or content myself with just a few. Both Shivbhai of Buva and D.K. Swami were incredibly supportive and complimentary. It can be a nice thing, sometimes.

I also realized yesterday, between footfalls, that Gandhiji cannot be understood politically. There's no sense in having a political discussion about Gandhi's ideas[2]. Ultimately, he is a mystic, a trans-rational figure, unconcerned with ego or earthyl peril. Many critics point out his tactic only worked because of the civility and kindness of the British. Orwell even notes that the British didn't mistreat him because they thought they were making use of him.

---

[1] "If you should stand then who's to guide you?
If I knew the way, I would take you home" from Robert Hunter's *Ripple*

[2] Again, Orwell points to this in his *Reflections on Gandhi*

What the critics fail to acknowledge is Gandhi's Magic Spell. The British tortured thousands of dissidents – why not Gandhi? If what he writes is true – and one thing all the critics agree on is that he lived his words – then he had virtually No malice. And, karmically, one without malice is one who can receive no harm. It is his deep civility, not theirs, that saves him.

In war, then, innocent victims are brutalized. They have done nothing. How? Do they perhaps still have violence in their hearts? Don't we all? A desire for vengeance but not the power to implement it? It is what Gandhi calls the non-violence of the weak – an outward peace and inward seething.

Rajendrabhai, whom I met last night, was fond of asking in his 'powerful' English:

"WHO IS I AM?"
"WHERE FROM I COME?" '
"WHAT IS MY WORK?"

Krishna is the easy way out, of course. *Krishna*, *Krishna*, and *Krishna*. If "God is one," like all the rickshaw drivers tell me, then "Jim threw Ankit the mango" becomes "*Krishna Krishna*-d *Krishna* the Krishna" and you might as well restrict your vocabulary to Allah or Jehovah or Sat or what have you. You might have trouble communicating at first, but ultimately Everybody would Understand. Ultimately: in the end, that is.

I cannot answer his first question beyond fuzzy intimations of being a giant marshmallow expanding to the membrane. And I don't know how to say that in Gujarati. As for the third question, I've filled out enough immigration forms to present an argument.

As far as I could tell, being social animals[3], we are here to love each other (and die)[4]. I think that's the extent of our duty on the planet. In the political realm, as Gandhi says. Outside the purely political level, we would have to love all Being.

Luckily, this is not hard or work *per se*, though it may seem so. Because this love is our true nature – not so much an action as a flowing, a loosening, a letting go. It's our natural state and the less we do – or entertain illusions of doing – the more we are in touch with

---

[3] As the early Marx often reminds us
[4] See the different versions of W.H. Auden's *September 1, 1939*

this reality, The Underlying Love Reality. Or, at least, that's the sense
I'm getting from this walk.

Again, as Gandhi conceives it, 'Truth is god'. And the only way
there, for him, is Love. To be totally loving – *ahimsa* – one must
control one's relations to sex, eating, possession, respect, and suffering
(to begin with). That's what all those vows are about[5].One must be a
seeker on the path. What's so revolutionary from one side and insane
from another is that following this ancient code is his political mission
– for Gandhi, non-violent *swaraj* can only happen when the masses
become enlightened. Gandhi's free India would not be an independent
state with its own military and political power, but rather another
version Jesus' Kingdom of Heaven on Earth.

These people have the best jobs. During the winter pilgrimage season,
Masiji says she's cooking all the time. All day *puja* and *bhajans* and
seva for the humans and for the trees. She feeds me pieces of coconut
blessed by the gods as she talks.

After my sunset meditation, I sit on the benches and talk with some
people who come for water. Like most temples and mosques, there is
free water here for anyone who will drink: water for the people. The
man I talk with is kind, calm, and listens. He can tell I understand
Gujarati better than Hindi, and speaks accordingly. He works in the
fields nearby and his son loves to read Vivekananda. I give him a
bookmark that Mukeshananda had given me back in Nadiad. Flow. I
gave Gulab's beautiful family all the posters they presented me at the
Surya Mandir. Without the flow, there is only weight.

The stewards of the temple serve me another sumptuous dinner:
the standard *kitcheree* plus *mung dal* and a new carrot *athanu*. For
the pickle, you mix equal quantities of *gor* and split mustard seeds with
just the right amounts of *haldi*, oil, salt. To this 'dressing' you then
add sliced carrots and mild green chiles, and let the whole contraption
marinate for a day. Basically a salad if you tread lightly on the salt
and oil, which they do here, oddly enough.

Today I've been resting and recuperating, reading Gandhi and playing the flute. After dinner I sit with *Maharaj* and his wife to sing. It
is easier, I have concluded, for me to be walking all day than sitting.

---

[5]See Appendix A

I have to face my indolence and mental lassitude on these days, to be aware of how little I focus when given the chance.

Now afraid of the temple at night, I sit on the pavilion by the gaudy statues of Gandhi and Kasturba. So very Indian. The bugs are starting to take over, and I'm scared I won't sleep again. Hopefully there will be wind tonight. I need the sleep. I try to remember Jayeshbhai always,

"Sleep is free medicine".

D.K. Swami told me, in his San Diego accent, two nights ago, "Many trips in One. The Road is easy."

It's hard to know what they mean, if they mean anything at all. I wanted to come to India and walk through farms and back roads, to find some notion of 'the real India', to get a sense of what is to be done[6]. I wanted to do this salt march, the Dandi kooch, out of respect and admiration for Gandhiji, to understand his path a little better. I wanted, also, to travel around Gujarat learning recipes from my people.

Magically, this trip has satisfied all those needs without any conscious intention. I am walking through farms and playing with villagers. I have learned that, as a man, there's no way I will get inside these kitchens. But I'm doing the best I can.

What more could I receive or ask for? All that remains is my contribution – to come back with composting kitchens and solar latrines for the masses. Surprisingly, no one has accused me of laziness or asked me get a job. A different India than I remember. Perhaps they treat me well because they think I'm a foreigner. Maybe it has to do with this mission. May there be a moral force to my proposition that silences negativity? Why else, after a lifetime riddled with nagging criticism, have there been no barbs from overbearing uncles and aunties?

Only one swami at the Santaram *Mandir* told me I could not do this forever. I have no plans to. Do I?

And where is this force coming from? It's not mine. All my relations can attest to that, to my lifetime of distraction and pleasure. It is a force yet in its infancy, a seed soaked in blessings and ancient knowledge, almost ready to sprout. The path I must walk has not yet begun: I have but a misty glimpses and clouded faith to go on, with eyes closed and fingers dancing, unconcerned about corners in the darkness.

---

[6] As in the novel by Nikolay Chernyshevsky.

Day 14

March 25, 2006

"We shall cease to think of getting what
we can, but we shall decline to receive
what all cannot get."

14.1   to Tralsa

Halfway home – or away from it – and for the first time I'm ready for all this to be over.

I pass half the night in sleepless hallucination, rampant and varying fantasies of traveling by bus and by plane, to a place far, far away. Eventually I end up at the N.Y.C. apartment of a friend who lives in Boston. It's hard to get food from the co-operative grocery store because the F-train doesn't run after 20h00 except on Tuesdays. So there's no way to share food after all and I would have to find the same desperate cocktail of planes and buses in reverse in order to get back and . . .

I wake up to realize I haven't moved at all. It's not yet dawn and I am being destroyed, once again, by mosquitoes. My hard night on the pavilion finally settle into sleep as the 4h30 alarm rings. I silence it, sleeping past Gandhi's rules and schedules to 5h45. Morning yoga, movement, prayer, shower, and *chai* in quick succession before the road I've missed so much opens before me.

I receive a deep *aashirvad* from *Maharaj* and the night watchman before I go. I continue along the same road that led me into town, knowing it is wrong and not having the effort or wit to ask for help. I leave Samni without visiting the broken-down *dharamshala* where Gandhi stayed, the second night-halt in a row where I skipped Gandhi's plaque.

The fields are full of cotton and *babul* trees – the monoculture doesn't look so aggressive or conglomerated with the trees there to break up the scene. I find the right road, eventually, and try to be open and loving towards the brothers and sisters I meet along the way. I cannot.

Thirteen days can be a long time.

I'm just beginning to realize how long, how arduous, a single night can be. What it means to suffer on a pilgrimage. It's probably fair to say the easy half is over. As I get farther from Ahmedabad and the press story gets older and my beard gets longer, I am no longer the blessed *yatri* they are looking for.

Except that I *am*. I'm the same human with the same *dharma*, if it were ever true. The same blessed angel, even though I look ten years older and meaner with a beard. I only have to remember the blessings come from within and I can choose to manifest them whenever I damn well please. To be loving without exception. To give the thumbs up and the smile without fear or reservation, even though my white shirt is torn and turmeric-stained.

I am beginning to understand, through experience, why people fixate on keeping clean and tidy: it has less to do with hygiene, and more to do with smiles. Smiles are good. I take the long way into Tralsa. This time, though longer, the road is peaceful and fields are green. I pass a Muslim farmer who adjusts my path. I gather the strength and attention to ask his name.

"Muslim."

Miscommunication. I tell him I used to live in Lebanon and I speak some Arabic. There's lots of Muslims over there. He's not interested.

"Lebanon! Lebanon!" I shout in Arabic, eager to connect. Maybe he's never heard of it. He thinks I'm crazy and walks away. It's a disaster. Kind of like Lebanon.

At the next turn there's a group of teenagers hanging around a group of motorcycles. They could be twenty-somethings, even. I've found here that men hold in a developmental stasis from puberty to marriage: there's no dating to move the emotional train along, and they generally live at home.

"What's your deal¿'

Just once I wish I could ask them first. But I'm too slow. They look around, stare down the road I walked.

"Are you alone?"

"No, no. How silly! I'm with all of you."

I give them the rundown: the Salt March, the duration, and the memory of Gandhi. They are totally uninterested in the Gandhian bits. I find it really sad and am too tired to engage them. It was only 50 years ago that India won her independence. It'd be like black kids in the states not recognizing Martin or Malcolm.

I get to Tralsa, tired and sleepy, at 10h00. It is a small village, almost empty. I passed a village yesterday so small it didn't send its kids to the school three kilometers away. Maybe fifteen houses and a dozen ox-carts.

In Tralsa, I walk without incident to the Gandhi memorial. It's open, for a change, across from the *panchayat* office. It occupies a small room on the ground floor of an abandoned two-storey concrete building (the former *dharamshala*).

I walk the few steps up to the room and enter. The steps themselves are covered with goat dung; Cobwebs and rat shit decorate the room. It smells strongly of urine. The memory is a mess. There is vinyl poster of Gandhi on a small platform, adorned with a soiled garland. Everything is covered with dust. A year's worth, I'm guessing. The platform is engraved with today's date in 1930. A few fingers have scraped the bottom in respect, pilgrims or locals since the big *yatra*. The filth and disrepair are all too fitting – I have an urge to clean it but decide it would be a lie, foreign and imperial.

Let my fingers grace his presence – I am no more than that.

To continue, I must learn about *ahimsa*, to establish myself in *ahimsa*, to live without expectation. It's not just not being violent or snapping at children or smiling, but a way of living without expectations, such that everything we are faced it becomes a blessing, perfectly fulfilling. It can be hard.

The afternoon passes me in twenty-minute segments, sitting by the dry town *talav*. I take turns watching the buffalo, meditating, playing with the flute and the children. I nap. I am still tired.

At the lake, I meet Ranchod. His name means *Krishna*, he is 31, has two *viga* of land and a few buffalo. He is too old to be single and fears he will never marry. I think there may be money involved. Ranchod offers me no *seva* besides his occasional company and I am happy that way. The kids bring me fruit and smiles from the trees. I don't feel much a need for anything else and notice a strange and subtle pride in *not* being cared for.

The wind changes course and brings me the burning body of a child. Before I can ask, I notice a procession and hear the wails. Ranchod returns and tell me the boy died this morning. I was wandering in a nearby temple when he found me – there is always a temple nearby – and had played an unwitting dirge on the flute. I can only remember Goenkaji's evening lectures from the Vipassana course, and wish the weeping and non-weeping alike the wonderful gift of the *dhamma*. Who would try to make sense of a child's burning body?

I am tired again and awake to the local popsicle man and a gang of kids. He offers me a cumin-flavored popsicle that I take with joy and trepidation. Buried in melting gifts. I eat the *jeera*-sicle, thankfully, and sit down to nap again.

The hunger comes.

14.2   to Derol

Thank you Dr. *Krishna*.

Today I ride a wild rollercoaster. I leave Tralsa at 15h45 with no free lunch outside the *jeera*-sicle. I play some good tunes on the flute, check out a nearby shrine (there is always a shrine nearby), and hit the road. When, two kilometers down the road, I ask for directions, the old peasant replies with concern -

> "Do me a favor: stay on the main road. Or else you'll get lost in those farms forever and never come out the other side."

The old man touches me: the most love I've felt all day. I follow his advice through cotton and confusion and come to Tralsi (not Tralsa) for water. The heat gets more jaguar furious every day and I can feel the pounding waves under my forehead. The good people give me water with pleasure.

A giant mango tree, loaded with fruit, beckons at the edge of town. I head towards it, zombie-like, until the huge fence comes into focus. Criminal! And yet so reasonable – with so many village urchins running around naked and poaching sour mangos, an unfenced tree doesn't bear a single ripe fruit.

I get to Derol at 17h00 with the grace of the gods, exhausted. Heat stretches space and time. A Muslim *ghazal* plays as I walk past the old cotton mills and new mansions. I pass through the town gates and stop to reorient myself. I can feel it won't be easy.

I've crossed into a different culture, I have become even more foreign. A different dialect has slowly emerged to temper my rising comprehension. The typical Gujarati overbearing care doesn't seem to exist here, at least for the unshaven wanderer.

In my Gujarat, any random person will attend to your basic needs, answer your silly questions, or – at the least – hand you off to somebody who will. Many strangers will take your errands upon themselves and do them for you, rather than merely tell you where to go.

> "You just come."

The angels I know wear second-hand spectacular t-shirts ('So many girls \ So little time') and love their families. I have passed whole afternoons drinking *chai* and doing errands with people I've barely met who, when my work is done, disappear with a smile into the cows and scooters of India's teeming streets.

Here in Derol, I see a grandfather and offer my standard opening: I am here on a pilgrimage, looking for where Gandhiji spoke and stayed during the Salt March. It's the only event for which their town is known, likely, so I assume everyone would know the answer.

He shrugs and walks away. There is no recognition nor leading by the hand. I ask another man, and earn the same response.

Maybe I smell. Gandhi was meticulous about hygiene and I have showered and washed my clothes ever yday, in an attempt to follow. I don't smell.

Someone points me to the town store, where a certain *dada* tends to relax. I enter, greet, and ask for him. He's not here. They tell me to sit ("You just sit here") and wait for him, so I put down my pack (which has only grown heavier with the heat) and observe their business. They are comically cheap and mean to their customers: frowning at women, and overcharging children, and insisting on being paid every last rupee.

Finally, *dada* comes. He is an old Muslim man in traditional garb, long and flowing white cotton pants and tunic. He was a child when Gandhiji stayed the night here. He tells me the school gave watermelon and dates to all the marchers, who stayed in the cotton mill next door. He was too young to remember much else.

"Cool."

The shopkeepers ask if I am looking for a place to stay, and I nod. I'm not exactly looking, but I'm open to one, and I don't know how to say that. I'm fine sleeping under a tree. Nobody offers anything, but they begin to joke that I should stay at the cotton jin, where the original pilgrims lodged seventy-six years ago. The old watchman can cook for me and do my laundry, entertain me.

The watchman arrives like they knew he would, and the merchants derive a sick pleasure from proposing their jest to him. He is uninterested, unwilling, and uncomfortable. I feel like sludge. They continue to harass him until flees, exasperated. Nobody seems to care and I'm only feeling sicker from the heat and the welcome. I get up to leave and wander around the town a bit. Before I can somebody orders the nearby kids to take me to a local temple.

It's less than a hundred meters away, enshrined in a small grove of trees, yet within the town. The priest is out so I drink water (thank the gods for free water) and play with his toddler. The birds are loud and cool in the shade. I sulk.

I am supposed to be offering people an opportunity to come together, not to cause fights and disputes. Where are the whole villages that walk with me?

A boy, Jignesh, returns to tell me to wait in the temple – my dinner has been arranged. I obey. The temple measures ten by ten meters, and has idols of gods on each of its four walls. It is equipped, I note, with many fans. I do not recognize the main idol. I attend the *puja* and talk to the men present, one of whom is calm and gentle with me. People can be very sweet. The man, who had come to bless his home with prayers and a coconut, gives me a piece of his sanctified fruit and shows me the water tank, so I can bathe. A rare bite of food.

Body and clothes washed, I speak to *Maharaj*, who affirms that someone from the town has taken charge of my dinner. My mother calls from the United States and, distressed to hear I missed lunch, offers to wire me money.

I decline and sit down to embrace my sadness. I feel the part of me that refuses, time and again, to give money to beggars. The part that says it's better to give food than money, yet seldom carries food to give. The part of myself that looks into the eyes of dirty children and tells them, 'no'. It is here with me, today.

Then the miracles start. I don't know if I failed, passed, or was reprieved the full extent of the test. I certainly didn't deal well with the hunger, uncertainty, and rejection (by man) that I had asked for. But nobody seems to care.

Maharaj arrives with a *thali* prepared by another faceless auntie. Eight oldish *rotli*, cold *kitcheree*, *athanu*, and one amazing *methi baggi thepla*. I slowly and gratefully take the bread of life into my body, acutely aware it could so easily not be so. Hunger is the best sauce[1]. Ten minutes of slow chewing wonder later, a boy – Ajay – arrives with another thali, basket, and cup. Ganshamkaka has sent me dinner. Who is Ganshamkaka? I have no idea, I can't keep these names straight. It must be the man who shared his holy coconut – he came here to ask, and went home to give. Or his wife did, at least.

---

[1]A Korean proverb

Six more fresh *rotli*, a bowl of curried *mung* sprouts, and a cup of fresh milk. I almost refuse the milk, automatically, and check myself, knowing at this point I have lost all power to refuse. Too many thanks to give. I eat what I can of the food and give the remaining *rotli* and milk to local animals.

What happened here? *Krishna* got a little late with one meal. Stuck in traffic perhaps? Hence the cold *kitcheree* and old *rotli* of the first meal. And then the next dinner, right on time. Nothing to worry about if you take the long view.

After dinner, as I sit practicing the flute, a young man coming to the temple carrying a large cloth. His name is Vaibhav. He stops to talk to me, then unfolds his cloth over the hard stone floor of the temple. Every week at this time there is a youth group which meets here. Do I mind? No, I do not mind. I am welcome to join. Yes, thank you.

Instead of writing alone, I am brought into society and meet a group of twelve young men, who come together each week under the tutelage of a charismatic young leader. Vaibhav keeps them occupied with exercises in creativity, personal growth, and social change. I sniff for the cultish side of it but judgment eludes me.

Vaibhav mentions Vinoba Bhave and I nod in ignorance. I can't tell if Vinoba is male or female[2].

> "Last week we discussed the life of this great personality, and most of these bodys didn't even know if he was male or female!"

I laugh. He must be a man.

This week they are practicing creativity and spontaneity. Vaibhav will tell half of a story and then we must go around the circle and each end it in different ways. Even me, in my elementary Gujarati. I listen carefully. He tells a story about a rich king and his various sons. Some socio-political problem about stability versus freedom. I don't quite understand, of course.

Some of their conclusions are funny, some are fast, some long-winded. Some love the spotlight and some push it away. They are like teenagers everywhere. When it comes to me, I articulate my response slowly, trying not to let my errors sabotage the communication, and

---

[2] *ba* as a suffix implies grandmother, but it might just be part of the name.

suggest giving the kingdom's material wealth away: "the true wealth of a kingdom resides in its people." A sort of anarchist fairy tale.

Everybody laughs at me. It's a good activity. We break with a closing *Om* circle. If Marx was closer to the truth than Sartre and god is other people[3], then the closing *Om* circle is exactly what I've been missing. The resonance, amongst us and in within the small temple, is amazing. Our vibrations tangle, flirt, become one.

We sit together a while longer and talk about my trip. I tell them the truth I'm living: I'm only alive because of the grace and love of the Gujarati people. Because of them.

"What are their deals?" I am able to ask.

Some study, some work. Those are generally the two options. Some are happy and some are trying to leave town. One of the boys, Rupesh, is a barber. He has just opened his own *saloon* and offers me a shave. Oh? A Shave? Oh, God, yes. Thank you *Krishna*. The only thing left on my list is dessert.

We walk back to the center of town, now a group of six. Vaibhav wishes us a good night, and goes home to his family. Rupesh unlocks the shop and greets his elders. They run a small store next door, selling an infinite variety of packaged snacks. They pass the evening in white plastic chairs, sitting and chatting together, men and women together. Rupesh is recently married but seems much more focused on spending time with his friends. I want to meet his wife. Not possible.

They are shocked I am unmarried at 26. They ask about America, how I can be American if I am Indian. I am and I'm not, American and Indian. I explain about black people, immigration, and the difference between the colors of papers and skins. They only see white people and beaches on TV. I explain about poverty and homelessness. Rupesh stops shaving me in confusion. Such is his sincerity.

"But it is such a rich country".

Yes. Yes it is. I can sense the shame he feels, on our behalf.

I am smiling to my half-bearded self in the mirror, caught between the worlds. Soon I will be young again, pure, and blessed to the eye. More like a pilgrim and less, according to all my relatives, like a terrorist. Maybe the garlands and trumpets will return[4].

---

[3] As opposed to the "Hell is other people" from *Huit Clos*.

[4] "Pity the nation that welcomes its new ruler with trumpeting, and farewells him with hooting, only to welcome another with trumpeting again," from Khalil Gibran's poem, *Pity the Nation*.

Rupesh finishes shaving me, carefully and precisely. He only cuts me once. The straight-edge is one of my favorite Indian tools, alongside the mortar and *velun*.

The boys walk me back to my temple. I have friends again, people I can touch. One boy will take me to the mill in the morning, and until then I can sleep under the stars and the *pipal* tree, next to the temple, huddled in cold contentment.

Day 15

March 26, 2006

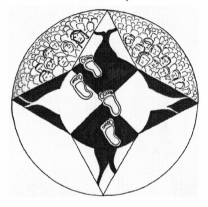

"I believe in thought-power more than in the power of the word, whether written or spoken."

15.1 to Bharuch

One of my friends from last night comes this morning for me, with a glass of hot milk. I drink it, and for the first time I like it. Fresh hot buffalo's milk with saffron and sugar.

He walks me out of town to see the mill where Gandhi stayed. I think of the caretaker from yesterday. He must still be sleeping. I should leave – I'm already late for Gandhi's schedule and, though there's no hurry, I like to leave when he did. My friend says goodbye and returns to his village.

I am walking, once again on the road. I am clean-shaven and new. I have started over. I have experienced hunger and love, understood that there is no scarcity, only delay. I can still taste the warm milk and I like it.

Half an hour of walking later a man coasts up on his motorbike and parks next to me. He introduces himself as Ranjeet and we walk together, in silence for a time. A rare joy, to feel accompanied and not invaded. He begins to ask me, kindly, about my walk, he exudes happiness and warmth, he is glad to have met me. As always, I feel honored and shy and use my words carefully and sparingly, trying neither to excite nor to disappoint. He seems to have considered many things, to have reflected on his life.

I do not encounter this humble reflection very often in the men here – those who know are often so Beyond, I have a hard time understanding how they got there. And there are so many others who know nothing beyond the accidents and contingencies of their upbringing. It is our global fortune that rural India's prejudices don't tend toward toilet paper or hatred, that – aside from its sexual politics – India's ignorance takes a peaceable shade.

"God is one"
"India is best"
"Just you come."

Even the traditional food here, the unexamined diet, is balanced, seasonal, and good for you: something to be said for a culture that has endured and evolved over thousands of years.

Ranjeet talks of his son growing up in changing times and eventually I put it together that his child was one of the students the night before. This father has gone to such great lengths to meet me – he rode his bike out of town and now walks along with me. I can think of no greater honesty, directness, compliment, or testament of his interest than the vision of his motorbike parked two kilometers back, knowing he must walk back alone.

Pilgrimage is every moment. It is more valuable than this quest I have inherited, or invented. This inheritance I have invented.

I continue in a blue shimmering daze through the outskirts of Bharuch. It's going to be a big city, I can tell. On the banks of the mighty Narmada river, they say. Hopefully this time there will be a bridge.

I receive a call from a man I've never met, Priteshbhai, the cousin of Mayurbhai from Ahmedabad. Mayurbhai is the brother of Janeshbhai, the Janeshbhai who gave me the very map that guides me. Of course. He, Priteshbhai, also knows my schedule and expects me today. Am I on schedule? Yes, I am on schedule. We will meet, then, where Gandhi stayed, at 11h00. I will come to his place for lunch. Yes, yes I will.

I walk past rickshaws and flat tire boys and *chai* stalls and all the trappings of a modern Indian city. Bus travel companies to take the devoted on day-long pilgrimages, crowded three to a seat, to a holy footprint of a blue-skinned god where they will get off the bus, worship, cry, and spend money they can't afford to, all in an hour, and rest elated for the dusty ride home to their newly blessed family. Pilgrimage's industrial upgrade. *En masse*, Indian style, with the senses and sentiments whole and intact. I have met the old women who take such trips. I know can scarcely imagine their devotion.

> "If you go with friends then you will have fun. Alone you
> can have no fun."

I see the irrigation canals turn into sewers, the shade trees which line the hot Gujarati road evolve into garbage patches and shelters for the homeless. I watch the world turn from farmers' riches to urban poverty. I walk by street children shining the shoes of policemen ('police-walla').

I only stop at a large florid park. There is an old man selling *chai* to an even older one and I ask them if I can enter the park.

> "This is not a park! It is a Muslim cemetery."

Oh, I see.

"Are you Muslim?"

No.

They smile. It doesn't matter. I should have a seat.

I go in to write and practice the flute on a bench, alone. A few minutes later the old customer comes in with *chai* for me. These people just won't stop with their beauty. He sends a child to buy *biscuits* (the Parle-G once again, oh how I've missed you) and we share those too. I put away my toys. He inquires about my journey and appreciates my task. He preaches the gospel of peace[1] in his everyday life. He sees no separation.

I do not cry but I want to be like him. I want us all to be like him. He is not innocent. To have suffered through half a century of partition and murder and retaliation and to know deeply and calmly that peace is not only the destination, but the way. He has played with the other options and found there are none.

Osho once said that his real *ashram* was connected with no building or *guru*, but constructed itself in each one of his disciples. I have another hour before me through the street cows and traffic to the *seva-ashram* here in Bharuch, where eventually I must meet Priteshbhai, but I feel I have found my stopping place. I have found where the Truth tarried, when it came to town.

---

[1] As in, the Essene *Gospels of Peace*

15.2   to Ankleshwar

I cannot wait to begin walking again, but I do. It's past 16h00 and I fear a late start and dark arrival, but Priteshbhai has assured me that Ankleshwar is just across the river and, more importantly, there is a bridge.

I sit alone in the second-floor waiting room of the local TV channel. I will be interviewed again. By now I know what to say. I have lived half of the journey, experienced the smooth and the rough, and have sound-bites at the ready:

> Thank you to the Gujarati people.
> Noting that nobody has any idea about Gandhi but it doesn't seem to affect their respect.
> Encourage everyone to take their life into their own feet and walk.
> Pilgrimage teaches you that the slower you go, the more you see.

Instead, they ask when I got the idea and, naturally, I don't quite know what to say. I first started reading Gandhiji in high school, scoffing at all but the communist and anti-colonial bits. Later the non-violence got to me, and finally his esoteric and alien behaviors: unsalted food, spartan schedules, celibacy. Gandhiji requires a lot of patience to make sense of, a commitment. Once again there is a play between time and causality – the understanding comes after the commitment, not before.

This morning, I wander around the *seva-ashram*, finding the plaque that noted the *yatris* passage. March 26, 1930. I have arrived an hour early, giving myself time to practice music and other meditations. As I sit in silence with my eyes closed, focusing on the heart whose existence Mukeshananda showed me (in all of us), I feel a sunflower of heat growing from my heart outward, first slowly and then rapidly, filling my entire being with light. My eyes open, startled.

Priteshbhai stands a few paces away.

We greet each other warmly and he shares how honored he is to meet me. I don't know the word for demure in Gujarati. I do know,

now, the words for 'innocent' and 'humble', because they throw those around me all the time, with no idea of how I am in English.

Priteshbhai takes me on his motorcycle to the newspaper office to make an appointment with the journalist, after which we continue to his home. He stops to buy *srikhand* on the way there. I protest, arguing that refusing to carry money is not an invitation to be treated. He is a good host and ignores me. *Srikhand* is my favorite dessert.

At home I can shower, rest, write, and play with his child as Priteshbhai's wife prepares lunch. At 11h30 another family arrives and we eat together. Young Aditya sits in his aunt's lap as mother and servant ('sister') bring out the food. Then mom sits too and the women eat together with the men. It's a feat as amazing and modern as the glass table we eat upon, or the home itself, a new condominium with tile floors and white walls. Maybe there is progress in development after all, equality mixed into the concrete and glaze.

Everything is very new, clean and young. Even the child. Priteshbhai has a good job with the Western Railway and a family he loves. Everything inside his home is pleasant and orderly, especially when compared with to the Indian exterior. A little white prefabricated sanctuary in a block of little white prefabricated sanctuaries. An effective filter for the intensity and overwhelming Eleven[2] that is India. It's oddly necessary: to be comfortable here you must sink into the chaos or defend yourself from it. The alternative, to feel that loud stinking conglomerate as Other, quickly turns to depression, illness, and disaster.

I eat too many desserts and collapse on the daybed, playing with Aditya and watching Aditya play with himself. Children are clearly the future. He learns, immediately, how to make sounds with the *bansuri*. It took me four months to learn all the notes. Yet it's impossible to be bitter with a child, and soon I stop trying.

After I rest the circus resumes. We get back on the bike and he takes me to a newspaper office, where I am photographed, pretending to walk down the busy street. I give the camera a solid Brazilian thumbs-up. I am shaven and beautiful again and the reporter loves it. I've always distrusted the media, have never been quoted correctly, and have a hard time seeing the value in the whole sordid operation. But, I must admit, having that Golden Passport has been an undeniable boon.

---

[2]You know, like in *Spinal Tap*.

After the newspaper, Pritesh kindly takes me to the TV. He has taken the whole day to ferry me around (it is Sunday), to make sure all my needs are met, even those I couldn't have possibly imagined. He is the very incarnation of youthful hospitality. After the interview he gives me one last ride, to the edge of town, near the bridge. I want to take up the journey from the *seva-ashram* where we met, but my fidelity to the salt march gets lost in the confusion. It's okay, though. I'm getting a sense of what this is about.

The bridge spans the Narmada river for a solid half-kilometer of rust. I walk alongside cars, scooters, bicycles, and goats, granting my own prayers of safety through careful footing. Far below me are the green banks of the Narmada and free herds of cattle lounging in bucolic glory. I have seen a portrait of them in the Louvre, broken into little dots, only to be reassembled by the eye. It's not so hot with the wind and I give thanks I don't have to swim. Tomorrow is another district, another dialect, another culture.

I walk over and off the bridge, up the hill that greets me on the Ankleshwar side. Less than a kilometer later I spot a man on a motorcycle waiting for me. It's easy to tell when someone is waiting for you. His name is Sanjaybhai, he waves and greets me. He is dressed in white western clothing, looks important, and sit atop a large motorcycle. Men here love sitting on their motorcycles. The seat cover on his motorcycle – every Indian motorcycle is styled with a seat cover – is a shaggy lion's mane. I am afraid he is a member of the media or the government.

Sanjaybhai wants to invite me to his house to stay tonight and, as always, I accept. He understands I am walking and doesn't even offer to give me a ride, but rather tells me to ask 'Fat Mehul' at the next roadside store to give me directions. I agree and he rides off. The road, for once, is surrounded by thick trees, with neither fat man nor roadside store in sight.

I assume my last host had called him and am both relieved and disappointed. After days of wanting peace and air, the mosquitoes have driven my desires around again: I must sleep in a house. It has been three days since I have slept well and I know that can only lead to sickness.

The store is a couple of miles away and 'Fat Mehul' is the largest Indian man I have seen so far. He is pleased in general and especially to meet me, a caricature of the jolly merchant. His tiny roadside stall stocks cheap plastic 'goods' and minor vices (tobacco, *sopari*, *chocolates*) and doesn't seem like it would provide enough sustenance to keep him round. The gods work in mysterious ways.

'Fat Mehul' tells me that Sanjaybhai has called and will meet me at the railroad crossing in Ankleshwar, right off the main road. I walk another hour and reach the crossing in the traffic of smog and sunset. It's a mess on all sides as bikes and cars line up directly across from one another, waiting for the train. They are stopped not by the idea of a crossing but only the physical barrier of the lowered wooden pole. A loose idea persists that one should slide towards the left. There are no lanes. Pedestrians and cyclists walk ahead and duck through even as the train approaches. We all wait and cough together.

The train flies through and the fleets start their engines in anticipation of the rising guards. Everybody goes at once, weaving through the other team like a giant mechanized game of 'Red Rover'. Nobody is hurt and I, too, cross in fear and wonder, carried through the smog by the tide. Sanjaybhai finds me on the other side and we walk together. Friends with video-cameras appear and they take footage of me walking for a few minutes in the last good light of the day. The flowers I picked for my hair have wilted in the heat. The cameras and cars continue as Sanjaybhai walks me the last few hundred meters to his house. He is not in the government, but has worked with the Congress Party in the past few years, helping out. Nobody told him about me but he was running an errand and saw me on the road and thought I looked interesting.

Really? Really.

It's a strange world, still. We sit on the roof in the twilight and he goes downstairs to make arrangements. I talk to his friend, a closed, elderly man. Another man comes up for an interview but I am already exhausted. I joke with him and refuse to give him the proper answers until Sanjaybhai works out a script for me, so I know exactly what to say. It's inoffensive and uninteresting and I follow it, knowing the whole affair will soon be over. It is. We eat dinner with his wife and daughter and they even turn off the TV to do so. Sanjaybhai lives a huge new *bungalow*, largely unfurnished. He is very proud.

After dinner we get on the bike and whip coldly through the neigh-

borhood, down to a 2500 year old temple complex, dedicated to both
Ranchod and Shiva. He warns me of the snakes and we walk carefully
through bushes and rubble to the temple, where an old *yogi* is presid-
ing, cigarette in hand. The *yogi* orders me a cup of *chai* and proceeds
to speak ceaselessly in an English I barely can't understand.

"Health is wealth."

Do I truly understand his wisdom? He clarifies:

"Health is money".

Is this from the ancient scriptures? I am too tired to pretend to
respect him, an enlightened wizard with textbook platitudes, who is
clearly not interested in this particular ego seated in front of him. I
am at the membrane with fatigue and smoky intolerance once again.
The *chai* is an acrid shade of terrible and remains ignored at my side.
I get up to go while Sanjaybhai faithfully has his consultation.

We are given holy milk and walk down to the rectangular temple
step pond, carved 2500 years ago. At the bottom, apparently, lies a
secret underground tunnel which allows water to flow directly from the
Narmada river, less than a kilometer away. The water in the Narmada
comes directly from the *Ganga*, Sanjaybhai says. All rivers comes from
the *Ganga*. Everything is connected. That which has taken me twenty-
six years to *begin to grasp* is the conventional wisdom in these parts.
We duck into a small cave tucked aside the pond and Sanjaybhai lights
some candles and *ghee* lamps. There is a stone *shivalingam* and bull in
the center and we take turns pouring the holy milk on it and praying.
We sing together and I play the *bansuri* tunelessly. In the echoes of
the small cave I can feel the power of the music regardless. Sanjaybhai
is impressd, the gods are happy, and we leave.

I am exhausted but agree when he asks if we can stop at his relatives' house. It was never up to me. We watch television, inhale
the smoke from a campfire on the front porch – an alternative to the
mosquitoes – and discuss the American spectacle. I refuse soft-drinks
and mildly offend them. We must draw our lines somewhere.

In our discussion I understand a bit more of how I see myself –
not the Indian they know nor the America they see on TV, but some
bastard child of the two. A possible future.

Before I can sleep we talk some more downstairs with Sanjaybhai's
daughter. He asks her to say her prayers for me. She does:

"Everyday, in every way, I am getting better and better."
"Everyday, in every way, I am getting better and better."
"Everyday, in every way, I am getting better and better."

I smile and try to avoid collapsing in laughter. I've heard that line before. It is a famous *mantra* used in self-help books and schools of Mind Power and confidence training. To help you get what you want when you want it. More hypnosis than prayer. And it works. Sanjaybhai excitedly tells me how it worked for him. For years he wanted a house of his own and would repeat to himself over and over, every night

"BIG *BUNGALOW*."
"BIG *BUNGALOW*."
"BIG *BUNGALOW*."

And now look! He lives in a huge three-storey house, a veritable Big *Bungalow* that cost 3.5 million *points*. How?

The power of the mind.

But how? I press him. His responds overshoots my comprehension. Something about a certain mineral ore buried deep in the ground, the Indian government, and making missiles. I'm not quite with him.

But listen! He quit his job three years ago to devote himself to practicing Mind Power and to teaching others. Anyone can have the same success. He can *easily* book an appearance of his *guru* in Ahmedabad, for me, if I want.

Sanjaybhai is unbearably genuine and has loved me in his mind and actions since he saw me walking down a crowded Indian highway. I stay the night under a mosquito net and a fan and sleep comfortably for the first time in four days. He is *Krishna* as Mind Power. Perhaps he has made his money in a shady deal involving Uranium that, generations later, all of humanity will rue. He's committed to teaching his daughter (female child, mind you) how to guarantee herself the manifestation of her wildest dreams.

There's really no way to process any of this.

While I'm trying, my host asks for my mother's phone number in the United States. Why? To call her every once in a while: he understands I'm her only child and am seldom there. I am bewildered and give it to him. I can't think of anything else to do than giving people exactly what they want, since that's what they seem to be doing with me.

Day 16

March 27, 2006

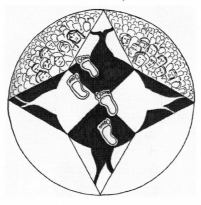

"Non-violence is not a cloistered virtue, confined only to the Rishi and the cave-dweller. It is capable of being practised by the millions, because it is the law of our species."

16.1   to Sajod

I don't know how to say twenty-seven. I've reached the limit of my vocabulaly. I ask *Krishna* for more words, and more Vitamin C.

Two weeks ago I woke up in Aslali, said goodbye to the incomparable B.K. Patel, and walked through Bareja to the Statesman's house in Navagam. Today is the 16th day. I'm over the hill, so to speak.

This morning I awake refreshed. After three nights of piss-poor sleep in outdoor temple style, *Krishna* treated me to a roof, screens, fan, and mosquito net. I sleep solidly from 11 to 5 and awake to yoga, a wonderfully cold shower, and my morning sit. When the social weight rises, the practices tend to drop, but I'm trying to keep everything in balance. Yesterday was full of *Krishna's* holy and frustrating society.

Masi prepares me warm milk with *bacri* (oiled like *parotha*) and Sanjaybhai leaves with me at 6h45. He wants to drive me to the building where Gandhiji stayed, now in a 'bad area'. Along the way he reiterates the power of the Mind:

"Everyday, in every way, I am getting Better and Better."

He tells me about communicating without speech. There is a special word for it in Gujarati. They call it 'telepathy'. He has not worked for three years and yet everything is taken care of. "*Krishna* even buys my gasoline," he laughs. I looked down over his shoulder, racing down the street, to see the gauge on empty.

There is no caretaker at the old house but the neighbors tell us a drunken old woman had occupied the building. She does not respond to our greetings. Sanjaybhai and I leave the building and walk together for 15 minutes. Upon leaving, Sanjaybhai gives me money. I am physically unable to refuse it. For the first time in two weeks, I am the proud holder of Indian currency. Gandhi and more Gandhi. Sanjaybhai instructs me to find Jyosisahib in Sajod and the *sarpanch* in Mangrol. He even gives me a card with some names for Rayma tomorrow. I haven't even looked at my map enough to know the names of these towns.

I am rich with objects. Twenty-one *points* from Sanjaybhai. Biscuits and *chevro* from Rupesh, the barber of Derol. I need to find someone to give them to before they become stale, a part of me. I am wearing a fresh shirt, a green and plastic women's ultimate jersey that has been with me for years. Sanjaybhai had good soap and a laundry brush and my *dhotis* are fresh and clean.

Yesterday at Sanjaybhai's relatives' house, I sat talking with a group of men, young and old, about the spectacle of America. They wanted it. They wanted to go there, to work there, to own there. I spoke some of my travels, of the beauty and peace of lives here, the lives that have escaped unscathed from the onslaught of marketing and desire. They laughed and made the usual joke that Americans want Indian culture and Indians want American culture. This time, I disagree.

The America they hunger for does not exist. It is an ideology, a dream, a marketing campaign. It is not a place itself, but thrives in various places. It is the America of Baywatch and remittances, where everyone is white and rich and plastic and loud. It is what I call 'the spectacle'[1].

The country I come from has a lot of the spectacle at play. It also has a lot of its own America, another country with culture and people who aren't made for TV or trying to be. In the American territory, yes, some people are interested in Indian culture. Others are interested in spectacular culture. The 'Matrix', as it were. Which is why I feel I am both of that land and not of that culture. More American than spectacular. In transition.

But in India, and in most of the rest of the world, people have no idea about the existence of my America. They only know the American version of the spectacle, that which they see on TV. They, for the most part, are interested in the American culture of wealth and whiteness. Many people can't understand how a brown person can be American. When I speak to them about inter-racial marriage and apartment buildings where people of all backgrounds live together, where your neighbor is cooking meat you can smell through the open window and the people downstairs let dogs into their houses, these people are horrified. Horrified. They do not want to move to the melting-pot salad-bowl America[2].

---

[1] See Guy Debord's *The Society of the Spectacle* and Raoul Vaneigem's The Revolution of Everyday Life for details. Those two books were the basis of my undergraduate thesis, *What is Subversive About Love*, and have affected me profoundly.

[2] As I put the final touches on this manuscript, we have elected a black president. This is *huge* for spectacular awareness. People who only knew Baywatch will now know Baywatch and Obama.

Most women here are not interested in wearing miniskirts and working in office buildings and never seeing their children. Many young men are relieved they don't have to date or take responsibility for living alone or choosing their spouse or planning their wedding.

What *do* they want, these people who stop me in the street and ask me to take them to America? Money. Objects. A camera, a car, a washing machine, a job. A big *bungalow*. And most of it would be to send back home.

Not a single young person I've met on this journey wants to go to America to *learn*, only to study or to work. They are generally only studying (here or there) as a means to get a job or a visa. They are not impressed by our universities or independent cinema or beaches or national parks. They are not interested in learning about two thousand different sects of Christianity or tattoos or maple syrup or the transgender activist movements.

These people don't even eat eggs.

I come down hard enough to give them an idea that America is a real place with real people and real differences. That if they live there and enjoy seeing women in bikinis they must know their daughter will be one of those women. That if they live there they will be spending their big salaries paying three and a half American *points* for a *chai* latte with no *buggia* in sight.

Watching American TV, Sanjaybhai's family concludes, is a lot less perilous.

I am still walking. I smile at a man on a bicycle and he gives me a look somewhere between "I bow to the god within you" and "How about a quickie in the cane fields?"

We are close enough to the river that the farmers are rich and the sugarcane is high. They smell sickly sweet after burning like the split juice from roasting pears. I begin to understand why civilization started along rivers – otherwise all you can grow is cotton. And eating cotton gets old. Here they cultivate millet and eggplant in secondary patches between sweet seas of cane.

I stop and hike off the road down a small irrigation canal, watching the last of the sunrise palette fade into blue. I can't quite handle the beauty.

The morning is haze wanting to be mist, without the help of clouds. The miracles refuse to stop. I am dumbfounded. Ever since the magic coconut offered two days ago, by Ganshamkaka in Derol, it has been a storm of blessings.

I am still amazed that Sanjaybhai's arrival was pure *Krishna*, natural and exotic, and had nothing to do with the news or some influential phone call. There was never a doubt in his attitude from the moment he saw me that he would take me in. And I am still amazed that after two weeks during which my very survival has been contingent on such miracles, they still amaze me.

Sanjaybhai demonstrates the success of 'Mind Power' and the inherent wrinkle therein. Now that people are beginning to understand that Anything is Possible with the power of the focused mind, it's time to educate ourselves as to how we should direct our wishes.

It's the Midas story again. Sanjaybhai could have anything in the world and he choose a Big *Bungalow*. I am given everything I ask and opt only for fruit and the occasional shave. Sanjaybhai pulled 350 million *points* out of a uranium mine. I impose myself on the charity of the rural poor.

Surely there's a better way, to benefit everybody involved, not waste our boons on trivia or private property. How do we train ourselves? What do we ask for?

Can I ask for a giant desalinization plant to offset the coming water crisis? Can we go to bed repeating

"Food Security"
"Food Security"
"Food Security"

and wake up conscious of the importance of supporting local farmers, eating in season, stopping the flow of pesticides and the erosion of topsoil?

Can Mind Power stop the War?

Another strange afternoon in India. Every strange is different, no time to accustom. Today it is the children. Sajod is a small village with a big school and, this week, a famous *guru* has been coming to give talks on the *Bhagavad Gita* every afternoon. After I pass a background

check, I am accepted as a guest of honor, housed, cared for, and made
to speak to the children.

I arrive in tiny Sajod, pass the school with its large tent sent up for
the big event, and ask for Joysisahib. At the correct house, I am made
to wait outside, and then – once verified – welcomed by Jyosisahib and
family. He proclaims the house to be my home – an open house, a
meeting place for all kinds of people. Only Hindus are people, I think.
He mentions the RSS which I only know as a Hindu fundamentalist
group associated with violence and bigotry: those are my prejudices,
anyways. So I ask Jyosisahib what the RSS is and he puffs up to
the membranes and discourses loudly (though no further away) on the
incredible love the RSS has for *Bharat*, the *seva* they do for the public,
and how their actions are so often misconstrued for political gain.

> "They are a *dharmic* organization and maintain Hindu
> *dharma*. They save bodies after dams break, they build
> houses after earthquakes. People fear them because they
> are decisive and efficient!"

I fidget at the fascist euphemisms.

Welcome to my new home. I spend the morning in the RSS safe-
house from 9h30 to 11h30, take an extra spicy *chai*, and learn music
and life from a large musical *brahmin* (they were all *brahmins*, with the
string) named Govindbhai. He plays many instruments, sings without
repress, and laughs so hard he seemed to be crying. Govindbhai even
teaches me how to play one of the most famous *dhuns* I've heard, on
my flute –

```
sa -- re -- | sa -- ni -- | da -- ni -- | sa -- -- --
sa -- re -- | sa -- ni -- | da ni da ni | sa -- -- --

sri ram | jai ram | jai jai | raaaaam
```

I stay with Govindbhai, soaking up the joy and the music, until
unseen voices call me to eat. We are so blessed to eat when we're
hungry, and even more blessed to eat when we're not. I eat with the
musicians hired for the *katha*, in the house where they stay. They
are here to play background music for the religious talks during the
seven day festival. It is day six and 1000 people have been coming each

day. The musicians are charming and open, smoking and joking about alcohol. Musicians. One of them still studies in high school and is eager to practice English. He practices by asking rapid-fire questions, not caring for responses.

> "In America what do the girls wear?
> "Do they all wear *saris*?
> "Do they only watch Hindi films?
> "Other films?
> "Do they know the Hindi film stars?
> "Will they speak Gujarati?
> "Which is the better language?"

We keep eating, courtesy of Vinod, the Rajasthani cook. He made *mung dal* and an onion/tomato salad dressed with salt and sugar, *dhokla* with lots of coriander and lime and *chass*. They give me extra lime (thank you *Krishna*, that was quick) against my running nose and I am called to give my speech.

The headmaster presents me as Sri Ankurbhai Shah. Formal, linguistic respect. A very strange phenomenon that the same word can be used for Ramana Maharshi, Ravi Shankar, and myself. Something is definitely wrong here.

Jyosisahib introduces me and the story of the *Namak Satyagraha* to hundreds of uniformed children – boys on the left, girls on the right, aisle in between. They clap and give their attention, garland me with flowers. They are seated 'Indian style' on the ground under the large awning built for the *katha*. There is no whispering or playing. I am scared to speak in my poor grammar but eventually tell them I've been on the road for 15 days out of respect for Gandhiji and faith in the divine, specifically the god in humankind. And after 15 days the god that is in the Gujarati people has proved to be alive and well, beautiful and bountiful, and shown me more love and respect than I could ever hope to reciprocate in my entire life.

It's all true of course, and exhilarating, but I feel disappointed. I know I could have used the podium to talk about Hindu-Muslim relations or the One Love or picking up trash or all the things that are so plain and so easy to change. But after having received so many sermons it didn't feel right to give one, and what can a foreigner say to a native anyhow in a tongue that is only partially his own? Another line I will not yet cross.

After my speech the kids are let out for lunch and a group of boys lead and follow me to the *talav* where the Gandhi plaque is. They call me Gandhikaka when they want my attention and are happy to play frisbee and fetch me cold water from the well. The water is pure, so sweet and so cold[3]. I ask them to sit in meditation with me under a giant mango tree and when I opened my eyes 15 minutes later, they had all gone. As it should be.

I still feel strange with kids, with groups, with groups of kids. I find myself trying to be aloof, holding back, refusing to play. I put effort out for them not to like me. Why don't I want to be their model.

I pray for fruit. As I finish my sit, alone, two young men arrive to take my spot under the mango tree, singing with sickles in tow. We greet, share water, and I give them the cookies. They left school at the 5th standard some years back and work in the fields. They earn forty *points* a day cutting cane and cotton. The cookies had cost Rupesh, the barber of Derol, ten *points*. They work alongside their father and drink together in the evenings. Just one glass of liquor. Five *points* a glass. It seems reasonable but his eyes are shot. Really just one glass? Prohibition and adulteration seem to go hand in hand. But everybody likes the coconut cookies and I feel good in the sun and the citrus, thank the gods for good health and digestion and the Hindu fundamentalists who take care of me.

---

[3]Like Williams' plums.

16.2   to Mangrol

I make it to Mangrol, which I expect to like from the name. It's a beautiful village so far – a perfect scene, the *talav* full of water, lotus, and lilies. A carpet of water chestnut is painted red across the lake's still surface. A temple or house or group of devoted musicians – one can't be sure – plays beautiful *bhajans* across the water. The sun readies to set. I'm parked on a well-groomed pasture next to a small *Dattatreya* shrine and some overgrown walls. It's neither hot nor cold and the light is for the painters and cameramen. Goats surround me, grooming the grass.

Eight pleasant kilometers to walk here – four on the unpopulated but well-paved highway from Sajod and another four southward on a smaller paved road. The last hour has been gorgeous, fluting across sugarcane fields, carelessly beckoning the invisible *gopis*. How different are the fields from the cities! Yesterday, walking through Bharuch, I passed the city Rotary Club, a huge concrete building on stilts above a fetid river of trash that could only be tolerated in a country as meditative as India. It rises from the filth like a lotus, a sculpture on paradox, a monument to imperial charity.

On the way out of Sajod, after my mangoed meditations, Jyosisahib invited me back to the pavilion to hear the *katha*. I was celebrated on the loudspeaker with the other honored guests, elderly Indian men dressed all in *khadi*, who walked slowly, drooping under the weight of gold and satisfaction.

The *katha* itself was crowded and fun. After the formalities the *guru* started into a thicket of the funny moral parables Gujaratis seem to love. They love moralizing. We love moralizing. I can remember only one of his stories:

> "A wandering sage is invited to dinner at a poor woman's house. Sages carry neither cash nor rice and are generally excited about any sort of invitation. The woman spends the whole day cooking, so excited that this holy man will bless her home with his presence. She prepares half a dozen curries, breaks out her favorite pickles from the larder, and makes both roasted and fried flatbreads. There is fresh yogurt for the meal and *srikhand* for dessert, with the sage's favorite sugar-soaked fried cheese-balls in his honor.

"The sage arrives, famished and humble, and seats himself on the floor in front of the magnificent spread. He is so full of joy that he becomes it. It oozes down his beard and becomes tangled in his matted locks. He acknowledges the feast and effort with a smile and blessing – it is not in his culture to say 'thank you' – and is about to begin when...

when
when
when

"...he notices a stack of fresh *pappadam*, yet to be fried, sitting on an end-table – the humble woman's sole piece of furniture – near the cooking area. His joy melts into desire. There is nothing better than starting a meal with a freshly fried *pappadam*, dark and salty, crispy and hot with oil. But she has not offered it to him – maybe there is not enough to share, maybe she considers it unworthy to accompany her grand production – and he is avowed never to ask."

I begin to relate.

"The sage is a great and clever man and begins to tell a story of his own, meditating in the jungles of Kerala, having tamed the tigers and elephants to lay next to him as he approaches union with the divine. One day, after timeless days of unbearable peace, he opens his eyes to see a giant cobra, vile and violent, about to strike.

"She shudders.

"And not only that! This cobra was so powerful, so huge, that it reached from here" – he taps his steel plate – "all the way to...to...to that table with the *pappadam* on it!

"She screams and leaps to her feet:

'*Hari Rama!*'

"She has always been afraid of snakes, ever since she was a little girl fetching water and once:

'I saw one so big it reached all the way to here!'

"she exclaims, reliving her fear, moving the table with the precious *pappadam* to the furthest corner of the house."

Yes, over *there*.

And the punchline, if I understood correctly, was either:

'The more you chase your desires, the further you are from contentment' or 'You should just ask straight up if you need something'.

I couldn't quite tell but the best part, clearly, was that my violinist friend Ignesh had been accentuating the entire talk, morality included, with subtle and dramatic cuts on his instrument. Oh, the violin.

I take out my flute to play for the goats. A thin bamboo reed with seven holes that will always be beyond me, that I will never exhaust. I must take my lessons from it. Another gift, a gift of harmony and mathematics and Chanoorbhai Atri, my teacher in Jamnagar. I am blessed, so blessed, and incapable, so incapable, of dealing with it. What can I do? I have been given so many gifts and miracles already in this life – spared so often from alcohol, from weather, from death – that I must do something. There are no options.

The sun reflects in the lake and lotus flowers. It's all too precious. I want to share this moment, this perfect moment, with all of my friends and teachers, all of the gods and blessings. I don't deserve it alone.

Luckily, in India, you are never alone.

Two gentlefolk from the town come to listen and compliment my plaing. They have clearly never heard a *bansuri* before. They give me some names in town and within an hour I am safely ensconced in a local temple, dedicated to the same Lord *Dattatreya*. The pujari, Daprat, is a kind man, living with his wife and children next to the temple, free lodging and a mere 800 *points* a month. He came four years ago from his native place near the Pakistani border. He tends to the humans, to the gods, and to the trees: *pipal, vad, shankpushpi, aso-palav*.

I sleep amidst altars and gods and regret not bringing a net. I was wrong. Fans are not enough. When you come here, bring a net. You deserve it, wandering pilgrim.

The town itself is clean, paved, and rich. They say only *brahmins* and *aadivasis* live here; the latter brought in for cheap seasonal labor. I have not been shown their neighborhoods. We talk until it is time for a *Krishna*-based soap-opera on television and I sit against the banyan tree to write. A local child comes to pray and we speak. He is in the 11th standard and wants to study 'commerce' in college. You can only study 'commerce' or 'science': 'arts' is for losers. He has never heard of Africa or the salt march. It has to do with the tracking, I guess. I talk to him about both before sleeping. There is no one to blame.

Day 17

March 28, 2006

"It gives me ineffable joy to make experiments proving that love is the supreme and only law of life."

17.1   to Rayma

I have become my environment. Jolted to consciousness before mechanical alarms by the unquestionable necessity to move my bowels. I jump the locked temple gate and scramble through the darkness as far as I can make it before succumbing to my humanity. Still unsure of whether it was the fields or the road but I now have some context for the piles of human excrement that seem to be everywhere in this country.

Mid-walk in the mid-morning and an endless line of cows continues along the road. I step aside, find a tree, and use their progress to time my meditation. Once again the world is too much for me: they parade far beyond the span of my attention.

The roads themselves have been greener and richer today and yesterday, full of calm and shade. Perhaps the timing of the sun has something to do with it, some phenomenon of its transit? I pass busy cane fields this morning, workers harvesting with huge cleavers onto sagging trucks, destined for large refineries. Where is the local processing? Where is the village *swaraj*?

Two consecutive nights of good sleep and the Fear is leaving, ushered away by a high power fan. Before breakfast with Daprat and family I take another powerful outdoor movement – there is no toilet in the temple compound – on a ridge at the end of the town field with a line of other morning shitters. A communal affair, reminding me of the social workers who built toilet blocks all over rural India, destined to disuse because village society had no interest in conducting its business alone.

I am convinced. Wherever I settle to build my *ashram* and farmhouse, there must be an outhouse.

Last night they eventually dragged me in to watch *Krishna* on TV – as a pilgrim there is no offer I can deny – and saw him whiter than white (he is supposed to be blue!), resplendent in gold, acting out fantasies ancient and modern for the masses to adore. *Masi* fed us a thin *dal* with *dhokla*, *bataka shak*, and *bacri*. You have nothing to lose but your chains, and a world of carbohydrates to win.

This morning's breakfast is *chai* with the *chevro* I brought, another gift from Rupesh in Derol. My host allows me to donate the 21 *points* Sanjaybhai forced upon me. I hope he takes it for his family. What if I had been smart enough to accept all the gifts and monies offered to me, declaring I would only pass them on to someone else? How much more valuable than refusal would that have been?

I sit to meditate again as the cows depart, and am soon jostled by the ringing of my phone. Today is its last day of service. My cousin is calling. She read the article today in the newspaper and wants to know if I can stop walking early to attend my niece's engagement ceremony. I love my niece and consider taking a train back to Nadiad – the ceremony is on my next rest day – and returning on schedule. It's a crazy scheme, utterly out of place in my isolated peregrine world.

Then I remember I have no money.

There is a tension here in the fields between flute and cattle, between families and ideas, presences and principles. Where must our loyalties lie?

Once you get over the whole 'living on the backs of the bruised' thing, it becomes hard to criticize the royal treatment. *Royale*. It feels pretty great, especially after you've been out in the dust and dirt and noise and jaguar sun all day and you can convince yourself you deserve it.

Then again, physical discomfort was never a downside of wealth.

Gandhi has a line somewhere about his rich friends and how he's not attached to their favors – that is, of course, the critical division, between acceptance and dependence, detachment and desire. Once we go beyond accepting hot showers and dark chocolate as mere (though pleasant) facets of the creation, and start thinking that somehow we have earned them, then we have traded humility for confusion. I can feel this idea of 'what do I deserve' swirling around me with all the blessings. I have earned none of this and nothing I do, nothing I say, nowhere I walk will earn me any of the smiles or blessings of these old women, and yet somehow I have a deep faith that we – all of us – deserve this life, this High, this touch of divinity.

We deserve everything and have earned nothing. The protestants would hate it.

I stop before Rayma to talk to a patel farmer (read: landowner) with kind eyes under his sunglasses (I knew it from the beginning). He is prepared to tell me all about India, the essence of India. I have been told by so many kind men and women about India, the true India, the essence of India that I can only conclude the true nature of India is exactly that – people excited to tell you the true nature of India.

Along the way, they tell you what America is like, the true nature of America, and what you are like, your own true nature. They tell you exactly what you should do with your short future on this long planet. This *kaka*, however, starts off more conversational than didactic, even listening at times. He takes off his sunglasses so I can see his eyes. But soon enough, in the shade of the willow tree, he veers towards the ancient knowledge of *Bharat*: the intercontinental missile technology developed in the *Ramayana* (perhaps already aimed at Pakistan), the unique property of *neem* and *pipal* trees to give oxygen around the clock and not just during the day, and even detailing *ayurvedic* treatments of diabetes – *neem* and camel's milk. Eventually he settles into the importance of standing up for yourself and doing your own work.

He discourses further on the *aadivasis* laborers who work for him and how limited and primitive they are, how they only care about pleasure and the worries of today, with no thought to long-term planning or commitment. They stop working when they can afford a bag of rice and come back when they have eaten it.

I sense a theme here, and it troubles me.

What is our work to be done and what is somebody else's? Who decides? Is it good that he owns land and they work it? Who is doing the work of whom? And can I really believe that 'these people' are *incapable* of thinking in certain ways? Are we fundamentally different? And if we are, are we really more advanced to be thinking about life insurance policies and ICBMs instead of enjoying our rice and coconuts every evening?

Or have they already thought about it, conducted the complex simulations in their minds, seen the inevitably trajectory from accumulation to hoarding to surplus-value to the hydrogen bomb?

I do know that histories – including my own journals – are written by the rich. I know that I can't even properly communicate with the poor, due to scheduling and dialect. I do know that when I walk into a town, I see a group of three-storey concrete houses with marble floors, where the landowners live – the very landowners who feed and house me – and that to get to them I must walk by villages of blue tarps that remind me of earthquakes and civil wars and refugee camps. I know that these tent cities are both provisional and permanent, that the labor supply is guaranteed year round, and that it's no worry because all the "big people" have houses, as *masi* told me this morning. "Big people", I think, means *patels*.

By *masi* I mean the three generations of women who me asked "What's your deal?" and "Are you really alone?" when I walked by their house this morning, then invited me inside for water and *chai*. They spoke little, but, then again, hospitality and classism require few words.

To get to Rayma you take the road onwards from Mangrol, through other two villages, and turn left at the sign for Valner (which I couldn't read), where the big people have houses and the small people play and stare at you from tents.

From Valner you walk, playing your flute, through sugarcane and cotton, pick wild *gorsimla*, and wave at schoolchildren. Five hundred meters north of Rayma an old man meets you on the road. Who had told him about me? The famed Hareshbhai Bhatt. Everybody had told him about him, from Sanjaybhai in Ankleshwar onwards.

In my limited experience when everyone tells you one man's name he is:

1. Rich.

2. Either awesome, or a jerk.

Which is to say you know nothing about him except that he's rich, and his wealth gives you no clue as to his actions. So judgment is out of the question, if not the field of desire.

With Hareshbhai, from his posture, smile, and gentle cradle of my *namaste*, I can tell he was a lover of humans, and he loved me, already. He welcomes me and gives me directions to his house, not bothering to offer me a ride I can't accept, and zips off on his scooter.

I can tell, now, how I will be received in a town and when I should center my attention to prepare for it. I can tell, now, the difference between good *chai* and bad – proportions of sugar and milk, tea to *masala*. All without even tasting. I can tell a man's attitude by how he reacts to my *namaste*. I can get any child to smile and give me the thumbs up. I can almost even tell *caste* by a man's face, structure, and cleanliness. Not all the way, but I'm getting there.

These are skills I don't think I've learned – there hasn't been enough time for that – but rather powers I seem to have been granted by a certain attunement, a certain harmony with my surroundings. They may be purely a function of walking, and I have no expectation to retain them when I stop.

In Rayma there is no need to make a special visit to the house where Gandhi stayed or spoke because that's where you are staying, too. Hareshbhai's family had the honor of welcoming Gandhi, and though they have remodeled a bit with cash sent from abroad in the intervening seventy-six years – putting in a grand spiral staircase, lining the floors with tile, and hanging giant, bland, nature photography on the walls – it's the same house.

Hareshbhai and his wife are divine and welcoming. A veritable feast of *puri*, fresh *tuved shak*, *basudi*, *dal*, *bath*, fenugreek-banana *buggia*, and *pappadam*. She forces me, with ease, to eat four bowls of milky sweet *basudi*. During lunch they tell me they have 50 acres of land, including 300 *chickoo* trees, now in season. We talk easily and pleasantly, I play the flute for them, and everyone is happy.

They are kind enough to let me nap and I fall asleep thinking of how royal this road has been since my two dinners in Derol: pure luxury. How overwhelming it is to be welcomed by a kind uncle as you walk into town. How only the *Krishnas* know what must follow. They are kind enough to let me nap and I fall asleep thinking of how royal this road has been since my two dinners in Derol: pure luxury. How overwhelming it is to be welcomed by a kind uncle as you walk into town. How only the *Krishnas* know what must follow.

17.2   to Umrachi

Two hours of One Love afternoon napping that Charak, the disciplinarian ayurvedic sage, would despise[1]. Feeling light and airy, I have enough alone time to practice 100 scales on the flute.

Courting tardy when I go downstairs and *masi* has prepared a spread of fruits for an afternoon snack: a *chickoo* milkshake with cardamom, a plate of dried *chickoo*, and a bag of fresh *chickoo* for the road. Grapes and *gorsimla* besides. I bathe in fruit and thanks: they are too kind, unwilling to let me leave. *Masi* starts crying when I won't take any money -

"You are alone! You have no plans, no places to stay!"

I haven't gotten lost yet!

"You have nothing."

But I made it here, to you!

It's to no avail, I cannot explain. They present me with a mounted copy of the latest newspaper article for me to take on my journey.

Hareshbhai warns me that I must cross the Kim river. There may or may not be a ferry and if there isn't I must walk an extra five kilometers to Vadoli, and then cross back up to Umrachi. We want to cross on the ferry of course, he repeats. Always the 'we'. In many parts of India the use of the first-person singular pronoun is non-existent. There is only 'we'. 'I' am only 'we'.

By the time I have crammed all the fruit into my pack and allowed to leave, I am late with the knowledge I have to walk an extra five kilometers. The afternoon is made of gold and beauty, the highway popular and full of trucks.

I traipse along in beauty's lap through fields of cane, banana, *tuved*, and a small edible gourd (*parvar*). It's idyllic and I sing and think and think about not thinking. The memory comes to me of Govindkaka, the *brahmin* musician, touching the flute to his forehead and eyes:

"With this tool, each breath is *Krishna puja*."
"In music, you lose yourself to the wonder of the world."

---

[1] In *ayurveda* the siesta is seriously frowned upon as bad for digestion.

That's the kind of getting lost I'm interested in.

Govindkaka. Holy fat people are unjustified to me in a country with so much starvation, privation, and lack of sanitation. A priest especially, a purported servant of god and thus the poor![2]

But a fat *brahmin* musician is different story. The jovial musician rolls in his own connection to the divine – he *should* be fat, he should be rewarded by god and man alike not merely for performing rituals and sacrifices on behalf of the poor, but for being himself a medium of interaction – music – between god and man. He doesn't stand between like the interpreter, he becomes the divine voice – the *swar* – for a time.

I make it to the Kim river bridge at sunset and stop to watch the show and finish my water. Then I lose my way.

It's the first time in 17 days I've walked in the darkness, and the first time I get lost. I miss the turnoff, and – in my hubris – refuse to ask for help, walking another three kilometers of obscure Indian road, alongside fading villages and rumbling trucks, until three people in a row tell me I have gone too far. Reluctantly, I turn around, past any other options, worried only that *masi* is waiting in Rayma for news of my arrival. She was right to cry.

As the night gets later and the trucks get louder it becomes increasingly clear that they could kill me. What are you supposed to do with your last moments, every time you hear an invisible truck lumbering on the highway behind you?

Sing the names of those you love, close your eyes, keep walking.

I find the turn-off and they (Who? The people who are everywhere, always, in this country) tell me Umrachi lies another two or three kilometers farther. I pray it's three and not the infamous 'two', which could mean anything.

I pass prohibited wine shops in the countryside, the only entertainment for exhausted laborers. They seem drunk and hostile when I stop to ask for directions, so I confine my focus to the stars; In 17 days I have never walked under the stars or felt the chill of the wind. Everything with its own beauty.

At the gate to Umrachi a motorcycled man asks my name. Yes, I am the *yatri*. Yes, I am alone. He scolds me for arriving late – it's nine o'clock – and leads me through town to a low earthen dungeon of

---

[2]For who else is god if not the masses? See the 'talisman' in 8.2

a house, crammed with so many people I can't record their names. So much for sending a postcard to each person I meet.

The women tell me to wash up and to sit, serve me *bacri* and *mung dal shak*. I eat in the kitchen under the long exposed timbers that hold up the metal roof. The walls and floor are made of mud, it's the biggest mud house I've seen yet.

When I finish eating, the men tell me to sit with them. We speak and play music until midnight, in the calm conversation of people genuinely learning and caring. A blind man plays the drum and sets the pace – so direct and sincere in his love, so well cared-for by his friends. They are present for him at every step and falter. At some point, the electricity goes and intimacy replaces it. Pravinbhai, the blind man, plays the *dhol* and his friends sing *Vaishnav Jan To* and *Sabarmati ke Sant*. I can only smile and cry.

They ask about my family and history, listen to my stories of the journey so far. It's so seldom that people listen and so seldom I feel like I have anything to say. I show them the Golden Passport – I love watching people's reactions after they've already met me. They light up with something beyond impression or surprise, but rather some species of gentle pride, for themselves and for me, that their friend has received such blessings. And I still have no idea what it says.

Day 18

March 29, 2006

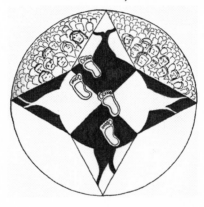

"A non-violent revolution is not a
programme of 'seizure of power'. It is a
programme of transformation of
relationships ending in a peaceful transfer
of power."

18.1 to Aarthan

The morning is cold and spaceless, no room for yoga or privacy for meditation. I quickly shower and notice the small cut on my face is pus-filled and tender. Last night was the first evening I didn't wash my clothes. With only two pairs of clothes there's only slight room for error. The nameless family feeds me *chai* and *bataka-poha* against the morning chill until my friends from last night come at 6h30.

All seven of them walk with me, first to the riverbank where Gandhiji's party had crossed. We touch the water with respect and walk back to their village in the very footsteps of the original *yatris*, seventy-six years ago. Ajitbhai, a teacher, asks me to speak at his school (on my way) this afternoon. Pravin and Yogendra (I did learn some of their names) are so proud to be walking the same path as Gandhi. My friends, giddy with excitement, find a camera and take picture after picture at the insistence of Pravinbhai (the blind man). We slowly walk the few kilometers to the highway, where they give me a map to Aarthan and bless my journey. So much love and respect, so much confidence in me. And so quickly. Faith.

> "Ankurbhai, this *yatra* of yours is the right way."
> "Ankurbhai, you are so young, maybe you will do something good."

At the highway I retrace yesterday's steps back to the intersection in front of the bridge, then follow the road west towards Surat. According to the program, I will reach Surat on one of the last days of the trip: even seeing the name is a shock.

Might this ever be over?

Trucks and humans stand aside as a Rabari shepherd passes with his huge heard of buffalo. I play for them until a motorcycle stops, fuel gauge on empty.

Sanjaybhai steps off to greet me. Sanjaybhai? The Mind Power *Krishna* from Ankleshwar with the Big *Bungalow* and open heart.

He is better in every way, I can tell. We embrace – a male pleasure – and I thank him profusely for his help and connections. He tells me he will prepare the media in Surat, give them my telephone number. I thank him without revealing my service has expired. We part in warmth.

Another bridge welcomes me (thank you civil engineering!) and I turn left thereafter, heeding the map Yogendrabhai gave me this morning. I walk a few gorgeous kilometers, by casual cane fields and smiling farmers. They cultivate *tindura*, *parvar*, *chori*, *karela*, *rai*, and *ringun*. I pass a makeshift village at the edge of town, the strong smell of shit on one hand versus the women washing clothes amidst the lily pads on the other.

At the entrance of town there is a temple, where I pause to attune myself to the new environment. I've noted I do a lot better with people if I give myself a few minutes to transition between walking the earth and talking to the humans. These omnipresent temples provide the perfect opportunity – nobody disturbs a prayer.

Pilgrims, take note.

I rise to a glass of water from the *pujari*, who has recognized me from the paper. We talk for a while in the gardens, along with a local teacher – a colleague of Ajitbhai, one of my friends from last night. They are loving, both, and the *pujari* tells me I will eat there and be taken around town. I negotiate some time for relaxation before the personal parade, to meditate and to write.

He lets me sit in silence with shut eyes between the shrine and the garden. I listen to the young mothers and their small boys giving offerings to *Mataji*, praying for success, wealth, and high marks on their exams. They must be beautiful young women with their own mothers in tow, calm and sincere in their affection. Nobody brings a girl.

The *pujari* decides it's time to see the town and we embark on tour. A woman has been waiting to invite me into her house since she heard of the *yatra* weeks ago. She plies me with fresh fruit and lemonade in congratulations.

Down the street a man understands I am from the United States and begins to harangue me about the WTO and corporate globalization. He is the first person I've met with whom I could potentially discuss these important topics, and yet he has no interest in discussion, only criticism. He treats me a foreigner citizen, not a person. The best part is that his insistence on criminal unfairness is totally tied to India's position in the global order – he would be more than happy if *his* nation were at the top.

The *pujari* helps me escape, to the house of a man whose father had worked with Gandhi. We read an interview together, in Gujarati, about Gandhiji's visit to Aarthan, today, seventy-six years ago. They serve me an unavoidable purple milkshake instead of *chai* and I can only give thanks for its coolness. It tastes a little 'off'.

I am starving and eventually my guide too gets hungry and takes me home for lunch. His wife is typically gentle and serves us both as I gaze into the gardens. It is unbearably hot and I have been asked – by Ajitbhai this morning – to speak to an elementary school down the road. I will have to leave at three to make it on time. Due to the heat, leaving before four is not recommended. It is, in fact, considered quite dangerous.

The *pujari* interrupts my reverie to present me with a gift, a simple white *dhoti* like my grandfather's. It is perfect – the turban I will need to ward away the afternoon sun. I am able to nap almost an hour in the temple as the *pujari* locks the gate, pulls down the curtains, and allows the gods their own afternoon *siesta*.

18.2   to Bhatgam

The jaguar is on the prowl. Over forty degrees of sunshine. I make it
to the school on time and without losing consciousness. Barely. The
sun was too much, even with the *dhoti* wrapped around my head, and
I can feel a fever coming on. I am cold.

They give me water and make me wait for my turn to speak. I am
seated under the sun next to some famous *ayurvedic* doctor, speaking from the podium. The principal once again introduces me as Sri
Ankurbhai Shah, the Dandi *yatri*. He instructs me to speak in English.

"It doesn't matter if they understand."

So I speak for a couple of minutes about American money and
cultural values and how they are inseparable or at least contagious,
to hundreds of kids who have no idea what I am saying. Hundreds
of quiet, well-behaved uniforms who have been sitting in the sun all
day. They give me a roaring applause and settle in once again for more
lectures on toothpaste.

The road to Bhatgam has welcome shade and looks quaint enough
to film a movie. I wonder, were roads quaint before movies?

I walk on, thinking back to Umrachi, consistently amazed at *Krishna's* love and generosity. I have experienced true hospitality. Not
the host who gives what he has, or what he thinks you want, or even
what you think you want, but rather the deep connective tissue love
that Knows and gives you exactly what you need and never thought
to ask for. In this case it's a journal, which I never dared to ask for
(to gods or to men) and was given last night by Ajitbhai, just as I
completed my first one.

It's been more than two weeks, and every day is different. Yesterday
was a glory and a trial, from the royal palace of Rayma to Umrechi's
long and winding road, through darkness to a dungeon, kerosene lamps
and the most interested and educated men I've met to date, all of whom
walked with me this morning.

My thoughts and the road dead-end into sugarcane fields; I continue through small trails as the afternoon slides into evening, finally
emerging onto pavement for the last kilometer. As usual the three-
storey bungalows of the rich rise into view as one walks through the
destitution of imported labor. I am shocked to see a woman bathing
topless in a fetid river – what most people in the world, India included

– would consider a sewer. I am more shocked at the shoulders than the sewer. It's been months since I've seen a woman's shoulders.

At Bhatgam, exhausted and sick from the heat, some men brusquely call me over before I can attune myself to the situation. They offer me water. I give them my story – now without fear, without thought – and they suggest, to no surprise, speaking with the *mandir* or *sarpanch*.

I conduct basic prayer and frisbee with the kids in front of the *mandir*, and the *sarpanch* kindly takes me in. It seems like he had been waiting – most of the 'big people' in town gather on the (sole) paved street that leads to their mansions, huge three-story affairs from a catalog of British suburbia. Half are empty, their owners working in a strange land. The landowners salute me and force me to consume a rose milkshake when I refuse their *chai*. It tastes a little 'off'.

I am given time to shower, wash my clothes, and meditate before the *sarpanch* walks me to the schoolroom that holds a permanent exhibition on Gandhi's life. Timelines and essays, old photographs and biographical sketches adorn the walls, well-organized and carefully transcribed.

Pareshbhai, the caretaker, reads me the text of Gandhi's speech the day he came here, seventy-six years ago.

"This very day!," he exclaims, surprised.

Yes, this very day.

It's easily the best preserved memory of Gandhiji I've seen on this road. The whole room – photographs, maps, texts – is water damaged, but it is still clear that somebody wanted it to be here, to be remembered.

My host comes to pick me up for dinner and conversation with the town, on someone's front porch. I have no hunger but eat anyways. All the men sit on the ground and talk on one porch, all the women sit on the ground and talk at the next one. We talk about organic farming and, to my surprise, two of the farmers (read: landowners) have recently switched over, back from the green revolution. Why?

"Good market."

It's the truth. In my mind, the growing organic consciousness is an attempt and opportunity for us to refashion our relationship to the land. That's the vision of the farm I work on back homes, thousands of miles and cultures away. Not everyone shares that opinion. They show me a newsletter of organic news and products, which I can't read. One day I'm going to come back literate and these people will really have to watch out.

They make me play the flute and it's terrible. I have no breath and am constantly sniffling. They are dressed in light cotton gowns and I feel cold. I dare to ask why the men and women don't sit together, why married couples don't hold hands in public, etc. I can't voice the etc., of course, but I want to know about it.

Even the women on the other porch hear my question. Men and women both smile and acknowledge the reality: that's how it is. They must know something I don't, for I can detect no desire for it to be any other way.

Day 19

March 30, 2006

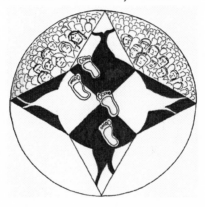

"There is no such things as defeat or despair in the dictionary of a man who bases his life on Truth and Non-violence."

19.1 to Sandhier

[writing on April 1st, 15h00]

The first words I've written in days. The worst is over.
Enshallah.

My head still hurts. I don't feel I've forgotten too much, probably
because not that much can happen when feel like you're dying. No
conversations, no insights. The last few days I witnessed with my own
mortality and frigidity – how starkly one's priorities and notions of the
self shrink under duress. As I witnessed earlier, in Napa, so it has been
proven to and through me – how can you be a lover under pain? Your
senses, your mind, your stature, your very consciousness contracts. I
didn't care to shower, I didn't brush my teeth for days, I didn't pray to
Krishna or to anybody else, speak the name of gods or my loved ones,
play the flute or sing songs, meditate. I could only focus on this body,
my exploding head, fragile bones, and shivering skin. Fever, delirium,
headache. Mental dysfunction. Cold. Vile green phelgm from my nose.

My mind is recovering. Slowly. I still can't remember which way to
walk after taking a break, or the names of yesterday's towns, but my
head hurts less. The traces of the illness remain, everywhere. Luckily
a steady diet of *ghee* is also everywhere to be found.

Level one of the fall must have been catching a cold trying to find
Amrachi at night, where I was eventually met with so much love. Level
two was acceding to Ajitbhai's wish that I speak at his school – a
disastrous afternoon walk through the jaguar sun. Level three was
likely some sort of poisoning from the rose milkshake or just too much
strange food in general or maybe that it's been twenty days and I am
in over my head.

I didn't sleep at Bhatgam – shivering and sweating and sniffling all
night – but felt a soreness in my bones so agitating I walked around
the deserted town in the middle of the night for an hour with neither
relief nor distraction.

In the morning I couldn't eat and from the first step felt tired
enough that I wanted to go home. I would try to focus on the moment,
that there was rest day coming up to work out all the illness, but ended
up muttering "I want to go home" for most of the morning. As in
'home'.

I had my first roadside diarrhea, at the edge of the pavement, unconcerned as a native, too painful to care. I was so dehydrated – I had

used all my drinking water to wash myself – by the time I got to where I was going that I went to a random house and asked if I could stay there. The woman at home went inside to confer and I took advantage of her absence to collapse on the daybed. I must have been asleep by the time she returned.

I can only barely remember the uncle helping me to my feet hours later, still unable to eat or drink *chai*, and showing me to the villa where Gandhiji had stayed. I have no idea of their names, only my disinterest and vague disappointment when he waved his blessings to me instead of carrying me to my next destination.

19.2   to Delad

[writing on April 1st, 15h00]

I recall the afternoon as slow and hot. I am shivering throughout. A long road to Delad that ended in another road, and then another one. Wandering through major intersections and traffic and tar and filth. I get lost once and am almost unable to Jedi the ordinary interaction necessary to find the path again. Even the most basic tasks overwhelm me. I am a foreigner again.

At Delad there is a cricket game to watch in confusion. During a break I show a young man – perhaps my age – the paper given to me (I don't remember when) with the name of someone to talk to. It's his father's name, so he walks me up the hill to the paved street with the nice houses and I collapse outside on a swing while they arrange the details. I can only hear the occasional rhythm of conversation, women's voices, men's glances.

A mist surrounds everything but the heat and I am guided to an empty room, a special place for pilgrims. I am given many blankets and shown the bathroom, downstairs. I am given water and fruit to eat. I remember no names nor anything I said to anybody.

Day 20

March 31, 2006

"Mutual trust and mutual love are no trust and no love. The real love is to love them that hate you, to love your neighbour even though you distrust him."

20.1 Rest Day: Delad

[deliria found in my journal from march 31st]

1.   It doesn't take a rocket scientist to understand,
That when the last rocket leaves your hands,
The only man with a stand-up plan,
Will be good ol' farmer Dan.

2.   Why ask men when you can ask gods? Similarly, why model yourself after man when you can model yourself after god? Especially when you've given up achieving and doing, when achievements and acts have given up on you? Why not imagine Jesus *Krishna* Gandhi Buddha? I am a psychedelic Gandhian, cartwheeling towards the moon. I will finish this *yatra* have a radio show and give sermons in Spanish churches while raising the goats.

3.   A few words for the media the next time they (I?) come to town. Everyone asks all the time if I am alone. It's a comfortable question. They return to it like a nest:

> "Your name?
> You are alone?
> Your country?
> No one with you?
> Your education?
> No friends?"

Finally you get the impression the international hand sign for '1' isn't working too well – we're dealing with a pre-numeric concern, the fear of solitude, atheism, and death.

And, no, I'm not alone. The entire village of Govindpura walks with me. An innumerable line of silent masis make *chai* without expectation of a smile. Three fat *brahmins* help me carry my flute. An agricultural reserve army of *aadivasis* plow the road before me, their blood and sweat filling my hosts' urns like so much sacrificial *ghee*. Two fishermen on the banks of the

Mahisagar ferry across anonymous civil engineers. The young men of Vasana and the old men of Matar give me their lives' strengths and stories. Rupesh, the barber of Derol, and his merry band of *bhaktas* question the gender of Vinoba Bhave and suggest new paths, turns, and endings for our *yatra*. The farmers of Amrachi and their blind drummer proudly guide me down Gandhiji's path from the river seventy-six years ago. I can see his footprints, still, in their hearts.

No, no, I am not alone.

4. I have learned, on this *yatra*, that the ancient wisdom is true. God is One. God is each of us. We, all together, only together, are one. I wouldn't have made it twelve hours without Mother India's Amazon-sized love to take care of me, whole platoons of young men, withered generals of colonial struggles, the large and silent corps of millet-wielding women, refusing to serve cold food to a stranger.

    All these men and women are my siblings, my own. I feel the love and strength pouring in great gushing waves, impulses of energy slave neither to spacetime nor bodymind, from across the dark oceans. From San Francisco and Buenos Aires and Barcelona and New Jersey.

    I am so blessed and lucky that, on the surface of a sphere, each point is the center.

    I shit in the woods with no water, sitting on an abandoned brickyard roadside. Stomach hurts and life is beautiful.

5. Oh *Amazon* – how much god in the Amazon! How much biomass? How much movement, noise, vibration, sensation, energy? This is the depth of the India/*Amazon* connection lurking this entire time – it's the presence of god. This country is religious like no other. Why? Because god is Being and there is a lot of Being in India and a long tradition of recognizing it. Biomass India. Sensation India. Energy = Mass = God(s).

6.   Dream in a bathroom in Berkeley, have to stand on tips of toes to piss in sink surrounded by all kinds of colored plastic feminine shower product bottles and it's very difficult to pee when your whole face is seared and blistered and burning and disfigured.

I just close my eyes to see a boy walking through the forest with the torso, head, and antlers of a large deer.

Day 21

April 1, 2006

"Non-violence is impossible without self-purification."

21.1 to Chaprabhata

[back to the present, already in progress]

Still at 15h30, 1 April.

And now, Ninaben. Ninaben just gave me a delightful half-hour talk on Amway, the ultimate goal of which was to get some relatives' addresses or phone numbers and turn them into Amway prawns. She fed me Amway vitamin C tablets and Amway *acerola* (Brazilian cherry) concentrate tablets at lunch, which was kind, and as I was washing my hands I noticed the bottle of Amway APSA-80 (pesticide) right next to them, which you do not want to give to your sick foreign guests.

After two days of unconscious mist in Delad, I was ready to leave. I felt no connection with the people there, because I could feel nothing. They had cared for me without questions. Is that what love is?

They seemed to understand when I awoke and could speak again, this morning, and plied me with fruit. I could eat, finally. They made no protest when I thanked them and left. I have no idea if they ever knew – or if I ever told them – what I was doing, where I was going, why I was sick, or why they should care for me. I just left.

I remember only a lumber mill from the morning's walk. I must have stopped afterwards, at a random house on the road, to ask for water. A boy was tying his shoes in front and called his father out. I asked the man for water and he ordered his wife to bring it, then asked what I was doing. He was amazed at my answer – I can speak again, and Gujarati at that – and made me sit.

Soon I'm back on the pilgrim track, eating an early lunch of delicious spicy Indian food. Food I had totally forgotten about. Food that not only exists in its cocktail and complexity of flavors, but is, in fact, the rule in this country. And vegetarian. And spicy. When I rose to leave he accompanied me to the road and, further, walked me clear to the next town, overjoyed to be a part of my *yatra*. And I, my strength still faltering, was overjoyed to have someone to lean on[1].

When we finally parted at Chaprabhata, the uncle told me we would meet again, at the ceremony in Dandi. Ceremony? Of course! Every year there is a ceremony to commemorate the Dandi march, a big affair with lots of famous Gandhians and speeches. The final act, as it were. I had never even considered that far ahead. I will see him there.

---

[1] As in the Bill Withers song

In Chaprabhata an elderly Gandhian – Ninaben's father-in-law – welcomed me into his home, feeding me and allowing me to collapse on his couch for a few hours of powerful recovery. As Jayeshbhai once told me, "Sleep is the best medicine".

It's also my only medicine, Amway respectfully excluded.

As I was leaving we walked by a grandfather so old he had no more stories, speeches, teeth, or memories left to share. As such he is forever locked into that kind two-handed gesture – arms raised, open palms facing down – of channeling bountiful cosmic energy onto the bare heads of passersby.

21.2   to Surat

Surat lies a worthy walk away. I cross into the city probably less than
an hour after leaving Champrabhata, toeing carefully across the Tapi
River Railway Bridge. It is the bridge I dreamt of three weeks ago.
I take the narrow two-way pedestrian pathway along its side, careful
of the loose and missing metal panels beneath me feet. Faith in the
kindness of *Krishna* keeps it going.

From there I walk an exhausting two hours (perhaps in a circle) to
the *Pranami Mandir*. I had entered the city without idea of where I
would go. Cities, naturally, present a whole different set of challenges
than villages. In a village, someone will speak to you in the street,
and the 'town hall' isn't more than five minutes away as a last resort.
In the city you have to know someone, to be pre-approved. Before, in
Anand and Bharuch, I had people to stay with and a phone to receive
their calls. Here, I have nothing, as I have wanted all along.

I wander to a group of tour buses – which tend to indicate a famous temple nearby – and sit down to think. Swaminarayan *Gurukul*,
Sivananda *Ashram*, Ramakrishna Mission: there are no dearth of temples. Then I remember my home in Jamnagar when I studied there
last fall, the Khijada *Mandir*. The Khidijara *Mandir* was built around
a pair of 400 year-old trees, where the sect's founder achieved Awakening. It is the central holy place of the whole sect, but they would
often mention a branch in Surat. Somebody would surely be visiting
and recognize me.

Sold. I only need to ask where it is. I notice, for the second time in
three weeks, that I am alone. The tour buses and streets are empty. A
fluke. I walk a block and see a shirtless man next to a woman, leaning
out a third-storey window. It's the most sexual moment I've witnessed
in India – could it be a brothel? – and I would rather wander aimlessly
than bother them.

Which is what I do. Surat is a modern city – as everyone has
told me – so nobody offers to help very much. They (everyone along
the way) told me it was a very clean city, like my cities in America,
because every night an army of displaced villagers sallies forth to clean
the streets. I couldn't tell.

But there are mangos (barely) in season now, at 200 *points* a kilogram (at five days' wages, they must not be local), and I stop to drool.
The merchant points me in the right direction and his friend offers me

a ride on motorcycle, which I refuse.

It seems, in India, there's always someplace to go even when there's no place to go. And you've always been invited there. Somebody will even take you in. As long as you can hold it together and Jedi your mind into cooperation. Remember: Mind Power. Big *Bungalow*.

The signs have been given to you.

You merely have to order them.

I make it, eventually, under assault of noise and particle pollution. The place is probably five kilometers out of my way and nowhere near where Gandhi was supposed to have stayed or spoken, but it never occurs to me to even look. I'm still sick, I guess. The *maha*-whoever gives me his blessings and allows me to stay, and walking up the stairs I run into my old friends from Jamnagar.

A lovely blessed reunion to bring my spirits up – for a moment I can stop feeling so foreign and alone, I can talk to people who know my name and not just my quest. I am a person, not a pilgrim. I have an ego. They are young men – some of them teenagers – who have dedicated their lives to god and the temple, to studying yoga and *vedanta*. We discuss the *Bhagavad Gita* and Gandhi, how profound Every Moment can be if we give it the attention, the chance.

I am able to shower and to scrub, slowly and meticuluously, my clothes. We eat dinner – *rotli*, *bataka shak*, rice, and *curdy*. Small quantities, no appetite or seconds. My teeth hurt while eating as wikipedia articles on scurvy, rickets, malaria, and polio fly through my mind. If it's affecting my head, appetite, joints, teeth, and it memory, I must have something bad. Something worthy of medical insurance, massage, or a blood test.

After dinner I lay on my thin mattress on the floor for hours, unable to do anything else. Yoga, meditation, and writing make me laugh in pain. I essay four minutes of tuneless breathless fluting before putting the *bansuri* down in shame and disgust. There are other pilgrims here. It is too hot to sleep and I lay naked under the fan for hours in impotent misery. My fear of sleeping only grows.

It is a torture, a way to destroy someone.

Day 22

April 2, 2006

"The whole scheme of the liberation of India is based upon the development of internal strength. It is a plan of self-purification."

22.1 to Dindoli

5h30 awakening to *aarti*, alarm, and digestive need. Some brief and painful *yoga*, a failed attempt at meditation. The neck, shoulder, and lower back are contentious rocks. My mind for days has been idling at a stage where the only words I write, I must first speak aloud in a reptilian growl. And this is a sign of great improvement. My head is still vicious.

I do six pathetic sun salutations and feel proud. I briefly hint at a warrior *asana*, and exhaust myself. I apply *triphala* to my facial wound – dating back to my shaving gift, infected, possibly related to my illness – and shower. The clothes I so carefully scrubbed and washed last night are now dry and still stained. I try a jumping jack in my hubris and nearly collapse. My head cannot take the pressure.

At 6h45 I am packed and out the door, asking directions to Dindoli. The first three people I query can only answer 'far'. The walk is long and dirty through the city of Surat, first to Udhana train station and then only towards Dindoli, perhaps in Gandhi's time a quaint village and now something of a suburb. In Surat, I pass dripping meat markets, offal, and the first intimations of violence and thievery I've encountered so far. Maybe it's my condition.

Surat also, being a city, has the most amazing fruit I've seen so far. Mango and jackfruit and papaya and different colors of oranges and bananas. Desire. I want the mangos. I begin to understand *tapasya* – the purification, the suffering offered as tribute – for the first time. For the first phase of the trip there was no issue. Then the day of doubt and hunger, and then the manifold blessings that followed. Since Rayma, though, it's been steady *tapasya*: illness at Bhatgam, deliria at Delad, suffering through my rest day, sub-normal functionality. A breakdown of my daily practices, my ability to communicate, the trivia of my pilgrimage.

The choice to continue is a choice to suffer. Every minute.

It's been long enough – the headache and heatstroke – that I wonder if this is my new consciousness. Welcome to the new me. Emotionally unconcerned, without the excess energy necessary for excitement. Unable to think properly, to analyze, to remember facts. No change in wisdom: the truths are all here, echoing in the empty cavern of my skull. Which can only mean they were never about me to begin with. I try to think what *ayurveda* would recommend I do for this fever, what my mom recommended.

I cannot recall.

My energy, however you define it, is low to not. Very little left to share. No conversation, barely able to ask for water. Twice I must sit on dingy concrete steps of yesterday's office buildings to gather strength. Finally I cross the tracks and approach Dindoli.

In Dindoli I turn left down the main street of the village and walk down the street until I'm tired. I don't get very far. There are no ostentatious houses like the last few villages, cobbled streets where only the *patels* may live. I ask an elderly man where the house of Vakkubhai Desai is, where Gandhiji stayed during the Salt March. The man smiles in response and invites me inside. His name is Chandukaka. He serves me water and *chass* – cooling for the body – and gives no notice to the article I proffer in eloquence's stead, for he is already sold.

After the *chass* it's 10h30 and he walks me to Vakkubhai's house. It's less than three minutes away but the sun is already deadly. He can see the fear in my eyes but we go anyways. We walk past a small one-room concrete shack where an even older man lives. He was but a child when Gandhiji came, but he saw him, saw him walk by, right over *there*! He leans out his door and points across the street, very excited, before going back to his television and bed.

Chandukaka works as a teacher, as does Vakkubhai's son. They open the house for me – it's normally empty and locked. Inside there is no furniture, no decoration but a few photos of Gandhi. It is a stagnant cave. Where does the family live, I ask my guide?

> "We have another house across the street. This side of the family all moved to outside."

Outside is the United States, Australia, Fiji, and England. The fabled America. Private property can't go with them, of course. How many empty houses are there in these rich farming towns? How many hard working immigrants live in basements in the first world to build empty mansions back home, where their laborers subsist in tents?

Oh, opportunity. Oh, capitalism.

The old men order me lunch and the old women serve me, seated on the front veranda near the swing. I have to lean, still, against the wall to avoid collapse. They smile kindly anyways: *dal* and *bath*, *curdy*. A mango pickle I should avoid: too spicy and sour for this heat.

Chandukaka was the first Gujarati teacher to win the national best teacher award. How they decide such a thing baffles me. He fought (non-violently) in the freedom struggle, broke the laws and went to jail. He has a simple home, gives me a coffee-table book of the freedom struggle, and allows me to nap.

I page through the book's photos, struck by the young brown faces, so committed they would go to jail before making a fist. Thousands and thousands of them. They are abused, tortured, jailed, shot. Everyone dies in the end, including Gandhi. I stop reading as I start crying, and sleep.

In my dream Chandukaka gives me a tour of Gandhi's life in the Brazilian wilderness, where the great social worker spent much of his time. There are huts made of vines and twigs, great snakes and jaguars all around.

For days now I cannot recognize myself. I am shorter and slower, stupid and lazy. I seem to have melted without the transcendence – instead of dissolving into God I have dissolved into dirt.

Maybe I have dissolved into the rough scarcity of this very earth, into the rich ritual and fatal inequality, as our own ancient practices and extended families dissolve into desire and automation.

22.2   to Vanz

In compensation for the industrial morning walk and in deference to my pounding (though thankfully somewhat less so) head, the afternoon road is gorgeous. A small two-way road winds the four kilometers to Karvasa, flanked by sugarcane, mango, and *chickoo* orchards. I take frequent breaks for water and rest and the by time I cross the river (reduced to a stream by irrigation – perhaps created with that in mind) it is almost six. At the river I turn right into Eden – a small one-lane road with mangos overhanging on both sides and stalls hawking local fruits: *jambu*, *keri*, *chickoo*, *srifal*. Fruit asking for money.

Speaking of which, it was a great idea to bring money. Two hundred *points* is not really enough to bail you out, so it doesn't impinge on your freedom ('No money, I am free!'). Yet, it's enough to satisfy small temptations, and thus challenge your will. It would have been easier to continue at the hardest moments had I no money, but that two hundred tucked away for the trip home really made it a decision every time, an opportunity to sacrifice, to suffer, to learn.

Whether it's actually enough to get me home remains to be seen.

I left Chandukaka this afternoon full of desire. The mind is returning and with it the image of a pomegranate: a sweet and astringent fruit would be great for my fever, according to *ayurveda*. I ask *Krishna* to no avail and wanted it so badly I almost ask Chandukaka. When I finally got up to brave the afternoon, auntie ran inside with four purple plum-shaped fruits.

And what is this?

Jambu. Sweet and astringent with a purple seed that cracks to reveal a bright green center. Juicy blue flesh.

As always, exactly what I needed, better than I could have imagined demanding. They saw my excitement and we went out back together, to the tree, to gather a large handful for the road. Juicy blue love bombs and you couldn't synthesize a better candy.

Kaka walked me to the road and showed me where the trio of trees (*vad*, *pipal*, *amla*) that Gandhiji had spoken under used to be. They have since been replaced by storefronts and garbage. It is a trend I've noted in many towns of this district – rich towns that have 'developed' right over their *ficus religiosa*, and their memories along with it.

Development. Such a curious word. Now the owning classes live in opulence with three-storey houses and faades that belong to the nowhere of American suburbia (generally the British flavor). But development? Education? Poverty? Health? Hygiene? Pluralism? Tolerance? These values are met from without or not at all. English-medium boarding schools for the children, and hired help cleaning the streets. Does the influx of remittances for development mean anybody understands more, cares more, or has internalized the virtues of education or cleanliness?

There's certainly not much in the way of integration.

I've noticed that with more 'development', the landowners are richer and the laborers are poorer. Which only serves to vindicate Marx and piss people off.

I get to Vanz at 18h30 and ask for the Patel Street. Literally, that's what I'm told to do. And apparently, I'm doing what I'm told. They point up the hill, to a short street with large flagstones. Maybe the granite is imported. A cluster of grotesque mansions and one crumbling temple comprise the entire town. A nice photo. At the base of the hill, in a pleasant feudal aesthetic, lies the impromptu tent village of the imported laborers.

I am quickly welcomed into a mansion and give thanks. I successfully decline *chai* and milk, trying to stay healthy, and gratefully drink my water. It's been a tough road regarding *chai* but I haven't been forced to drink it since Sandhier, and, as I had forced my entire being on that household, it wasn't right to complain.

My kind hosts serve me a plate of grapes and another of watermelon. India and I finally understand each other. The father of family has left to attend 'business' of some kind and his son, Mayur, sits down to talk with me.

Mayur's just a kid, who studied computer science like I did, and is now working in Mumbai. Nobody can believe I'm actually educated but he doesn't seem to mind the comparison. He's applying for an H1-B temporary work visa to go to New Jersey or Fremont. Maybe we want to exchange lives. I certainly don't need to spend any more time in New Jersey or Fremont. Mayur has a job in Mumbai – a thing of envy – and tells me that working is okay but not great. He puts in his eight hours each day and goes to his rented apartment, only looking forward to the weekends when he can come here – a three-and-a-half hour train ride away.

> "The only real enjoyment is at home. That's where your friends are, your family."

I think of all my friends who couldn't wait to go to college, to get out of their hometowns and away from their families, who will never tire of the joys of New York City. Then why are you applying to go abroad?

He smiles shyly and doesn't answer. I don't understand.

Soon Mayur has to go, is replaced by two more personalities in the endless cast: Mohanbhai and Solanki. Mohanbhai is the *sarpanch*, which – across districts and dialects – people still cannot mention without raising their fist in a symbol of power. Solanki is the *NRI* philanthropist, back to visit his native land. Together with Mohanbhai and Solanki, we slowly pass the hours in traditional harangue.

Mohanbhai is a member of the BJP, and I must fight my prejudice during our entire conversation. He is a good politician and has raised a lot of money for his village, I am told, and yet, like most politicians I've met, seems deeply involved in the Power and the Glory[1]. He is deeply committed to the notion of the Wall: love within and dust without. Perhaps that's what it means to be a good politician, as opposed to a good social worker, good father, or good neighbor. That's what the *sarpanch* of Dabhan thought at least, the one who looked up to George Bush for 'making sure his people have what they need'.

Solanki lives in Leicester, England. He calls himself as a philanthropist. He seems to loves charity at least as much as man and repeats himself in the interest of my comprehension. He is from Vanj, this village, and has committed himself to village improvement for years. Though he only earns a humble pension of two hundread British pounds monthly, he is committed to village improvement, to helping the people of this village, Vanj, and gives 30,000 *points* a year to his village, Vanj, from his humbly monthly pension of two hundred British pounds, monthly.

They are patient with me in my slow recovery and take the time to make their points clear, if not succinct. I am almost ready for it. They have come to honor me, to receive me into their village, to teach

---

[1]Simon's appeal to Jesus in Andrew Lloyd Webber's *Jesus Christ Superstar* comes to mind.

me, and to share this life, these breaths. My own negativity frustrates
me; They hold up a mirror in the guise of pomp and bombast.

A male of the household calls me to dinner. The father had run
out on important business as I arrived, so – for the first time – I am
not properly introduced to the family. Love and obligation have such
different textures. We eat a traditional Gujarati meal with a *shak* of
fresh beans (so green, so rare) and he is generous with his food and
wife's effort, imploring her to refill my plate time after time. Finally
I can accept no more and forcefully decline her, usually the last step
in the hospitality game. But this time he orders her in the 'I am your
husband, I own you' tone of voice to serve me more food, against our
wills.

There is a delicate balance to the food game. You have to try
everything. And you are served more of what you eat, like a feedback
loop. And even more of what you openly admit to liking. First refusals
never stand, so you must plan in advance.

So if I want to eat X flatbreads (*rotli*, *bacri*, *thepla*, *parotha*, *chappati*, *puri*, etc.) I have to say, "No, auntie, that's enough" at flatbread
number X-2. She should smile and ignore me.

Then, at flatbread number X-1, I have to say, again, "No, auntie, I
can't have any more" to which she will generally respond, "Last one,"
to which I should respond, hesitantly, "Okay, auntieji".

At that point I should be set. When she offers me flatbread number
X, I immediately say "No more," allowing us to negotiate until she
agrees it will *really* be the last one. I must still be careful that there is
not an extra flatbread already on the griddle cooking – they are clever,
these women – and I still have to fend off further attempts to offer me
flatbreads. But at least, after this protocol, I have the right to say
"no".

The force of the husband, however, is a bit of a trump card. He is
quite insistent, expressive, and attentive. His expression of attention is
so micromanaged it goes from comic through annoying to comic once
more. A helix. Each question merits three tries:

> "More food? More food? More food?
> "Bathroom? Wash hands? Bathroom? Bathroom?
> "Clothes washing? Washing soap? Clothes brush?
> "Hair brush?
> "Cold water here.
> "Hot water coming. Hot water coming. Hot water coming."

He instructs me from above, as I squat and soak, how to rinse and how to scrub my clothes. How to squeeze them, how to beat and how to hang them. Has he ever even washed his own clothes? Only the flimsy aluminum outhouse door saves me from further instruction.

We talk more about India and computers – there is no interest in Gandhi – and finally it is time to sleep. The whole family sleeps on daybeds in the living room (this seems to be true of rich and poor alike) though there are many empty rooms in the large house. I will not, however, sleep here.

Natuarbhai – that is his name – shows me out and we walk across the street to an older, mustier house, conspicuously out of place on the opulent patel street. The large mansions we pass are stuck together, half of them locked and unoccupied. Where have all the Indians gone?[2]

"Outside."

Once again gone to the USA, the UK, Canada. So many homeless and so many houses to occupy.

My lodgings are fittingly dank and dismal, with low ceilings and cobwebs. I don't know why I've been put here alone. Perhaps it's the privacy whose lack I've been lamenting this entire journey. Luckily I can still enjoy it. He shows me where the lights are and which bed is mine, three times each. He leaves twice only to come back to make sure I know which switch is which, to reassure me he will be here at six in the morning. I don't doubt it.

"What time do you wake up?
"Do you need anything?
"*Sarpanch* will be here at six in the morning?
"There is your bed."

His care maddens and perplexes me. Am I the victim of a joke? I imagine the actual pilgrimage to be over – I am now walking through an ironic remix of Indian culture. Everything I value about this experience has been marshaled to asphyxiate me. I must now renounce my renunciation, return to the Matrix. Wine turns to vinegar in the mouth.[3]

---

[2] cf Pete Seeger's *Where Have All the Flowers Gone?*
[3] A quote from Raoul Vaneigem's *Revolution of Everyday Life.*

Day 23

April 3, 2006

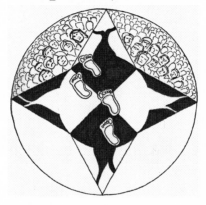

"The moneyed classes have got to learn
how fight, either with arms or with the
weapon of non-violence. For those who
wish to follow the latter way, the best and
most effective mantra is: 'Enjoy thy wealth
by renouncing it'."

23.1   to Dhaman

I wake up at Gandhi's 4h30 and set my alarm to meditate for half an hour. Ten seconds after it rings at five, Natuarbhai enters to sit down across from me.

"So. Are you up?"

I'm having an increasingly difficult time remembering the names of these villages, remembering to care where Gandhiji was and why he came here, remembering I am an ambassador of pure love and kindness. Perhaps this morning, along with renewed health and renewed vigor, comes a renewed ego, a feeling that all these people are insufferable. It's a funny feeling.

Yes, uncle, I am up. Jai sri *Krishna*.

"Yes. Hot water?"

No, thanks.

"Yes, yes, Hot water."

An unprecedented degree of nagging and micromanaging that surpasses every member of my family I have met to-date. I am simultaneously impressed and dismayed. He is so vocal and hyper and active at every moment that I cannot act without interruption – a life-sized interference pattern. A new way to wake up.

I bathe with hot water behind the house. At six, the *sarpanch* and the Philanthropist arrive to walk me to the next town. They take me by the old tree where Gandhiji spoke. We take *darshan*. A hint that I'm actually on the path.

We walk together – it's always nice – and the Philanthropist discourses at length on the silence of the mornings and the sounds of the birds, the value of discipline and consistency. I choke on the irony but am recovered enough – through sleep, time, and *jambu* – that I have the mental and physical fortitude to deal, to observe. *Krishna* gives us exactly what we can handle, when we can handle it.

The Philanthropist greets and questions the poor children and parents on the outskirts of the village. My mind is polluted enough that everything he says seems patronizing. Their glum responses confirm my prejudice. What more harm can you do to a man than call him important or in-charge?

They walk me to four kilometers to Oopdi and introduce me to the town. *Chai*, lemonade, formalities. I continue walking, alone, thankful, once again drowning in the love. How so can many people who've never met me be so kind? There is hope for us all.

The Indian roads continue to be quiet and beautiful. My health continues to return. I continue to give thanks. Let's call it the spring[1]. Exactly what I need. *Krishna* gives us exactly what we need. The material plane is a mirror, nothing more.

I arrive to Dhaman, a ghost town. In India? I can't find anybody and am thankful for the solitude, the lack of stress and effort that every human interaction requires. I play the flute at the town school – there are no students – and eventually fetch water from a well and walk back to a temple under construction at the entrance to town.

It is a large *Jain derasar*, a white marble affair with a junkyard of scrap marble around the perimeter. The workers welcome me and show me their art. It has been under construction for twenty-four years and will need at least another decade to finish. Hell of a time commitment.

I talk to a young man who has been working on the temple for the last few years, a few months at a time. The money is good enough that he can travel around, enjoy himself until the money runs out, and come back to work. The road goes on forever and the party never ends[2]. I have never met anyone like him in India, so concerned with his own exploration and pleasure. So selfish. He is, like me, the future.

We are the future. That's what I want to tell these parents who look at me as a strange throwback to India's independence or ancient yogis. I want to help them understand I'm no more concerned with the past than Gandhi was. I want to show them what I've lived. Their dreams of wealth will consume them, spit out selfish egotistic children who – on the other side of hedonism – arrive at the essential ever-present Unity of spiritual existence[3] not because anybody told them

---

[1] "When spring came, even the false spring, there were no problems except where to be happiest. The only thing that could spoil a day was people and if you could keep from making engagements, each day had no limits. People were always the limiters of happiness except for the very few that were good as spring itself." from Hemingway's *A Moveable Feast*

[2] As always, with Robert Earl Keen

[3] As in Teilhard de Chardin's: "We are not human beings having a spiritual experience, we are spiritual beings having a human experience".

to, but because they can't live without it.

And we've tried.

They serve me food without speech or ritual, unconcerned with my mission. To them I am a pilgrim among other pilgrims, and all pilgrims deserve simple, bland, warm food. The Jains really get it, it's true. I give thanks for the sustenance and anonymity, and go outside to rest on a stone bench across from the *derasar*. I mediate. I write. I nap. Before I play more scales, an elderly bearded *guru*-figure emerges from the temple to preach to me in Hindi (which I still do not understand). He tells me I know nothing about Gandhi, the real Gandhi, and thus should be shown around the temple.

I sigh in acquiescence – if there is no Self, there's no one with whom to argue – and follow him to towards a pile of scrap marble where he drops to the ground and pees.

"Wait."

I go back to my bench to await further instructions. This time he motions to follow him inside the temple, which I do. He is nowhere to be seen. Another man materializes outside a side chapel – the eternally unfinished ringing of the hammers add to the dreamlike ambience – and approaches me. He has lived in Oklahoma for seventeen years ('a very nice place') and will give me (another) tour.

We part, friends, at four-thirty. I never did find the peeing, bearded, glsguru again. I sit on my bench, lean forward, and prepare to go. No shirt in the afternoon breeze. I feel better! Not one-hundred percent, naturally, but better. Slight tension in the head and real fireworks when I try any inverted postures but otherwise great. I walk a straight line at a normal pace. I can think again, wonderful thoughts. I know it's the third of April. 56 x 29 = 1624.

23.2   to Navsari

The ten kilometers to Navsari start out beautifully with *amba* and *chickoo* orchards on both sides, but eventually turns from pretty to wild as I enter the city to the tune of the setting sun. I walk on auto pilot with my recently healed monkey mind for the ultimate hour and only deep into the city do I realize I am lost.

I am still shy from sickness to talk with people, and this far south few people have heard of my journey. Young men give me directions to a large temple on the lake side of town and even offer to motorcycle me there. I can only thank them, walking an hour through the city past the devil's own temptation, a fruit market at dusk, ripe with post-haggled prices.

At the temple I submit myself at the lotus feet of *Krishna*, at once sad that in the cities no one offers *seva* to this pilgrim and grateful for the institutions that have been established to do so.

Maharaj, however, is anything but open, claiming there is no room and I must talk to the office, which is closed. In India you are never alone and there are enough of the devoted around to have their own heated discussion without my presence. I take a walk to explore the large marble grounds and meditate in peace and darkness. It would be a cool night outside if they don't let me into their guest quarters, but nothing I won't survive. I still have grapes and *chickoo* and no longer believe in scarcity.

An accountant by the name of Gandhi had called one of the trustees by the time I got back, and permission was granted. The watchman, satisfied, resumes his post by the door, the faithful leave in peace, and the *pujari*, still grumbling, invites me to dinner.

It turns out there are three rooms empty out of eight and I have a lot of space to clean. I sweep and mop, wash my body and clothes, practice music and read Gandhiji.

maharaj eventually calls us – another old *saddhu* and myself – to eat, thick *rotli* smothered in *ghee* and a *shak* whose only discernable vegetable was oil. We share the same life and the same bounty – the topography of our riches wholly dependent on the gifts of others.

I eat as little as possible and retire.

"No tension," as they say. I can feel my face healing, my headache receding, my fever retreating. I sit in *vajrasana*, writing and reading. Tomorrow is the last day I won't reach Gandhi. Dandi, that is.

It's clear to me by now that what peace needs to happen between men and dogs must start with a balance between humans and our environments. Humans and soil. This change in our relationship to the land must start in our hearts. If we can first practice *ahimsa* with a partner as forgiving as the earth, we will one day be ready for each other. The real battle is in humans' hearts – what we allow ourselves to feel, to think, and to imagine.

This would, of course, require a total reorganization of the food system, a return to valuing and to working with the land, an understanding that in developing a perfect system for maximizing quantity we have lost all quality.

It's world peace through individual love,

Individual love through abundance,

Abundance through land reform.

Day 24

April 4, 2006

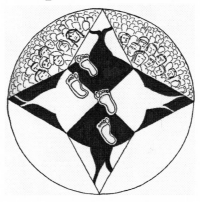

"The root of Satyagraha is in the prayer. A Satyagrahi relies upon God for protection against the tyranny of brute force."

24.1   to Vijalpur

I return to the health. Excellent godsgiven health and I can almost smell the sea. There is yoga and meditation and the familiar cold shower. My body remembers not to complain. I'm folded and packed by six-thirty, eat a *chickoo* as I head down the stairs and leave the rest for *Maharaj*.

The road out of Navsari, to the West, circles around a beautiful lake. There are men jogging and listening to music, like any other city in the world. I find the early morning traffic – in India we are never alone – and cross the railroad tracks amidst a haze of humans, animals, and vehicles.

The Indian version of a strip mall is a thin concrete faade over rural life. Busy bus agencies and stainless steel emporiums. Whole complexes of technicolor textiles. All in a hard grey line along the all-important road, crossed by cows seeking the narrow alleyways to their rivers and pastures, dusted with trash and excrement, just on the other side.

I don't normally look – all the trappings of money have gradually disappeared from my visual field as they are no longer relevant – but today I have a renewed appreciation for industry. I appreciate them like a low-budget horror movie – I'm too old or too young to be scared.

My walking takes me to a busy intersection where my instincts guide me to turn right, to the West. I pass well-landscaped private schools – I can't read the signs of course – and thirst for water. I am ready to walk towards the sea. I turn without seeking counsel from the multitudes and soon walk into the idylls of the past, large state-owned demonstration farms, asphalt that seems soft from low-traffic, a shaded welcome after the mutter and opportunity of the city.

Highway 77 leads me to a fork between Karadi and Dandi where I stop to drink water and check my schedule. Karadi is listed at the night-halt for April 4th, which means I must have accidentally left Vijaypur behind me. A short day.

The tine to Karadi takes me 1.3 kilometers to the much signaled "Gandhi Smirti Mandir", around the *talav* and into a nice commemorative park. I arrive at nine in the morning, famished and excited.

Gandhi's *jhopri* is still here – the shack of lashed-together branches where he stayed for a few weeks after the termination of the Salt March. The shack – perhaps a reconstruction? – sits in the shade of three huge mango trees. I sit before them and ask permission, then pick one green mango from the tree and another off the ground. They are hard and tart and full of *mangitude*.

I sit in meditation in Gandhiji's shelter. We are very close now. I have felt him this entire trip, stronger and stronger. When people ask what I was studying, I would merely say "Gandhi is my teacher" and smile. The word and walk together can make truth[1].

After writing inside the shelter and out, I walk around the strangely modern water tower next door. None of its angles can distract me from the fading baby blue paint job. We are still in India.

I spot a kind-looking man walking around; he receives me warmly and welcomes me into his office, an *ayurvedic* care center complete with steam bath and medicinal plants, photos of Gandhi and human anatomy. It's the kindness I'm really looking for, surviving on.

The good doctor brings in an old freedom fighter to talk to me, now a trustee of the park we enjoy. We look through a book of photographs and he tells me the story.

Gandhi stayed here the night of April 4th and walked the remaining six kilometers to Dandi on April 5th. On the morning of the 6th he broke the law, picking up salt crystals that had dried from the ocean. Afterwards his party returned here to strategize and wait for the British. On May 4th the authorities arrived to arrest him, where I had meditated, under the mango tree. The freedom struggle went on from there.

We finish the photographs and the doctor returns with news. "There is no facility" for me to stay here, so I will be lodged in a house in the next village, on the main road, with another freedom fighter.

We walk to his motorcycle and the doctor gives me a mini-lecture on old Gandhian men, walking richly around their villages in pressed white *khadi* without much connection to their grandchildren or washerwomen. They continue, however, to dispense advice weighty as blessings: *caveat peregrinator*.

"Heavily thickening into empire," some might say[2].

---

[1] "Hands that work are holier than lips that pray," as the Gandhians like to say.

[2] A reference to Robinson Jeffers' poem, *Shine, Perishing Republic*

24.2   to Karadi

We get off the motorcycle where I turned off highway 77 towards the Gandhi Smirti *Mandir* in Karadi, at the Kakavadi Memorial House. The house is old and full of photographs and memorabilia in plastic and Gujarati. There is a lifetime of information amidst the dust.

The good doctor walks me behind the museum to a single-storey wooden house among mango and guava trees. There I met a true family – an old threesome of nagging Indian freedom fighters.

Vallabhdada – the name of my own grandfather – has eighty-four years with him; his wife has eighty-five. Vallabhdada's sister is an ardent eighty-one and does her best to take care of everyone involved.

When I arrive they are already entertaining guests: three women, young and modern, with their driver in tow. Students of architecture from Ahmedabad, the metropolis I left over three weeks ago, coming to do research for the Dandi Heritage Project. They would help decide which sites should be preserved, recognized, memorialized, and otherwise funded.

The girls shock me by smiling and speaking in English. They are not afraid. They wear no veils to pull over their eyes as I approach. They are sexy, even.

Ah, yes, modern India once again.

I stand at the porch railing, next to the driver, observing. The old threesome ceaselessly harangue and harass the girls – do this, sit here, not that, more here, eat this – who smile effortlessly. True Indian culture. I am watching a movie of my life, or better yet, an instructional video on how to behave. Throughout it all the elderly hosts, who are all mostly deaf, communicate to each other exclusively by yelling.

The family serves us a course of *chai*, then *mamra*, then water. The girls eat with polite reluctance. Then one grandmother brings out a tray of tea cups full of orange *chai*. Orange *chai*? No. The last bottle of last year's mango juice, home blended and bottled from the tree that shades our conversation, even now.

Oh what sweet ungodly heaven. Ask and you shall receive. Has there been anything I haven't received? Sugarcane juice, perhaps. And that's my own fault. I remember asking for fruit, mangoes, a book to write in, a shave, a piece of cloth. Did I need anything else? Does anybody? Green vegetables. I've been getting plenty.

Vallabhdada announces he will take the girls to a local monument, leaving me to rest with the two grandmothers. We exchange contact information before they leave; I agree to give them some recommendations for their project, since they have visited virtually none of the towns on my route.

Dada leaves with the girls and I play *Krishna* with the old women, practicing the flute tunelessly to their deaf delight. I am made for this life, I have little doubt.

When I finish, Firemasi (my name for the younger of the two) sits next to me somberly to ask "What does heritage mean?" She speaks English well, taught in schools for many years, and has a fat *American Heritage Dictionary* with print too small for her to read. We look up heritage:

> "Something that is passed down from preceding generations; a tradition."

She is satisfied and begins to use the word with increasing frequency in our conversations, like a new *mantra*. *Dada* comes back alone and we talk a little bit about Gandhi and his own history. For decades he has made and sold *retiya* – spinning machines to make thread out of raw cotton – and has a house full of cotton and cloth. We eat at two in the afternoon, a simple meal of *bacri*, *mung shak*, rice, *curdy*, and an excellent tamarind chutney. I am given the bottle of mango juice to finish.

All the while I focus on Firemasi, trying to figure out what's going on. She is firmly in control, yelling, ordering, and silencing *dada*. A powerful woman.

After lunch *dada* leads me onto the porch to teach me *retiya*. In Gandhi's *ashram*, all the inmates practiced spinning for an hour a day. It was their time of meditation – for Gandhi it represented the source of India's renewed spiritual and economic power. So much so that they put the *charkha* – the simple spinning wheel – at the center of the flag during the Independence movement.

The classical Indian teaching method, I learned, consists of alternate sessions of careful watching and fruitless effort. Watch. Try. Fail. Watch. Try. Fail. *Dada* tried to help by yelling commands while I tried but the vocabulary was too specific for me to understand.

It is something I will one day have to master. We take a nap, after which I am allowed to write and walk around. I feel lost that my walking finished at nine in the morning – I am restless and want to continue. I could get there today – to Dandi, Gandhi, and the sea.

In the evening we watch the television news – which seems to be all about different *mandirs* – yell lovingly at each other, and eat again. I have found the logical extreme of the Indian relationship: three octogenarians who care deeply about each other and are only capable of communicating through yelling simple commands.

Dinner is exactly like lunch, but the yogurt has become slightly more astringent. And *gor*: moist, sticky, *gor*. After dinner I read and watch *Dada* arrange a *khadi* mosquitero. We both sleep in his storeroom, surrounded by bedsheets, pillowcases, spreads, and *dhotis*. A *khadi* emporium, the collected wares of a lifetime of service. There is a fan for me and I sleep under it, atop two blankets and a wooden board. Tomorrow I will see the ocean and finish this chapter. There is nothing to keep me awake.

Day 25

April 5, 2006

"You cannot build non-violence on a factory civilization, but it can be built on self-contained villages. Rural economy eschews exploitation altogether, and exploitation is the essence of violence."

25.1 to Dandi

4h30 wake up, back to Gandhiji's schedule in time for the end of days. Yoga *asana* and meditation, relaxation and shower. A good morning movement. A breakfast of sour yogurt, *mamra*, and *gor*, before walking the road with *dada*. The last road and an 84-year old man who is my grandfather alongside me, unafraid, giving me his time, his blessings, his energy, his very life.

Dada turns back after ten or fifteen minutes, and it's time to walk alone.

There's no excuse not to walk this part of journey, the curving road empty of traffic and fields brown with salt and scraggly cows. I don't see how you couldn't. All the way from the start of this highway 77, the Vijaypur that I missed, should be mandatory walking. It's too beautiful not to. They should put a parking lot for the scooters and tour buses at the turnoff and the humans can take it from there. You can feel the salt and the history in the air. You can feel the strength it takes to stand up to empires within and without, the discipline to confront the violence inside you.

It's the last stretch for me. I have to get home tomorrow, materialize a magic ride out of the white *khadi* cocktail party that awaits me. Faith always. And my 200 *points*.

I walk past the town, where I know I must turn to stay, and go directly to the beach. There is stand selling coconuts and ice cream and even places to park for the holidaymakers but it's too early yet in the day and the year – the beach is empty, waiting for me. I set my backpack and clothing on the beach, strip down to my *dhoti* and shorts. The Indian Ocean, brown as I am, awaits me.

I wash my body in its salt, wash my *dhoti* of the road, and swim. The surf is rough and welcoming. Nothing feels real. There must be somewhere else to go. There is no further, from here.

I return to the beach to collapse in meditation, to open my eyes and take in the light. I am exhausted and can finally let the exhaustion wash over me. I straighten myself and collapse again under the weight of the realization:

I want to go home. I want not to be alone anymore.

I have never wanted to go home before. I have never wanted to come home early, descend from the heights, or turn around. During the fever, sure, I could crawl into welcome arms and have soup. But this is my first time I've been homesick and listening.

And what could that mean but *the hacienda must be built?*[1]

I am finally ready and have nowhere to go, no-one to go to.

So I walk back to the high school in Dandi to meet the teacher and rector. They recognize me and treat me like the prince of pilgrims, give me a room of my own and a feast for lunch. My room is full of windows and empty of locks, and the curious students inspect my every move, surround me every time I dare to read, write, or put the *bansuri* to my lips.

I sit in meditation for fifteen minutes, until I have vision of two men walking towards me. They stop in front of me and speak:

"Okay. Time to get up."

I open my eyes, hear *thalis* ringing a few seconds later, and, one minute after that, two students come to fetch me.

At lunch the hundred or so boys sit obediently on long mats they unfurl after sweeping and mopping the hall. The rector and I preside from a wooden table across the room, attended by a few of the older students. They are overjoyed to meet me, to serve me, to be next to me.

Respect. Privilege. Dominance. They are yoked together here – I have come to understand the importance of craving distinction against the entropy towards oneness, for the sake of discipline. But while eating? Shouldn't there still be a togetherness, a joint submission to god and our fragile mortality, an awareness that we all must eat together, serve each other, and die? How do the authorities think their status is something other than a game?

Or perhaps they don't, perhaps it's all a kind and elaborate charade for my benefit, the wandering homegrown foreign guest?

Rotli, bataka ringun shak, athanu, pappadam, dal, bath, tomatoes. More than I can handle, and gladly. After lunch they allow me to clean my own plate – a huge benefit of Gandhian institutions – before returing to my room for a school-wide *bansuri* practice, a public Gandhi reading (in English), a nap, and another (school-wide, once again) practice, and *chai*.

---

[1] The phrase is taken from a Situationist article, *Towards a New Urbanism*, by Ivan Chtcheglov.

When young children bring hot *chai* to your room on the top floor, no amount of poisonous refined sugar can veto. I have no choice but to take advantage of the comedy: my room is standing-room-only with students, others poking brown faces through interior windows, the door, and the roof to stare. I have never felt so surrounded, and so surrounded by myself, a twisted fun-house mirror of short black hair and wide black eyes.

I order them to bring me chalk and give an impromptu world geography class on the stone walls, drawing continents around the room. I explain the mathematics of circles and time zones. I make them place Dandi in Gujarat, Gujarat in India, India in Asia, Asia in the world.

They stay with me through the novelty and math and missteps, and eventually leave to study for exams. In India, I've noticed, students are never in class: they are either walking uniformed through the streets or studying for exams.

I am given a few eternal moments to read and to write. At five it's cool enough to go outside and I walk down the road – oh, precious walking – to the local Gandhi museum. It is cool and empty for me to read, cry, and write in the guest book. I can never get through a story of sacrifice without crying – whether it's Martin Luther King Jr. or Che Guevara or Archbishop Romero or Jesus. They who give everything they have are inevitably murdered in the end.

And they know it.

Eventually I can leave the large photograph of millions upon millions of mourners walking through Delhi for Gandhiji's funeral procession, but I cannot escape Nehru's baffled despondence:

> "Friends and comrades, the light has gone out of our lives, and there is darkness everywhere, and I do not quite know what to tell you or how to say it. Our beloved leader, *Bapu* as we called him, the father of the nation, is no more. Perhaps I am wrong to say that; nevertheless, we will not see him again, as we have seen him for these many years, we will not run to him for advice or seek solace from him, and that is a terrible blow, not only for me, but for millions and millions in this country."

I salute the over-sized statue outside, daze back to the beach across the salt flats to swim and witness the sunset. I am confused into thinking Gandhiji has just come here, broken the law, liberated India, and been murdered, all today.

The light is incredible, our sun still two and a half fingers high above the approaching water, the ocean's shimmering fat tongue licking closer and closer. From this angle the water can even be blue under its muddy brown halo of haze.

The sun is orange, sinking, topped with yellow, and now a striated chiogga beet as it swings through the skies and my salutations. I finish and sit as it enters the grey-blue grime over faraway Pakistan.

I return to a waiting dinner and rector in the empty hall. I will never accustom to the kindness of these people. Tuved *shak* and *bacri*, then rice. I finish reading my book of Gandhiji's writings, right on time. It is the slowest book I have ever read – so powerful and true that I often couldn't take more than a paragraph at once without leaning backwards onto a banyan tree in exhalation and wonder. I have been convinced, in series, that Mohandas Gandhi was a fool, a leader, a *loco*, a saint, a prophet.

I now understand his non-violence has nothing to do with passivity and nothing to do with politics. He didn't want political freedom for India; He wanted total freedom for everyone. Enlightenment. *Ahimsa* is the code of conduct of the Enlightened Warrior, and he sets it as premise, path, and terminus to trick us into our true destiny, already in progress.

The door knocks. Dhirubhai, the principal and founder of the school, has come to visit me. He talks some about his inspiration for starting this school, the Gandhian values India needs both to prosper, and to stay true to itself. I listen. Dhirubhai tells me that tomorrow is also the birthday of Lord Ram, as well as the anniversary of the *Namak Satyagraha*, so he doesn't expect a huge turnout at the event tomorrow. In addition there is an eye camp to offer free cataract surgery and a huge banquet for all the Gandhian dignitaries who would attend. He says he is proud to have me and will either find me a ride home or buy me a train ticket, so there is nothing I can worry about. He also requests me to speak tomorrow, he can find a time, though the program is, as I can only imagine, extremely crowded with important figures. I thank him.

Dhirubhai dresses well, wears *khadi*, and speaks softly. He is an educated man recognizes what almost nobody else does – that Gandhiji's face, name, political legacy, and actual thinking are all separate entities, siblings in a family of myth. And his thinking has, naturally, been locked out of the inheritance of popular culture.

Every thing is so good to hear. Shortly thereafter a physics teacher comes to see me with his colleague, wife, and child. He asks about *asteya* and I explain how I see the principle applied in an injust society. When so many are cold and starving, how can it be moral not to give everything we have – time, energy, and objects alike – directly towards the welfare of all? I ask about the bicycle knife sharpener on the road to Ras and he explains to me how dynamos work.

This is, fittingly, as good as it gets. Humans who care, whom I can understand. The language finally feels smooth and supple. Well-fed with time to meditate. Yoga on the beach. Not afraid of children, women, rich, or poor. Of anyone. Is that peace – not being afraid of anyone?

I take some time to write before sleeping, and the kids come in two batches to check out my strange handwriting. They think it is Arabic. I bid them goodnight and stare out the window as they leave – if I really knew this language, I could really share something with them. I finally feel as if I have something I can offer, I am worthy of their attention. The fear has melted away and left room for the spirit of play.

Right on schedule.

Day 26

April 6, 2006

"One person who can express Ahimsa in
life exercises a force superior to all the
forces of brutality."

26.1 Dandi-*sur-mer*

The dream is over. No place to go. No salt to pick-up. No more hallu-cinations. No more begging for food nor housing. No more walking in the sunlight. Guaranteed rest. No more walking the *dharma*. No more golden passport. No more truth and connection and god and purpose and Gandhiji and suffering.

Money. No more freedom.

Long meditation this morning. No answer. Now what? *Krishna* was going to tell me. Maybe I out-planned him. So much happening. I can carry money again. Buy some credit for my phone. Get in cars. Eat ice cream. Smoke. Drink. Sex. Eat *paan*.

No desires, of course. Yet. I just want to play music and memorize other peoples' prayers. Type up some thoughts and send out thank-you cards. Thumbs-up all around. Stay put. The thought of travel repulses me, for the first time.

Thinking of going back to Ahmedabad tires me. It's not home. All the commitments are waiting there: speaking, media, interviews, visits. *Darshan*. I want some "me time" already. Where is the 'me time'? Gandhi? Meditation. Spinning. Spinning. Spinning: it's the 'me time'.

> Golden light on door.
> The sun, he is rising up!
> Where is my long night?

The march is over.

Gandhiji picked up a handful of salt seventy-six years ago and kick-started the struggle for independence. Broke the back of the British empire. How is it possible? For Gandhiji, how was it not possible? How could everyone *not* see the truth of purity, the purity of truth, that love is that truth, one with god and themselves.

Today will be ceremony and commemoration. I will be asked to say a few words in Gujarati and will do so, haltingly. The sun has risen over a Thursday. Maybe I'll go back to the ocean. Maybe I'll never leave. Meditate further. Pray. What else is there? My new life lies open before me. The one thing about the road is there is no going back. You can go around and go the way you came but it's always the other side and there's no finding that back, it's somehow elsewhere, spinning in its own relative frame, a fly on a spinning-wheel.

It's not what you think, young pilgrim – time is relative and there's no going back. There is only the oneness. The names even disappear – the one road that twists upon itself, bites its own tail. The One Love consciousness that nothing is apart from the you-part of god, the me-part of god, the them-part of god. The one rose in her many truths, her many gardens, her many roses, colors, and dresses[1]. One road, one love, one truth all slip away into the awareness.

That's the only future to interest me. The path of abundance. The others are flavors of anarchy wrestling for commodities – plutonium, oil, or paternal affection. The birthright future is the future of abundance – the abundance we create and maintain in our minds. Oh, most fertile of seed-flats.

The material world is a showcase, irrelevant, spectacular. The experiment is to align our egos with our nature and the spirit of abundance. To show how easy it is, how everyone can do it. Wealth will be the love of simplicity – how much weight and wealth can the planet afford, after all?[2]

I still can't tell the texture.

I spend the morning meditating and lying in bed in reverie. At 9h15 I go down to check out the scene. Important Indian people milling about in preparation for an important Indian event. No possibility of escape. Many of them recognize me and want to talk. One kid has come from England to run the NGO offering free eye exams and cataract surgeries. He speaks decent English. The largest man finds me immediately and sits me down with him. Maheshkaka Kothari. He has a soft sweet voice and kept me safely under his care. I have little idea who he is except respected and yet I felt it is important to stay with him. The last day of these duties, this respect, after all.

We wait out the alternately boring and comical opening ceremonies, with *khadi*-clad octogenarians failing to light *ghee* lamps despite a polyphony of comments and commands. He suggests I go with him to another ceremony down the road for an hour and come back. Why not? I can ride in cars today.

It actually happens, and we roll with his driver in an A/C van to a school for the deaf, back in the Vijaypur, across the street from a school for the disabled. Both of which I remember from my walk (now

---

[1] Remembering "Is the rose naked, or is that her only dress?" from Pablo Neruda's *Book of Questions*.

[2] In Gandhi's words: "Earth provides enough to satisfy every man's need, but not every man's greed."

over) two days before. We stop for an hour to relax with a friend of
Maheshkaka's from South Africa, who tours the world doing karate and
professional pilgrimages at 70-80 kilometers a day. He drinks American
soda and I take some water. I am now apparently in some sort of club.

It turns out that Maheshkaka is the dean of service for the young
children of the world. He founded both of the schools we visit and
tomorrow will inaugurate new ground for a school for the blind. More
guests come, he sets them up, and we go to the ground-breaking ceremony for the statue of a colleague of Maheshkaka's who died last year,
at 101. It is also Maheshkaka's birthday and his servants, who abso-
lutely love him, give him flowers and kind words. Today also is Lord
Ram's birthday and either the birth or death anniversary of another
famous freedom fighter, Ravishankar Maharaj.

It's time to roll to the other ceremony and we get back in the car.
My new uncle shares some wisdom with me.

He tells me he went to South Africa four years ago to organize
a *katha* with Muraribapu[3]. They spent a day on Gandhiji's Tolstoy
Farm, in a state of disrepair. Muraribapu wanted something done to
preserve it, and put Maheshkaka in charge.

He tells me he spent seven years in Japan giving talks on Gandhi,
as part of Gandhi-Buddhist society there. He was first sent to Japan
by Prime Minister Nehru for a world peace conference in 1959. Nehru
was a friend to Maheshkaka's parents and when he came to inaugurate
the museum I visited yesterday, in 1961, he stayed in the Kothari's
one-room shack.

Amazing and inspiring stories from a generation with which I have
no connection. How did this happen?

"Do you know about Vinoba Bhave?"

I almost blush. No.

"When I finished college at 21 years of age I didn't even wait
for my exam results but left to join Vinoba right away."

Vinoba Bhave, apparently, was a prominent Gandhian reformer.
Maheshkaka tells me his story – he was a student of Gandhi's who,
when *Bapu* passed away, decided to enact land reform in India, through
Love. He walked all of India various times, over 26 years, asking the

---

[3]One of the most famous Hindu televangelists around.

rich to donate land for the landless. And received 40 million hectares in response.

It's a pretty good story.

> "I spent 10 years walking with him. He would get up and walk at 2h30 in the morning, reach the next village at 9h00 or 9h30 – walk 20 miles in 6 hours because it was too hot to walk after 9h00. At 11h00 every day we would talk to villagers and have a report compiled for Vinobaji at two. At four there would be a prayer session[4] and afterwards Vinobaji would speak and offer some solutions to whatever issues we encountered. He did this for twenty-six years."

We arrive. My role is to stand at Maheskaka's side and look cool, a non-servant accomplice to make him look good. I talk to some people who read about me – apparently there was an article about my night in Vanj. No surprise given the power and efficiency of the *sarpanch*. I look around when I notice only the dignitaries are talking. Hundreds of students are all seated, wildly gesticulating to each other in passionate conversation. It is a college for the deaf.

We look pretty, pray, and leave. A *brahmin* has been hired for the ceremony, arrives late, and finishes on time. On the way back I ask Maheshkaka more about Vinobaji and land reform.

> "There are two ways of accomplishing land reform: through politics or through love. Vinobaji tried through love."

At Dandi the eye camp is winding down and everyone is eating. The tables are full and they unroll mats on the floor but of course I am called to sit at the main table with Maheshkaka. Lunch is a feast to celebrate Ram and Gandhi and Maheshkaka and Ravishankar Maharaj and everone else: *mung shak*, *ringun shak*, *lapsi*, *shiro*, *dal*, *bath*, *athanu*, *pappadam*, and surprisingly perfect *chass*. I spend more time trying to avoid being served than actually eating, and still end up with too much *lapsi*.

There is too much to focus on and I escape. Outside I run into the good doctor from Karadi, frothing at the mouth. He takes me to the museum I've already been to, complaining violently about the same

---

[4]They recite the same prayer, oddly enough, that I started with at the beginning of the journey. It was written by Vinoba himself.

old men. They have closed minds, live rich irresponsible lives, and think wearing *khadi* is enough to make them Gandhian. Apparently. I don't doubt it but it's hard for me to get worked up at this stage in the helix, full stomach and tired legs and all. So he rants to people in the museum and I look at the pictures (they haven't changed since yesterday) and cry.

Outside the doctor motions to the empty field between us and the ocean and tells me how the owner of this house spread manure over these two acres before Gandhi came to hide the salt field from the authorities. When Gandhi came the British were waiting at a different location to arrest him. The owner called the pilgrims over and pushed aside the dung to reveal the salt field. Gandhi's group could therefore break the law without interruption, sending a powerful signal throughout the subcontinent. A nice photo shoot as well and – bonus points for world peace – the owner of the house was Muslim.

My good doctor drops me off where the speeches will be given. There is a photo exhibition, some book stalls, and seating arranged in the shade of a large *vad* tree. The photos are of desolate *Kutch*. I meditate off to the side until all the benches are full and society nudges me out of consciousness. We sit through an afternoon of actionless, motionless Gandhian talk, the three hours interrupted by two sweet songs and one inspiring woman.

She is 93 and spoke of meeting Gandhi when she was 17 years of age and barely literate. He asked her to write to him and when she did, he sent back the original missive circling five errors in four lines. They started a correspondence that was to teach her the importance of proper spelling and grammar. She then spent her entire life teaching literacy to children and adults, in jails during the freedom struggle and in schools after independence. She considers herself a true daughter of Gandhi.

Towards the end, I am introduced and speak to the gathering briefly in Gujarati. I remember that god is love, and, in my short *yatra* – I am now conscious of its brevity, one day for each year that Vinobaji walked – I trusted each person as god and was handsomely rewarded for it. All I could really offer is thanks, to everyone there, the people of Gujarat, and the human spirit.

Everyone has a good time. I run into the uncle who walked with me to Champrabhata, just as he foretold. I say my goodbyes. After the ceremony they give me leave, once more, to walk to the ocean one more time, to say goodbye.

It's still brown. Various people offer to public my book, give me scraps of paper and business cards, tell me important names. I remain skeptical that I could write anything worthy of their presses. It would be too jumbled, too mystical, too arrogant, too American.

> Sunsets on journey
> must mean a new beginning:
> I'm ready for home.

Appendix A

Sabarmati Ashram Observances

by Mohandas K. Gandhi

The object of this Ashram is that its members should qualify themselves for, and make a constant endeavor towards, the service of the country, not inconsistent with universal good.

A.1 Truth:

Truth is not fulfilled by mere abstinence from telling or practising an untruth in ordinary relations with fellow-men. But Truth is God, the one and only Reality. All other observances take their rise from the quest for, and the worship of, Truth. Worshippers of Truth must not resort to untruth, even for what they may believe to be the food of the country, and they may be required, like Prahlad, civilly to disobey the orders even of parents and elders in virtue of their paramount loyalty to Truth.

A.2 Non-Violence:

Mere not-killing (the animals) is not enough (for this observance). The active part of non-violence is Love. The law of Love requires equal consideration for all life from the tiniest insect to the highest man. One who follows this law must not be angry even with the perpetrator of the greatest imaginable wrong, but must love him, wish him well and serve him. Although he must thus love the wrong doers, he must never submit to his wrong or his injustice, but must oppose it with all his might, and must patiently and without resentment suffer all the hardships to which the wrong doer may subject him in punishment for his opposition.

A.3   Chastity (Brahmacharya)

Observance of the foregoing principles is impossible without the observance of celibacy. It is not enough that one should not look upon any woman or man with a lustful eye; animal passion must be so controlled as to be excluded even from the mind. If married, one must not have a carnal mind regarding one's wife or husband, but consider her or him as one's lifelong friends, and establish relationship of perfect purity. A sinful touch, gesture or word is a direct breach of this principle.

A.4   Control of the Palate

The observance of Brahmacharya has been found, from experience, to be extremely difficult so long as one has not acquired mastery over taste. Control of the palate has therefore been placed as a principle by itself. Eating is necessary only for sustaining the body and keeping it a fit instrument for service, and must never be practised for self-indulgence. Food must therefore be taken, like medicine, under proper restraint. In pursuance of this principle on must eschew exciting foods, such as spices and condiments. Meat, liquor, tobacco, bhang, etc are excluded from the Ashram. This principle requires abstinence from feasts or dinners which has pleasure as their object.

A.5   Non-Stealing

It is not enough not to take another's property without his permission. One becomes guilty of theft even by using differently anything which one has received in trust for use in a particular way, as well as by using a thing longer than the period for which it has been lent. It is also theft if one receives anything which he does not really need. The fine truth at the bottom of this principle is that Nature provides just enough, and no more, for our daily need. Hence it is also a theft to possess anything more than one's minimum requirement.

A.6 Non-Possession or Poverty

This principle is really a part of (5). Just as one must not receive, so must one not possess anything which one does not really need. It would be a breach of this principle to possess unnecessary foodstuffs, clothing or furniture. For instance, one must not keep a chair if can do without it. In observing this principle one is led to a progressive simplification of one's own life.

A.7 Swadeshi

Man is not omnipotent. He therefore serves the world best by serving his neighbour. This is swadeshi, a principle which is broken when one professes to serve those who are more remote in preference to those who are near. Observance of swadeshi makes for order in the world; the breach of it leads to chaos. Following this principle, one must as far as possible purchase one's requirements locally and not buy things imported from foreign lands, which can easily be manufactured in the country. There is no place for self interest in Swadeshi, which enjoins the sacrifice of oneself for the family, of the family for the village, and of the country for humanity.

A.8 Fearlessness

One cannot follow Truth of Love so long as one is subject to fear. As there is at present a reign of fear in the country, meditation on and cultivation of fearlessness have a particular importance. Hence its separate mention as an observance. A seeker after truth must give up the fear of caste, government, robbers, etc. and he must not be frightened by poverty or death.

A.9   Removal of Untouchability

Untouchability, which has taken such deep root in Hinduism, is altogether irreligious. Its removal has therefore been treated as an independent principle. The so-called untouchables have equal place in the Ashram with other classes.

A.10   Varnashrama Dharma

In the Ashram, caste distinction has no place. It is believed that caste distinction has caused harm to the Hindu dharma. The ideas of the superior and inferior status and pollution by contact implied in caste distinction serves to destroy the dharma of non-violence. However, the Ashram does believe in Varna and the Ashram dharma. The division of Varna is based upon occupation. One who follows that division lives by his parents' occupation, not inconsistent with larger dharma, and spends his spare time in acquiring and advancing true knowledge as well as performing service.

The Ashram believes, as in the Varna, so in the four Ashrams of the Brahmacharya, Grihastha, Vanprastha, and Sanyasa. But the Ashram does not believe that life of renunciation can be lived in a forest only, or by giving up performance of one's duties. The Ashram believes that dharma of renunciation can be and should be observed while leading a normal life and that it alone is true renunciation.

A.11   Tolerance

The Ashram believes that the principal faiths of the world constitute a revelation of truth, but as they have all been outlined by imperfect men, they have been affected by imperfections and allowed with untruth. One must therefore entertain the same respect for the religious faiths of others as one accords to one's own.

A.12 Physical Labour
(this was added afterwards by Gandhi)

Man can be saved from injuring society, as well as himself, only if he sustains his physical existence by physical labour. Able-bodied adults should do all their personal work themselves, and should not be served by others, except for proper reasons. But they should, at the same time, remember that service of children, as well as of the disabled, the old and the sick, is a duty incumbent on every person who has the required strength. Keeping in view this object, no labourers are employed in the Ashram, and if at all they are inevitably employed, the dealing with them would not be of an employer-employee.

Appendix B

Songs in English

B.1   Vaishnav Jan To

He is the true Vaishnava who knows and feels another's woes as his own

Ever ready to serve others who are unhappy, he never lets vanity get to his head

Bowing to everyone humbly and criticising none

He keeps his speech, deeds and thoughts pure; blessed is the mother who begets such a one

He looks upon all with an equal eye. Having rid himself of lust, he treats and reveres every woman as his mother

His tongue would fail him if he attempted to utter an untruth. He does not covet another's wealth

The bonds of earthly attachment hold him not. His mind is deeply rooted in renunciation

Every moment he is intent on reciting the name of the Lord Rama. All the holy places are ever present in his body

He has conquered greed, deceit, passion (lust) and anger

The sight of such a Vaishnava, says Narsinh, saves a family through seventy-one generations

B.2   All Religions Prayer

Om Thou art that, Thou art Narayana, God in the form of man;

Thou art the Embodiment of perfection and the perfect master. Thou art enlightened Buddha; Thou art Subramanya and Ganesha, the remover of obstacles; Thou art the Sun-fire

Thou art Brahma, the Creator; Mazda, the Great One; Thou art Jehovah and the Divine Mother, the creative Energy. O Lord! Thou art the Father of Jesus.

Thou art Rudhra, the Transformer, and Vishnu, the Preserver; Thou art Rama and Krishna; Thou art Rahim, all kindness, always giving and expanding; Thou art the Tao.

Thou art Vasudeva, the Sustenance of all, omnipotent and omnipresent; Thou art Hari, Destroyer of illusion, the blissful Spirit.

Thou art unparallelled, beyond time and fearless of adversities; Thou art Shiva, Creator of the lingam, Symbol of the formless Absolute

Appendix C

Dandi Kooch Programme: 386 km

day	date	starting	mid-day	night	distance (km
1	12 march	ahmedabad	chandola lake	aslali	21
2	13 march	aslali	bareja	navagam	14
3	14 march	navagam	vasna	matar	16
4	15 march	matar	dabhan	nadiad	24
5	15 march	nadiad	boriavi	anand	18
6	17 march	rest day anand			
7	18 march	anand	napa	borsad	18
8	19 march	borsad	ras	kankapura	19
9	20 march	kankapura	mahisagar	kareli	18
10	21 march	kareli	gajera	ankhi	18
11	22 march	ankhi	jambusar	amod	19
12	23 march	amod	buva	samni	19
13	24 march	rest day samni			
14	25 march	samni	tralsa	derol	16
15	26 march	derol	bharuch	ankleshwar	21
16	27 march	ankleshwar	sanjod	mangrol	19
17	28 march	mangrol	rayma	umrachi	16
18	29 march	umrachi	arthan	bhatgam	16
19	30 march	bhatgam	sandhier	delad	16
20	31 march	rest day delad			
21	1 april	delad	chaprabhata	surat	18
22	2 april	surat	dindoli	vanz	19
23	3 april	vanz	dhaman	navsari	21
24	4 april	navsari	vijalpur	karadi	14
25	5 april	karadi	karadi	dandi	6
26	6 april	dandi			

Appendix D

Map to Dandi

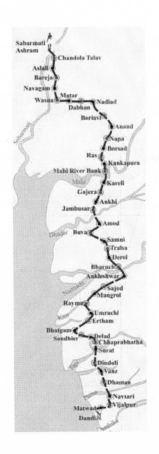

Glossary

aadivasi indigenous people of India, many of whom still retain their traditional lifestyles and traditions, and many of whom supply cheap seasonal agricultural labor.

aarti worship offered to a god or saint with fire and incense, usually performed at sunrise and sunset.

aashirvad blessing.

aditi deo bhavana "guest is god".

ahamkar ego.

ahimsa often translated as "non-violence" or "love": one of Gandhi's eleven ashram observances (See Appendix A).

Akshardam the main temple of the Swaminarayan sect.

Allah the word used in Islam to denote the concept of God.

Amazon the author's understanding of the totality of all Being, a conjunction of Love and Death, generally incomprehensible through reason but most easily apparent in the overwhelming sensation and power of the Amazon ecosystems in South America. Salient features of Amazon (as opposed to "the Amazon") include a love so broad as to be inescapable, power so great it can kill you at any moment, perfect extension through time and space, and a visceral rawness of presence beyond the mind's capability to grasp.

amba mango (mangifera indica).

Ambaji Mataji in a benign form.

ambavadi mango orchard.

America thi aiva a phrase meaning "he came from America.

amla Indian gooseberry, a fruit important to ayurvedic medicine.

ananda bliss, the ground of Being beneath the fleeting pleasures (sukh) and sufferings (dukh) of our material sojourn.

asana one of the various positions and stretches in the science of Yoga.

ashram an ancient Indian idea of intentional community including notions of conservatory, monastery, and eco-village. Each ashram sets its own rules for its residents ("inmates") and may or may not have a guru to guide things along.

aso-palav a tall tree famous for its ayurvedic uses.

asteya non-stealing, one of the Gandhi's eleven vows (See Appendix A).

athanu pickle, often made from lemons or unripe fruit (especially mango). Generally very strong in taste, either spicy, either sweet, or sour.

atman the soul.

ayurveda ancient Indian medical science, "remembered by the gods" over 5000 years ago.

babul tall tree in the acacia family, whose branches are traditionally used as toothbrushes.

bacri traditional flatbread made from medium-coarse wheat flour, usually dry-roasted and served with ghee.

bajra pearl millet, a major grain crop.

bansuri Indian bamboo flute, association with Lord Krishna.

bapu "father". Mahatma Gandhi is popularly known as Bapu or Bapuji.

basudi milky rice pudding flavored with nuts, cardamon, and saffron.

bataka potato.

bataka-poha savory breakfast made from potatoes and rice flakes (poha), often spiced with curry leaves, mustard seeds, and turmeric.

bath plain steamed rice.

Bhagavad Gita The Song Divine, a section of the Mahabharata that is regarded as the most concise and beautiful elucidation of Hindu dharma and ethics.

Bhagawan God as total knowledge, complete understanding, enlightened awareness.

bhai brother.

bhajan devotional song.

bhakta devotee.

bhakti devotional love.

Bharat India.

bhavan a nice word for house or domicile.

bidi small smelly hand-rolled Indian cigarettes.

bike motorcycle.

bilva tree.

bindi okra, ladyfinger.

biscuit cookie.

brahmachariya chastity, one of Gandhi's eleven ashram observances (See Appendix A).

Brahman God as the everything, "The one without a second".

brahmin the top of the caste system, devoted to society's religious (including musical) needs.

buggia savory fritters, usually made from besun.

bungalow a freestanding house.

caste the traditional Indian system of social organization, theoretically based upon merit, and practically oppressive by birth.

chaavani a home, refuge, or meeting place.

chai tea. Indian tea is brewed in milk or half-milk and half-water, often with a mixture of spices including ginger, cardamom, clove, black pepper, and holy basil.

chappati the most common whole-wheat flatbread in North India.

Charak Samhita one of the central texts of ayurveda, named for it's author, Charak.

charkha the spinning wheel, for spinning thread from carded cotton. Gandhi adopted the charkha as the symbol of Indian economic and political self-sufficiency.

chass buttermilk, the whey after separating the fat out of yogurt.

chevro a spicy snack mix.

chickoo a small round brown sweet fruit.

chillum traditional clay pipe for hashish or marijauna.

chocolate candy. Doesn't usually mean "chocolate".

chori a kind of bean.

chula outdoor wood-fired cooking stove.

cuchumber salad, possibly derived from "cucumber".

curdy a savory buttermilk soup, spiced with curry leaves and thickened with besun.

curry patra curry leaf, used as a spice all over India, with a unique and sublime flavor.

cycle bicycle (cf bike).

dada paternal grandfather (wife is dadi).

dal split lentil or pulse, often used to mean the traditional split lentil soup. In Gujarat, dal and rice are the second course of the meal, and the dal is often quite sweet.

Dandi kooch the pilgrimage to Dandi.

darbar a caste designation.

darshan glimpse. Can be used in the context of visiting a temple, idol, holy place, relative, or friend.

daru alcoholic beverage.

Dattatreya God as the conjunct of Vishnu, Brahma, and Shiva, usually seen with three heads riding a horse.

derasar Jain temple.

dhamma Pali for dharma.

dharamshala rest house for traveling pilgrims.

dharma one's path or duty, "The Law". Similar to the concept of the "Tao".

dhokla savory steamed cake, made from a fermented mixture of rice and lentil flours, then spiced with some combination of sugar, mustard seeds, chiles, coconuts, cilantro, and lemon.

dhol a large, loud drum of plastic and metal.

dhoti the thin male cotton skirt.

dhun a devotional song of call-and-response nature.

dungri onion.

enshallah "God willing" or "I hope so" or "maybe" (arabic).

ganga the Ganges river, often personified as a Mother figure.

ganja marijauna.

gerba traditional Gujarati circular dance.

ghazal some kind of song.

ghee clarified butter, traditionally made by first churning the fat out of yogurt to make butter, then heating the butter until all the water has gone and only the fat remains. Ghee keeps indefinitely and is a major component of many Hindu rituals and ayurvedic medicines.

gober a pleasant word for cow dung.

gobi cauliflower.

gopis sixteen thousand young milkmaid consorts who expressed divine love for Krishna.

gor jaggery, unrefined evaporated sugarcane juice.

gorsimla a tamarind-like fruit, but sweeter.

gram swaraj village self-sufficiency, one of Gandhi's long-term goals.

gulab rose.

guru a teacher, one who leads you from the darkness to the light.

gurudwara Sikh temple.

gurukul residential school, usually religious.

haldi turmeric.

Hari a name of Krishna, commonly used as an exclamation or chant.

harijan "children of god", used by Gandhi as a replacement for "untouchable".

harmonium traditional Indian accompaniment instrument, similar to a small organ or accordion.

hingu asafetida.

Holi a two-day festival of fire and color to celebrate the victory of good over evil, as well as the spring.

hotel restaurant.

imli tamarind.

Jain a member of the Jain religion, which holds ahimsa as its central principle and follows the teachings of Mahavir, a liberated soul who lived in the 6th century BC.

Jalaram a saint and social reformer from the 19th century, famous for serving food to the hungry.

jalebi fried sticky sweet dessert, made from white flour, white sugar, and orange food coloring.

jambu fruit.

japa type of meditation, involving repetition of a name of God or mantra, usually accompanied with a rosary.

jeera cumin.

jhopri a small hut.

ji suffix giving respect, generally added to a first name, ie "Judithji".

jivatman a techinical term in Indian philosophy, roughly meaning "soul" in beings we understand as having "life".

kaka paternal uncle (wife is kaki).

kaliyuga the last of four great ages of time in Hindu chronology.

kaman a type of dhokla.

Kanaiya Krishna.

karela bitter gourd.

katash astringent, one of the six tastes defined by ayurveda.

katha public lecture or explication, usually of a holy text.

keri mango.

khadi handloom cotton.

khajur the fruit of the date palm.

kitcheree a Gujarati specialty of mung dal and rice cooked together to a near porridge consistency, usually eaten at night with curdy.

Krishna God as love, the eigth incarnation of Vishnu, often represented playing the bansuri, stealing butter, and flirting with gopis.

Kutch grassland and desert region in Northern Gujarat.

ladoo a big ball of sugar and ghee. Dessert.

lapsi dessert.

Laxmana Rama's brother and faithful devotee.

limbupani lemonade, generally made with sugar, salt, and cumin.

madrasa Islamic school, often attached to a masjid.

maha great.

maharaj literally "great king", often used for servants and priests.

mama maternal uncle (wife is mami).

mamra fried snack food.

mandir Hindu temple.

mangitude the author's understanding of the essential quality of a mango, beyond such spectacular characteristics as color, firmness, or sweetness.

mantra a syllable or phrase, often repeated for meditation.

masala spice.

masi maternal aunt (husband is masa).

masjid mosque, Islamic center of worship.

Mataji God in the form of the mother, often worshipped in many forms and names.

methi baggi thepla wheat flatbread with fenugreek leaves mixed into the dough, cooked with oil on a hot griddle.

mirchi chile.

mitai a general term for sweets.

mitai-walla one who sells sweets.

Mohammedan a common term for 'Muslim'.

mori bland.

mugus intensely sweet dessert made from besun and ghee.

mung green gram, a type of lentil, considered the healthiest by ayurveda.

namak salt.

namaste a traditional greeting, honoring the divine essence in another.

Narayan God as pure consciousness.

nasila tobacco.

nasta a word for both snack and breakfast, almost always offered with chai.

Navratri nine-day dance celebration to honor different forms of Mataji, usually around October or November.

neem a tree famous for its uses in medicine and farming.

nilgiri eucalyptus.

NRI non-resident Indian, a general term for Indian citizens who have emigrated abroad or foreign citizens of Indian descent.

Om God as the original sound of the universe.

Osho "The Master." An enlightened soul famous for controversial styles of meditation and large numbers of foreign disciples.

paan originally an ayurvedic concoction of various herbs and spices wrapped in the leaf of the betel tree, paan later evolved into a drug-vehicle for chewing tobacco and the betel-nut. Associated with constant spitting of red nasty liquid.

pack a shot, generally of whiskey.

panchayat village governing body.

pappadam light roasted appetizer, usually made from pounded lentil flour.

paramatman God as the over-soul.

parotha usually triangular wheat flatbread, rolled and cooked with oil to achieve a flakier consistency.

parvar a type of small gourd.

patel a caste designation.

pathak one who can recite the holy texts at will.

peon employee of low rank.

pipal one of the grandest and most important trees in Indian culture, in the banyan family (ficus religiosa).

point the author's understanding of currency, independent of national character. One point equals one rupee in India, one peso in Argentina, and one euro in France.

police-walla policeman, or he who sells policing services.

prana God as energy or breath.

pranami a sect of Krishna-worship.

pranayama branch of yoga dealing with controlling and developing the breath.

prarthna bhoomi prayer ground.

prasad food first offered to god then distributed to the devoted. Prasad is never refused.

puja worship in the Hindu family of religion, which may take a dizzying variety of forms.

pujari he who performs the puja.

puri small deep-fried wheat flatbread.

rai the seed of the mustard plant.

raj kingdom or government.

rajbhog a feast fit for a king. Also a flavor of ice cream.

Rama God as righteousness, the seventh incarnation of Vishnu.

Ramayana ancient Indian epic telling the story of King Rama's adventures.

rasmo alfalfa, perhaps.

rastra pitta father of the nation, usually referring to Gandhi.

retiya travel-size spinning wheel.

ringun eggplant, aubergine.

rollo line of thought (spanish).

rotla large thick bajra flatbread, hand-rolled.

rotli thin wheat flatbread.

Sabarmati Ashram the ashram Gandhi established in Ahmedabad, Gujarat, and lived in until beginning the Salt March in 1930.

saddhu literally "pure", often referring to one who has given up attachment to the material world to wander the earth and seek truth.

sadhaks one who is deeply into her sadhana.

saloon hair salon, generally for men.

salwar-kameez traditional panjabi women's outfit of pants, a long loose shirt, and scarf (dupatta).

samsara the material life, the creation.

sanyassi a seeker, one who has renounced the material world in pursuit of the true nature of reality.

sari a traditional womens outfit made of a single piece of cloth, usually five meters long.

sarpanch mayor, the leader of the village panchayat.

sarva dharma prarthna all-religion prayer, written by Vinoba Bhave with holy words from many religious traditions (See Appendix B).

sasro father-in-law.

satsung philosophical discussion, generally meaning the discourse of a guru.

satvic see satva.

satya truth, one of Gandhi's eleven ashram observances (See Appendix A).

satyagraha soul force, Gandhi's term for a non-violent civil disobedience campaign based on fearlessness, love, and humility.

satyagrahi a participant in satyagraha.

saudade a feeling of longing and desire for something lost that may never again be found.

saunf fennel or anis. I can never keep it straight.

seva selfless service, can also refer to employment.

shak vegetable or vegetable curry.

shankpushpi a sacred tree, used in rituals for the god Shiva, and a strong ayurvedic medicine.

shanti peace.

shastri one who knows the scriptures and understands what they mean.

sherbet flavored sugared drink or ice ball.

shiro dessert or breakfast made from roasted cream-of-wheat, ghee, and sugar.

shivalingam phallic sculpture representing Lord Shiva.

shivasana yoga asana commonly known as the 'headstand'.

siesta afternoon nap (spanish).

Sita Rama's wife, an incarnation of Parvati.

sopari betel-nut, a common legal stimulant, mainly chewed by itself, with tobacco, or in *paan*.

sou-babul exotic short tree of the acacia family, now a plague in the countryside.

srifal coconut, "holy fruit".

srikhand creamy dessert made from draining the water from yogurt and blending it with sugar, literally "oh beautiful holy sugary sweet".

standard grade, year in schol.

surya God as the sun.

swadeshi the ideal of using locally-made goods to satisfy your needs and support the local economy.

swami a term and title for a saddhu or sanyassi.

Swaminarayan a rich sect of Hinduism.

swar a musical note.

swaraj self rule, political independence.

tabla pair of drums common to North Indian classical music.

takkor a caste designation, usually associated with agricultural work.

talav town season lake, providing water for animals and irrigation during the winter and dry seasons.

taluka county, administrative subdivision of a jilla. One taluka includes many villages.

tamaco tobacco.

tapasya penance.

thali stainless steel plate, used to mean a traditional lunch.

thepla traditional flatbread made with herbs and spices, then roasted
   with oil.

tikka mark placed on one's forehead to indicate attendance of puja.

tindura small gourd-like vegetable.

toran auspicious garland of aso-palav leaves hung over the entrance-
   way to a home or temple.

triphala a common ayurvedic remedy, combining three fruits: amalaki,
   haritaki, and bibhitaki.

trust charitable foundation.

tubelight fluorescent light.

tulsi holy basil (ocimum sanctum).

tuved pigeon-pea, a common legume used in curries (fresh) and dal
   (dried).

urea the most common chemical fertilizer applied to crops.

vad banyan tree (ficus bengalensis).

vadi orchard.

vagar culinary technique critical to indian cuisine, for flavoring various vegetables or lentils. To vagar an item, first heat oil in a
   small curved dish, then fry a variety of seeds and spices (mustard,
   cumin, fenugreek, ajwain, hingu, whole dried chiles). Different
   styles of vagar may also incorporate onions, garlic, ginger, and
   green chiles. After the oil has been flavored, you may add it to
   a dish of already cooked lentils or vegetables. Continue cooking
   the vegetables along with the vagar, adding more spices (some
   spices do not take well to being fried at such high temperatures)
   cooking together to meld the flavors.

vajrasana yoga asana, performed by sitting upright with your legs folded at the knee ("Japanese style"), recommend for twenty minutes after eating.

vas neighborhood.

vatana peas.

vedanta a branch of ancient Indian philosophy.

velun Indian rolling pin for making flatbreads, whose center is fatter than its ends.

viga a measurement of land equally one fourth of an ancre.

vohra patel a Muslim community of the patel name.

walla the one who has, or the one who sells. Can be used with almost anything: chai-walla, bansuri-walla, police-walla,etc.

yatra journey, pilgrimage.

yatri traveler, pilgrim.

yoga Indian holistic science of well-being and union with the divine.

yogi one who studies and practices yoga (yogini for women).